The COMPLETE IDIOT'S GUIDE TO

Learning Spanish on Your Own

by Gail Stein and Marc A. Einsohn

alpha books

A Division of Macmillan General Reference
A Simon & Schuster Macmillan Company
1633 Broadway, New York, NY 10019-6785

International Standard Book Number: 0-02-861040-7
Library of Congress Catalog Card Number: 95-083359

98   8

Interpretation of the printing code: the rightmost number of the first series of numbers is the year of the book's printing; the rightmost number of the second series of numbers is the number of the book's printing. For example, a printing code of 96-1 shows that the first printing occurred in 1996.

Printed in the United States of America

This book is dedicated to:

My tremendously patient and supportive husband—Douglas

My incredibly loving and understanding sons—Eric and Michael

My proud parents—Jack and Sara Bernstein

My superior consultant and advisor— Roger Herz

My wonderful student—Alexandra Bernal

Gail Stein

and also dedicated to:

My wonderful parents—Sidney and Florence Einsohn

My significant other—Meredith Ripps

Marc Einsohn

Publisher
Theresa Murtha

Development Editor
Nancy Mikhail

Copy/Production Editor
Charles K. Bowles II

Technical Editor
Wigberto Rivera

Cover Designer
Kim Scott

Illustrator
Judd Winick

Designer
Kim Scott

Cover Designer
Michael Freeland

Indexer
Craig Small

Production Team
*Heather Butler, Angela Calvert, Daniel Caparo, Christine Tyner,
Pamela Volk, Megan Wade*

Contents at a Glance

Contents

10 Finally, We're at the Airport 93

11 Let's Get to the Hotel 109

Introduction

Today, more than ever, the acquisition of at least one foreign language is essential for both business and pleasurable pursuits. Sophisticated improvements in travel and communication have made the world our neighborhood. The world is now accessible to everyone: to you, to me, and to the generations that will follow.

Learn Spanish and you will enter a world that can provide you with endless opportunities, intriguing experiences, and exciting challenges. Learn Spanish and you will have the key that opens the door to a different lifestyle, a distinctive culture, and a unique outlook on life. Learn Spanish and you will possess a valuable tool that will serve you well when you least expect it. Open up your mind and immerse yourself in the beauty of the language and the culture. Study Spanish purposefully, with patience and love. You will be rewarded again and again.

Right from the start you'll feel that this book was written with *you* in mind. It is extremely user-friendly and will make your language learning experience pleasant, satisfying, and entertaining. You'll find the approach to be easy-going and clear-cut, enabling you to start communicating almost instantly with a reasonable amount of skill and an encouraging sense of achievement.

Why and How This Book Is Meant for You

This book takes you from the most basic material to a deeper understanding of the patterns of the Spanish language, and finally to a higher level of expertise and accomplishment. This book is unique—it is a phrase book, a grammar book, a cultural guide, and a dictionary all wrapped up into one. Its goal is to enable you to handle common, everyday situations proficiently and competently. Whether you are a student, traveler, businessperson, or simply a lover of languages, this book will provide you with the knowledge and skills you need, in a format that is simple to understand and easy to use. Thematically linked vocabulary, useful expressions, and grammar, as well as practical activities for mastery and enrichment are presented in every chapter. Authentic materials will immerse you in the Spanish culture and give you a thorough understanding of the people. Here's what you can expect to find in this book:

Part 1, "The Very Basics," shows you why Spanish is a language that you should learn. The simple, phonetic pronunciation guide will have you pronouncing the language properly almost immediately. You'll see how much Spanish you already know based on your knowledge of English. Don't fret over grammar—basic, elementary terms and rules are painlessly presented along with high-frequency idioms, slang, and gestures indigenous to the culture. Right from the start you'll be asking and answering simple questions and even engaging in basic conversations.

Part 2, "Travel," enables you to plan and take a trip to a Spanish-speaking country. When it's time to introduce yourself, you'll be able to express greetings and salutations, describe yourself and those traveling with you, and talk about your job. If you're the curious type, asking questions will prove to be quite easy. There are chapters to help you find your way to the airport, obtain necessary ground transportation and even rent a car. Don't worry about giving or receiving directions, that will be explained too. Lastly, this section will help you acquire a room with the creature comforts you prefer.

Part 3, "Fun and Games," enables you to go out and have a great time in any Spanish-speaking country. Everything that makes for a superb experience is covered in this section: food, sports, museums, tourist attractions, musical events, and leisure activities. You'll learn to plan your daily activities around the weather, offer suggestions, and make your opinions and preferences known. The food chapters will help you stick to your diet or go all out. If you love to shop, there's a chapter that will help you buy anything from typical native artisanry to a tropical Guayabera shirt. Conversion charts for sizing clothes are provided to help you make correct selections.

Part 4, "Problems," prepares you not only for the simple, minor inconveniences, but also for problems that are more serious in nature. Consult this section when you need a haircut, a stain removed, your camera fixed, a replacement contact lens, new heels on your shoes, prescription drugs, or a package sent.

Part 5, "Let's Get Down to Business," was written to meet the needs of those who want to conduct banking transactions, which include making deposits and withdrawals, opening a checking account, and taking out a loan. A mini-dictionary of bank terms is included. This section will help you rent or buy property and express your present and future needs.

If you persevere and study this book from cover to cover, you will learn and practice skills that will allow you to enjoy a significant amount of confidence in both social and business situations where Spanish is required. If you have the time and the patience, and if you are willing to make the effort, you will be able to successfully communicate in a new and beautiful language in a relatively short period of time.

Extras

In addition to the grammatical explanations, the useful phrases and expressions, and the vocabulary lists, this book provides a wealth of interesting and informative facts formatted throughout the text as sidebars. Look for the following icons that set these tidbits apart:

As a Rule
These boxes will help you quickly understand the grammar or refresh your memory with rules from previous chapters.

Pitfall
Read these warnings to avoid making any unnecessary or embarrassing mistakes.

Cultural Tidbit
Useful facts about Spanish-speaking countries and their customs appear in these boxes. Use these tidbits to increase your understanding of the culture and to make your trip more fulfilling.

Acknowledgments

The authors would like to acknowledge the contributions, input support, and interest of the following people: Charles Bowles; Héctor Cardwood, head pastry chef of the San Juan Marriott; María Chin and Brenda Dávila of the San Juan Marriott; Nancy Chu; Gabriel Cruz; Trudy and Richard Edelman; Angela Felipe; Barbara Gilson; Michelle and Stephen Gordon; Robert Grandt; Christina Levy; Anne Marie Loffredo; Marion Meitner; Nancy Mikhail; Jennifer Nicholson; Max Rechtman; Dr. Angel Rueda; Herbert Waldren.

Part 1
The Very Basics

Chapter 1

The Top Ten Reasons Why You Should Study Spanish

In This Chapter

➤ What Spanish has to offer you

➤ Where Spanish can be used

➤ Developing a learning strategy

➤ Why you shouldn't be afraid

If you haven't already purchased this book, you're probably leafing through it at this very moment wondering: "Can I *really* do this?" No doubt you're deciding if you'll have the time, if you have what it takes to stick with it, and if, indeed, it'll pay off in the end. Just like Dave on late night syndicated television, I'm going to give my top ten reasons why you should study Spanish:

Reason #10   You want to impress your date at a Spanish restaurant by ordering in Spanish.

Reason #9   You loved *Man of La Mancha* so much that you want to read *Don Quijote* in the original.

Reason #8   When you meet Paloma Picasso on the street you want to be able to ask her questions she'll understand.

Reason #7 You want to buy time-sharing property on the beach in Puerto Rico.

Reason #6 When you get pulled over for speeding in Tijuana, you don't want to wind up in jail.

Reason #5 You want to study flamenco dancing in Madrid.

Reason #4 You can get a discount on Cuban cigars if you order them in español.

Reason #3 You want to sing along with Richie Valens when they play "La Bamba" on the oldies station.

Reason #2 You want to run with the bulls in Pamplona, but they don't understand English.

Reason #1 One word: Cancún.

Seriously Now

Now that we've had a little fun, it's time to seriously consider why you should study Spanish. Let's take a look at some of the more credible reasons that should convince you that you've made the right choice:

Real Reason #10 You love music, especially music with that native beat. It just makes you want to move your feet. And although your friends are into all the modern stuff, you have to admit that you really find Casals' cello pieces and Segovia's guitar solos very relaxing.

Real Reason #9 You love to dance. The music starts to blare and you can't help it, your hips start to sway and your feet start to move. Let's face it, you've got rhythm. You want to mambo, cha-cha, salsa, even tango. Just reading this makes your feet start tapping.

Real Reason #8 You're an aficionado of Spanish movies and really would enjoy watching them without having to read those distracting, poorly translated, sometimes invisible subtitles.

Real Reason #7 You're an artist at heart. You long to spend time at El Prado admiring the works of Zurbarán, Velázquez, Murillo, and El Greco. Picasso's Guernica brings tears to your eyes and Dalí's surrealistic paintings really make you wonder what was going on in his mind. You truly are a cultured person and Spain has a lot to offer.

Real Reason #6   You are definitely not money-hungry, but you'd like to improve your chances in the job market. There are so many fields open today where a knowledge of Spanish would be a real plus. Here's your opportunity to get that little extra that will put you above all the others who are competing for the job you want.

Real Reason #5   You want to live in a warm climate, and the countries in Spanish America have a lot to offer: the landscape is beautiful, the people are friendly, the food is delicious, and you won't need an expensive winter wardrobe.

Real Reason #4   Speaking of food, you love to cook. You want to learn how to make an authentic paella valenciana or a truly hot and spicy salsa picante. If you want to do it right, you have to go to the source. And besides, you probably won't be able to get all the spices and ingredients you'll need in your hometown.

Real Reason #3   You hate to cook but you love to eat. And you like it hot and spicy. You're a fan of tropical fruits and you dream of sipping an ice-cold piña colada on a white sandy beach in Mexico. You're tired of the same old stuff and you want to sample all the different types of food available to you in countries that are really quite close by. You can plan your next vacation accordingly.

Real Reason #2   You want to prove to yourself that you are smart. Foreign languages have always had the reputation of being impossible to learn. How many of your friends and acquaintances have studied one in school for 2, 3, or even 4 years and then claim: "But I can't even speak a word!" That simply doesn't have to be the case. Learning a foreign language can be easy and fun. Try it. You'll be pleasantly surprised.

Real Reason #1   You're a traveler. You want to see the world and all it has to offer. And so you make sure that for each vacation, you never go to the same place twice. If that's the case, keep in mind that Spanish is spoken by more than 300 million people throughout the world in over 20 countries. You have an awful lot of trips ahead of you. Just look at the following maps to see all the countries where Spanish is the primary language.

GUATEMALA   HONDURAS   *MAR CARIBE*

EL SALVADOR
NICARAGUA
COSTA RICA
PANAMÁ

Barranquilla
Cartagena
Caracas
Lago de Maracaibo
Río Orinoco
VENEZUELA

Manizales
Cali
Bogotá
COLOMBIA

GUAYANA
SURINAM
GUAYANA FRANCESA

OCÉANO ATLÁNTICO

ECUADOR

Quito
ECUADOR

Iquitos

Río Amazonas

PERÚ

ANDES
Lima
Machu Picchu
Cuzco
Ayacucho
Lago Titicaca

BRASIL

BOLIVIA
La Paz
Sucre
Potosí

Río Paraná

PARAGUAY

CHILE

Salta
Asunción

Iguazú

OCÉANO ATLÁNTICO

OCÉANO PACÍFICO

Río Uruguay

URUGUAY

Santiago
ARGENTINA
Buenos Aires
Montevideo

AMÉRICA DEL SUR

ISLAS MALVINAS (Br.)

Estrecho de Magallanes

TIERRA DEL FUEGO

0   1000 km

0   600 miles

NIGERIA

ÁFRICA

CAMERÚN

Malabo

GUINEA ECUATORIAL

ECUADOR

GABÓN

ÁFRICA

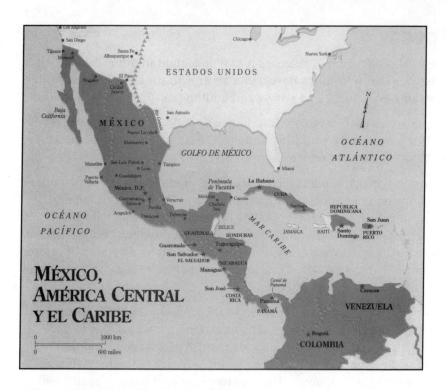

MÉXICO,
AMÉRICA CENTRAL
Y EL CARIBE

ESPAÑA

Full Speed Ahead

The best way to become proficient in a language is to plunge right in. Immerse yourself in anything and everything that is Spanish. Have a love affair with the language and culture. Follow these suggestions to ensure a long lasting and fulfilling relationship with Spanish:

➤ Examine your goals honestly, evaluate your linguistic abilities and pace yourself accordingly. Don't rush—take your time studying the language. Set aside special time each day that you devote only to learning Spanish.

➤ Invest in or borrow a good bilingual dictionary. Keep in mind that pocket varieties may be too skimpy and not appropriate for learning a new language. Carefully check what is available in your local bookstore or library before purchasing a dictionary. Current, popular, easy-to-use dictionaries that provide a comprehensive listing of current, colloquial vocabulary words are published by a number of companies (the best include those by Simon & Schuster and Larousse) and can be found in any bookstore to fit any size pocketbook.

➤ Take advantage of any opportunities to listen to the language. Rent Spanish movies and try not to read the English subtitles. If broadcast in your area, listen to public service radio or television stations that provide Spanish programs. In addition, search bookstores and public or college libraries for language tapes that will help you hear and master spoken Spanish. Then try to create your own tapes and use them to perfect your accent. Also, ask to use language laboratories and computer programs that are available in many high schools and universities.

➤ Read everything you can get your hands on, including: fairy tales, children's books, and comic books. Try to also read Spanish newspapers such as : *El Diario/La Prensa*. And, if you're not too bashful, read aloud and practice your pronunciation and comprehension at the same time.

➤ Set up *un rincón español* (a Spanish corner) in a convenient place in your home. Decorate it with posters or articles. Label items whose names you want to learn and display them for easy viewing. Keep all your materials together and organized in this special Spanish spot.

There's Nothing to Fear

Some people are truly afraid to study a foreign language. They think that it will be too much work, too hard, and too time-consuming. However, in reality, if you take it slow, and don't allow yourself to become overly concerned with the grammar and pronunciation, you'll be able to manage very well. To help you feel more at ease as you begin your task, remember the following points:

➤ Don't be intimidated by the grammar. Everyone makes mistakes, even in their native language. And besides, very often, only one or two correctly used words (especially verbs) will enable you to be understood.

➤ Don't be intimidated by the pronunciation. Put on your best Spanish accent, don't be shy; and speak, speak, speak. In any country, there are many different regional accents. Certainly yours will fit in somehow.

➤ Don't be intimidated by native speakers. They are usually helpful to anyone who makes a sincere attempt to communicate in their language.

➤ Don't be intimidated by the reputation foreign languages have for being difficult. As you will see, right from the start, Spanish is fun and easy.

The Least You Need to Know

➤ Whether for business or pleasure, there are many reasons why you should learn Spanish.

➤ The best ways to learn a new language are to take your time and listen and read everything you can in the language.

➤ There's nothing to fear when studying a language. Just don't let the grammar and pronunciation intimidate you. You'll be able to make yourself understood, even with limited vocabulary.

➤ You can become proficient in Spanish if you learn to love the language and become totally involved in it.

Chapter 2

Pronounce It Properly

In This Chapter

➤ The stress of it all

➤ Finding fluidity

➤ Getting the accent

➤ Phonetically yours

So you've decided you want to learn how to roll your r's and to purr like a wild *tigre*. You also want to learn how to make your v's sound like b's and silence some letters while emphasizing others. Lose your inhibitions, put on your best Spanish accent, and repeat and practice the sounds of the language. Remember that although Spanish is a foreign language to you, it is very *phonetic,* and therefore, very easy to pronounce. That's right, just read what you see and pronounce it the way you think it should be pronounced. Chances are, you've got it perfectly. Let's take a look at just a few rules that will help you sound like a true Spanish-speaker. You're going to find that you'll be purrrrring away in no time at all.

Think of this lesson as a verbal workout. Just like any skill you might want to perfect, proper Spanish pronunciation requires a certain amount of practice and dedication.

So don't hesitate to sit down and talk to yourself, read aloud, or sing along with your favorite Spanish singer. If you want to be successful, exercise slowly at first and then gradually increase your efforts, until you find yourself working at a comfortable pace. Avoid burning out by trying to accomplish too much, too soon. Remember, practice makes perfect.

Don't Get Stressed Out

Pronounce each syllable of a word with equal emphasis unless there is a written accent. Unlike English words, which often contain many silent letters, Spanish words are pronounced exactly as they are written. The songlike flow of Spanish is just one of the reasons why it is considered one of the romance languages.

Pitfalls

CAUTION

If you want to sound like a native Spanish-speaker, remember to maintain an even keel by using, more or less, an equal amount of stress for each syllable. Keep in mind that overemphasizing letters, syllables, or words will make you sound like a "gringo."

To Accentuate or Not to Accentuate?

Don't worry that you'll have trouble sounding great. Spanish is a relatively simple language to pronounce. Sure, there are accent marks, but don't let them trouble or confuse you. Luckily, there are only three in the language:

➤ The most common accent, the ´ only requires that you put more stress on the letter. For example: mamá (mah-mAH), interés, (een-teh-rEHs), terrífico (teh-rrEE-fee-koh), avión (ah-bee-OHn), único (OO-nee-koh).

➤ The ~, which only appears over an *n* (ñ, which is considered a separate letter), produces the sound **ny**, as in the *ni* in *onion*. For example: *mañana* (mah-NYah-nah), tomorrow or morning.

➤ The ¨ may be used in diphthongs (combinations of two vowels), and indicates that each vowel is to be pronounced separately. This last accent is very rarely seen. For example: *vergüenza* (behr-goo-ehn-sah), shame.

As you can see, accents in Spanish really create no problem at all. You'll get some practice with them in just a little while.

Developing Your Best Accent

Did you ever notice how some people can pick up another language and sound authentic with very little effort at all, whereas others just can't seem to lose their native, hometown accent? Those of you who are lucky can sound great by simply imitating the Spanish speakers you've heard on T.V., in the movies, on the radio, or in your neighborhood. Right from the start you'll be able to reproduce accentuation and pronunciation with minimal effort. Positive feedback will be immediate and a feeling of accomplishment will be yours with little practice. How lucky for you. You probably have a "good ear" and are somewhat musically talented too. You could probably skip a large part of this chapter and maybe even ignore some of the phonetic spellings in this book and manage quite well.

There are those, however, who view foreign pronunciation with trepidation. If you were born with a "tin ear," chances are that words and phrases you speak just won't sound right at first. You'll need to spend a bit more time practicing your pronunciation. But if you keep at it, eventually you'll get the hang of it.

Remember, no matter how you sound, you'll make yourself understood if you use the correct words. That should be your goal. Nobody is going to laugh at you. In the end, your level of competence in pronunciation is no big deal. So relax, try your best, and, above all, don't be discouraged.

Wow! Same Five Vowels

Unlike the English alphabet, the Spanish alphabet contains 28 letters. Five of these 28 are vowels: a e i o u.

The pronunciation of these vowels is shown in table 2.1

Table 2.1 Pronouncing Vowels Properly

Vowel	Sound	Example	Pronunciation
a	ah	artista	ahr-tees-tah
e	eh	egoísta	eh-goh-ees-tah
i	ee	isla	ees-lah
o	oh	objeto	ohb-heh-toh
u	oo	uno	oo-noh

As a Rule

Remember that if an accent is placed on one of the five vowels, you must stress that syllable for correct pronunciation.

Accented Word	Pronunciation
mamá	mah-mAH
té	tEH
magnífico	mag-nEE-fee-koh

The other 23 letters of the Spanish alphabet are consonants. The three letters that are not contained in the English alphabet are *ch*, *ll*, and *ñ*. (*ch* and *ll* are no longer considered separate letters in the Spanish alphabet, but Spanish dictionaries have not yet noted this change.) The letter *w* is not considered part of the Spanish alphabet because it is used only in words of foreign origin: watercloset, week-end, western, wharf, whisky, and wintergreen, for example.

Table 2.2 illustrates the Spanish consonants. Note the sounds and the sample words associated with them with their phonetic spellings. After studying the chart, repeat the sample words aloud to practice your pronunciation.

Table 2.2 Pronouncing Consonants Properly

Letter	Sound	Example	Pronunciation
b	same as English	bebe	beh-beh
c	soft c (s) before e and i	centro	sehn-troh
	hard c (k) elsewhere	catedral	kah-teh-drahl
ch	ch	cheque	cheh-keh
d	d	dama	dah-mah
f	f	fiesta	fee-ehs-tah
g	soft h before e and i	general	heh-neh-rahl
	hard g elsewhere	gala	gah-lah
h	silent	hispano	ees-pah-noh
j	h	Julio	hoo-lee-oh
k	k	kilo	kee-loh

Letter	Sound	Example	Pronunciation
l	l	libre	lee-breh
ll	y	llama	yah-mah
m	m	mamá	mah-mAH
n	n	necesario	neh-seh-sah-ree-oh
ñ	ny	niño	nee-nyoh
p	p	papá	pah-pAH
q	k	Quito	kee-toh
r	r (slightly rolled)	radio	rah-dee-oh
	rr (r rolled two or three times)	carro	kah-rroh
s	s	salsa	sahl-sah
t	t	toro	toh-roh
v	less explosive English b	vigor	bee-gohr
x	English ks (sinks)	exacto	ehk-sahk-toh
y	y	yoga	yoh-gah
z	s	zoo	soh

As a Rule

The Spanish *r* is always rolled. At the beginning of a word, or after the consonants *l*, *n*, or *s* the *r* requires two or three trills, just like the double r (*rr*).

Cultural Tidbit

Even though Spanish is the common language spoken in Spain and in most South American countries (notably, Portuguese is spoken in Brazil), people from different regions have their own individual speech and pronunciation patterns. For example, in some countries, it is common to not pronounce the final *s* of a word. The most commonly known speech pattern is that of the Castilians, where the *z* sounds like **th**.

15

Imagine that you're about to visit Spain. Before you go on vacation you decide to get your accent down pat. Here is a series of words for you to read aloud in order to help you pronounce the sounds of the Spanish alphabet.

Word	Pronunciation	English Meaning
bajo	bah-hoh	short
barato	bah-rah-toh	cheap
cada	kah-dah	each, every
carro	kah-rroh	car
casa	kah-sah	house
chica	chee-kah	girl
chocolate	choh-koh-lah-teh	chocolate
doctor	dohk-tohr	doctor
delicioso	deh-lee-see-oh-soh	delicious
fruta	froo-tah	fruit
fuerte	foo-ehr-teh	strong
generoso	heh-neh-roh-soh	generous
garaje	gah-rah-heh	garage
hablar	ah-blahr	to speak
hora	oh-rah	hour
lindo	leen-doh	pretty
libro	lee-broh	book
llover	yoh-behr	to rain
llave	yah-beh	key
moda	moh-dah	style
mesa	meh-sah	table
norte	nohr-teh	north
nueve	noo-eh-beh	nine
niño	nee-nyoh	child
pequeño	peh-keh-nyoh	small
papa	pah-pah	potato
playa	plah-yah	beach
regla	reh-glah	rule
razón	rah-sOHn	reason
perro	peh-rroh	dog
siempre	see-ehm-preh	always
serio	seh-ree-oh	serious
tela	teh-lah	cloth
tarde	tahr-deh	late
zapato	sah-pah-toh	shoe
zoo	soh	zoo

Dealing with Diphthongs

The Spanish language contains many diphthongs. Your curiosity is getting the best of you: "So what's a diphthong?" Well, a *diphthong* is a combination of two vowels, one weak and one strong, that appear in the same syllable. The *a*, *e*, and *o* are the strong vowels. That means you pronounce them with a lot of emphasis. The *i* and the *u* are the weak vowels, so say them softly. Use table 2.3 to practice pronouncing diphthongs.

Table 2.3 Spanish Diphthongs to Say Aloud for Practice

Diphthong	Sound	Example	Pronunciation	Meaning
ae	ah-eh	aeropuerto	ah-eh-roh-pwehr-toh	airport
ai	ah-ee	aire	ahy-reh	air
au	ow	autor	ow-tohr	author
ei	eh-ee	seis	seh-ees	six
eu	eh-oo	Europa	eh-oo-roh-pah	Europe
oi	oy	oigo	oy-goh	I hear
ia	ee-ah	seria	seh-ree-ah	serious
ua	wah	lengua	lehn-gwah	tongue, language
ie	ee-eh	siesta	see-ehs-tah	nap
ue	weh	cuenta	wehn-tah	check (bill)
io	ee-oh	avión	ah-bee-OHn	airplane
uo	oo-oh	continuo	kohn-tee-noo-oh	continuous
iu	ee-oo	ciudad	see-oo-dahd	city
ui	wee	cuidado	kwee-dah-doh	be careful

Practice Makes Perfect

Now that you are an expert on the Spanish alphabet and Spanish diphthongs, read each of the following sentences aloud to practice and improve your pronunciation.

El país es grande.
Ehl pah-EEs ehs grahn-deh
The country is big.

Oiga, hay seis respuestas.
Oh-ee-gah, ah-ee seh-ees rehs-pwehs-tahs
Listen, there are six answers.

Mi abuelo es viejo.
Mee ah-bweh-loh ehs bee-eh-hoh
My grandfather is old.

Paula va al cine.
Pow-lah bah ahl see-neh
Paula goes to the movies.

El anciano tiene cien años.
Ehl ahn-see-ah-noh tee-eh-neh see-ehn ahn-yohs
The old man is 100 years old.

17

The Least You Need to Know

➤ To sound natural, don't be afraid to slide one word into the next.

➤ Don't stress any syllable unless it includes an accented vowel.

➤ You must practice often if you want to improve your pronunciation.

➤ If your accent is poor, you'll still be understood.

Chapter 3

You Know More Than You Think

In This Chapter

➤ Cognates and comprehension

➤ The tricks of the trade

➤ Pitfalls and traps

Do you love chocolate? How about potatoes and tomatoes? Do you take a taxi often? When the weather is nice do you sit on your patio? Can you play the piano? Perhaps you have a sweater made from the wool of an alpaca. And I know that you've been stung by a mosquito more than once in your life. Well look at that, you know some Spanish already. You're probably totally unaware of the fact that your vocabulary is filled with words and phrases that we've borrowed from the Spanish. And there are other words and expressions that are so similar to ours that you'll be able to use and understand them with very little trouble at all. By the time you finish this chapter, you'll be well on your way to creating simple, correct Spanish sentences that will enable you to express your ideas and opinions.

What You Already Know

My husband makes frequent trips to the video store, especially in the summer when all the stations show reruns. He takes his time and often spends an hour or more trying to pick out the perfect film for the evening. His taste is very eclectic: one night we'll watch a Japanese samurai warrior film and the next night we could be viewing a French romantic comedy. It seems that more often than not, he picks out foreign films. He claims they are very interesting and so different from what we are used to. And although he only speaks English, he also enjoys the experience of listening to native speakers. I guess he feels that I should, too.

I loved it when one night he rented *Like Water for Chocolate,* a wonderful, but sad, Spanish love story. We sat in front of the T.V. for about two hours totally involved in the tale being told. At one point I noticed, to my great astonishment, that my husband wasn't reading the titles. I thought that perhaps he was bored by the romance. But that wasn't the case at all. When I asked him why he wasn't reading, he said that he understood what the people were saying. How could that be? He took French in college. He replied that the words sounded just like English to him. I gave it some thought, and I immediately understood his point, there is a logical explanation.

And that explanation is cognates. "What's a cognate," you ask? Simply put, it's a word that is spelled exactly the same, or almost the same way in two different languages and has the same definition. In many cases, we've borrowed the word from the Spanish and have incorporated it into our vocabulary, without giving much thought to the word's origin. Naturally, cognates are pronounced differently in each language, but the meaning of the Spanish word is very apparent to an English speaker.

It's time to take a closer look and see how much you really know before you even get started.

As a Rule

When you look at the following list of cognates, you will notice that all Spanish nouns are marked by a definite article, *el* or *la*, which both mean "the," and indicate the gender of the noun (masculine or feminine, respectively). This may seem strange to you at first because we do not have anything similar in English. For now, just remember that if you want to express that Spanish is easy, you must say: "*El* español es fácil."

Although the gender of nouns is easily identifiable in Spanish, it is best, for those rare exceptions, to learn the noun with its corresponding definite article. See Chapter 6 for more details. For now, just remember that *el* is for masculine singular nouns and *la* is for feminine singular nouns.

Perfect Partners

Table 3.1 provides a list of cognates that have exactly the same meaning in both Spanish and English. The column on the left will provide you with adjectives that you can use to describe some of the nouns shown in the middle and last columns. Using the skills you learned in the last chapter, take your time pronouncing the Spanish words and compare them to their English equivalents. Your goal is to sound Spanish.

Table 3.1 Perfect Cognates

Adjectives	Masculine Nouns El (ehl)	Feminine Nouns La (lah)
horrible (oh-rree-bleh)	color (koh-lohr)	banana (bah-nah-nah)
natural (nah-too-rahl)	chocolate (choh-koh-lah-teh)	fiesta (fee-ehs-tah)
popular (poh-poo-lahr)	doctor (dohk-tohr)	alpaca (ahl-pah-kah)
sociable (soh-see-ah-bleh)	hotel (oh-tehl)	plaza (plah-sah)
terrible (teh-rree-bleh)	soda (soh-dah)	radio (rah-dee-oh)
tropical (troh-pee-kahl)	motor (moh-tohr)	
	taxi (tahk-see)	

Near Cognates

Near cognates are words that look so much alike in both languages (although not exactly the same) that their meanings are unmistakable. Perhaps a letter or two is different, or there might be an accent mark on the Spanish word, but essentially, the words are the same. Look at table 3.2 and see if you can figure out the meaning of all the words. Are you up to the challenge?

Table 3.2 Near Cognates

Adjectives	Masculine Nouns	Feminine Nouns
americano (ah-meh-ree-kah-noh)	aniversario (ah-nee-behr-sah-ree-oh)	aspirina (ahs-pee-ree-nah)
confortable (kohn-fohr-tah-bleh)	automóvil (ow-toh-moh-beel)	bicicleta (bee-see-kleh-tah)
curioso (koo-ree-oh-soh)	banco (bahn-koh)	blusa (bloo-sah)

continues

Table 3.2 Continued

Adjectives	Masculine Nouns	Feminine Nouns
delicioso (deh-lee-see-oh-soh)	ciclismo (see-klees-moh)	catedral (kah-teh-drahl)
diferente (dee-feh-rehn-teh)	diccionario (deek-see-oh-nah-ree-oh)	computadora (kohm-poo-tah-doh-rah)
difícil (dee-fee-seel)	grupo (groo-poh)	dieta (dee-eh-tah)
elegante (eh-leh-gahn-teh)	jardín (har-deen)	familia (fah-mee-lee-ah)
excelente (ehk-seh-lehn-teh)	limón (lee-mohn)	hamburguesa (ahm-boor-geh-sah)
famoso (fah-moh-soh)	mecánico (meh-kah-nee-koh)	lámpara (lahm-pah-rah)
grande (grahn-deh)	parque (pahr-keh)	medicina (meh-dee-see-nah)
importante (eem-pohr-tahn-teh)	plato (plah-toh)	guitarra (gee-tah-rrah)
imposible (eem-poh-see-bleh)	presidente (preh-see-dehn-teh)	mansíon (mahn-see-ohn)
interesante (een-teh-reh-sahn-teh)	programa (proh-grah-mah)	música (moo-see-kah)
magnífico (mahg-nee-fee-koh)	menú (meh-noo)	nacionalidad (nah-see-oh-nah-lee-dahd)
moderno (moh-dehr-noh)	restaurante (rehs-tow-rahn-teh)	opinión (oh-pee-nee-ohn)
necesario (neh-seh-sah-ree-oh)	salario (sah-lah-ree-oh)	persona (pehr-soh-nah)
ordinario (ohr-dee-nah-ree-oh)	supermercado (soo-pehr-mehr-kah-doh)	región (reh-hee-ohn)
posible (poh-see-bleh)	teatro (teh-ah-troh)	rosa (roh-sah)
probable (proh-bah-bleh)	teléfono (teh-leh-foh-noh)	turista (too-rees-tah)
rápido (rah-pee-doh)	televisión (teh-leh-bee-see-ohn)	universidad (oo-nee-behr-see-dahd)
sincero (seen-seh-roh)		

The Complete Idiot's Reference Card

20 Important Words and Phrases

Please.	Por favor.	pohr fah-bohr
Thank you very much.	Muchas gracias.	moo-chahs grah-see-ahs
You're welcome.	De nada.	deh nah-dah
Excuse me.	Perdóname.	pehr-doh-nah-meh
	Con permiso.	kohn pehr-mee-soh
My name is...	Me llamo...	meh yah-moh
I would like...	Quisiera...	kee-see-yeh-rah
	Me gustaría...	meh goos-tah-ree-ah
I need...	Necesito...	neh-seh-see-toh
	Me falta(n)...	meh fahl-tah(n)
Do you have...?	¿Tiene Ud....?	tee-yeh-neh oo-stehd
Please give me...	Déme, por favor...	deh-meh pohr fah-bohr
Could you help me please?	¿Podrías ayudarme por favor?	poh-dree-ahs ah-yoo-dahr-meh pohr fah-bohr
Do you speak English?	¿Habla Ud. inglés?	ah-blah oo-stehd een-glehs
I speak a little Spanish.	Hablo un poco de español.	ah-bloh oon poh-koh deh ehs-pah-nyohl
I don't understand.	No comprendo.	noh kohm-prehn-doh
Please repeat.	Repita, por favor.	reh-pee-tah pohr fah-bohr
What did you say?	¿Qué dijo Ud.?	keh dee-hoh oo-stehd
I'm lost.	Estoy perdido(a).	ehs-toh-ee pehr-dee-doh(dah)
I'm looking for...	Busco...	boos-koh
	Estoy buscando...	ehs-toh-ee boos-kahn-doh
Where is the bathroom?	¿Dónde está el baño?	dohn-deh ehs-tah ehl bah-nyoh
Where is the police station?	¿Dónde está la comisaria de policía?	dohn-deh ehs-tah lah koh-mee-sah-ree-ah deh poh-lee-see-ah
Where is the American Embassy?	¿Dónde está la embajada americana?	dohn-deh ehs-tah lah ehm-bah-hah-dah ah-meh-ree-kah-nah

alpha
books

CLOTHING MEASUREMENTS

MEN

SHOES

American	7	8	9	10	11	12	
Continental	39	41	43	44	45	46	

SUITS, COATS

American	34	36	38	40	42	44	46	48
Continental	44	46	48	50	52	56	58	60

SHIRTS

American	14	$14\frac{1}{2}$	15	$15\frac{1}{2}$	16	$16\frac{1}{2}$	17	$17\frac{1}{2}$
Continental	36	37	38	39	40	41	42	43

WOMEN

SHOES

American	4	5	6	7	8	9
Continental	35	36	37	38	39	40

DRESSES, SUITS

American	8	10	12	14	16	18
Continental	36	38	40	42	44	46

BLOUSES, SWEATERS

American	32	34	36	38	40	42
Continental	40	42	44	46	48	50

METRIC WEIGHTS AND MEASURES
SOLID MEASURES
(APPROXIMATE MEASUREMENTS ONLY)

OUNCES	GRAMS (GRAMOS)	GRAMS	OUNCES
$\frac{1}{4}$	7	10	$\frac{1}{3}$
$\frac{1}{2}$	14	100	$3\frac{1}{2}$
$\frac{3}{4}$	21	300	$10\frac{1}{2}$
1	28	500	18

POUNDS	KILOGRAMS (KILOS)	KILOGRAMS	POUNDS
1	$\frac{1}{2}$	1	$2\frac{1}{4}$
5	$2\frac{1}{4}$	3	$6\frac{1}{2}$
10	$4\frac{1}{2}$	5	11
20	9	10	22
50	23	50	110
100	45	100	220

LIQUID MEASURES
(APPROXIMATE MEASUREMENTS ONLY)

OUNCES	MILLILITERS (MILILITROS)	MILLILITERS	OUNCES
1	30	10	$\frac{1}{3}$
6	175	50	$1\frac{1}{2}$
12	350	100	$3\frac{1}{2}$
16	475	150	5

GALLONS	LITERS (LITROS)	LITERS	GALLONS
1	$3\frac{3}{4}$	1	$\frac{1}{4}$ (1 quart)
5	19	5	$1\frac{1}{3}$
10	38	10	$2\frac{1}{2}$

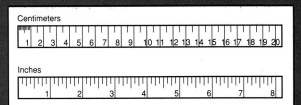

To convert centimeters into inches, multiply by .39.
To convert inches into centimeters, multiply by 2.54.

As a Rule

In Spanish, adjectives agree in number and gender with the nouns they describe. Until a more detailed explanation in Chapter 9, use adjectives ending with *o* to describe masculine nouns, those ending with *a* to describe feminine nouns, and adjectives ending in *e* to describe either masculine of feminine nouns.

Spanish words that begin in *es* are often near cognates too. You can easily guess the meaning of many Spanish words that begin with *es* by simply dropping the initial *e:*

Word	Pronunciation	English Meaning
escarlata	ehs-kahr-lah-tah	scarlet
escéptico	eh-skehp-tee-koh	skeptical
escultor	ehs-kool-tohr	sculptor
espacio	ehs-pah-see-oh	space
España	ehs-pah-nyah	Spain
especial	ehs-peh-see-ahl	special
espectáculo	ehs-pehk-tah-koo-loh	spectacle, show
espía	ehs-pee-ah	spy
espiral	ehs-pee-rahl	spiral
espléndido	ehs-plehn-dee-doh	splendid
esquí	ehs-kee	ski
estudiar	ehs-too-dee-ahr	to study
estupendo	ehs-too-pehn-doh	stupendous

How Much Have You Learned?

Practice reading the following Spanish sentences and then figure out what they mean. (The pronunciations of the Spanish phrases are provided in parentheses next to the phrases themselves.) Keep in mind that the Spanish word *es* means is.

El piano es grande.   (Ehl pee-ah-noh ehs grahn-deh)

El actor es horrible.   (Ehl ahk-tohr ehs oh-rree-bleh)

La información es terrible.   (Lah een-fohr-mah-see-ohn ehs teh-rree-bleh)

El profesor es sincero.   (Ehl proh-feh-sohr ehs seen-seh-roh)

El tigre es cruel.   (El tee-greh ehs kroo-ehl)

El cereal es delicioso.   (Ehl seh-reh-ahl ehs deh-lee-see-oh-soh)

Yes, You Can Write in Spanish!

Try writing and saying these sentences in Spanish. You may take a peek back at your cognate list to make sure that you are using the correct article (el or la), and to check your pronunciation:

The president is elegant.   The hotel is large.

The computer is interesting.   The color is magnificent.

The information is important.

Verb Cognates

There are many Spanish verbs (words that show action or a state of being) that are so similar to their English counterparts that there should be no difficulty in immediately recognizing their meanings.

Spanish verbs are also governed by certain rules that will be explained shortly. For now, look at the three major verb families (verbs ending in *ar*, *er*, and *ir*). Any verbs belonging to a family are considered regular, while those that do not belong to a family are designated as irregular. Each family has its own set of rules that will be explained in Chapter 7. All irregular verbs must be memorized. Look at the three major families and see if you can determine the meanings of the verbs presented:

AR Verbs

acompañar	entrar	negar	reparar
adorar	explicar	observar	reservar
celebrar	ignorar	pasar	terminar
comenzar	invitar	practicar	usar
declarar	marchar	preparar	verificar
eliminar	modificar	refusar	

ER Verbs

comprender   responder   vender

IR Verbs

aplaudir   dividir   omitir

decidir   persuadir   recibir

describir   preferir   sufrir

You've Got It Now!

As a matter of fact, you're such a pro now that you can easily read and understand these sentences without any problem at all.

Juan prepara el menú.   El programa termina.

El mecánico repara el carro.   Marta celebra su aniversario.

El turista usa la información.   José adora el programa.

Give Your Opinions

Pretend that you are a tourist in a Spanish-speaking country. Use what you have learned to express these feelings to a fellow tourist:

The program is excellent.   The theater is modern.

The park is popular.   The program is magnificent.

The dish is famous.   The actor is dynamic.

The restaurant is large.   The hotel is comfortable.

Cultural Tidbit

Many English words have infiltrated the Spanish language. We politely refer to these words as *spanglish*. Some examples are los jeans, el bloque, el CD, la soda, el bistec, el rosbif, el champú, el cóctel, la hamburguesa, el sandwich, el béisbol, el fútbol, el básquetbol, and el boxeador.

False Amigos

Although you may think that you've mastered it all, every rule has its exceptions. An example of such exceptions is called a *false friend*. False friends are words spelled exactly the same or almost the same in both Spanish and English, but have different meanings in each language. They might even be different parts of speech. Don't automatically assume that every Spanish word that looks like an English one is a cognate. Nothing is ever quite that simple. Beware of the following false friends listed in table 3.3. You want to use them correctly.

Table 3.3 False Friends

Spanish Word	English Meaning	Spanish Word	English Meaning
asistir	to attend	hay	there is (are)
caro	expensive	librería	bookstore
comer	to eat	joya	jewel
fábrica	factory	pan	bread
flor	flower	sopa	soup

The Least You Need to Know

➤ All Spanish nouns are preceeded by the definite article, el or la, which is a marker for the gender of the word.

➤ Cognates are words that look exactly or about the same in English and have the same meanings.

➤ Watch out for false friends; words spelled exactly the same in Spanish and English but which have different meanings in each language.

BUENOS DÍAS MI AMIGO.

Chapter 4

Good Grief, It's Grammar

In This Chapter

➤ An overview of very basic grammar

➤ How to use a bilingual dictionary

There's more to speaking a foreign language than merely translating words from one language to another—a technique that has been used throughout the years in school. We have finally realized that in order to communicate effectively you cannot simply walk around with a dictionary and read from it. Instead, you must learn to use the language and its patterns the way native speakers do.

For any student of a foreign language, probably the most difficult concept to grasp is that languages follow different grammatical patterns. Trying, therefore, to translate word for word from one language to the next often produces awkward results and in many instances, becomes an exercise in futility. To truly sound like a native, a student must have not only a good grammatical understanding of the language, but also a good colloquial, idiomatic command of it.

Oh No, Not Grammar!

Does the word "grammar" send chills up your spine and bring back bad memories of the days when you sat in school learning the parts of speech and verb conjugations, as well as diagramming sentences? Well, that was then and this is now. To learn a foreign language you really don't have to become an expert grammarian. All you're going to need to know is some of the simple parts of speech: nouns, verbs, adjectives, and adverbs. So don't panic—just follow along and see how simple it is.

Nouns

Nouns refer to people, places, things, or ideas. Unlike English, all nouns in Spanish have a gender (masculine or feminine), but just like English, they also have a quantity (singular or plural). Articles that serve as noun identifiers often help to indicate gender and number. You will learn more about this in Chapter 5. Like English, nouns may be replaced by pronouns.

Verbs

Verbs are words that show action or a state of being. In both English and Spanish, we conjugate verbs. In English, this is so automatic (because we've been doing it practically since birth) that we don't even realize that we are doing it. *Conjugating* refers to giving the correct form of the verb so that it agrees with the subject. For example: In English we say "I am," but "you are," "he is," etc.; "I look," but "she looks." It is improper to mix and match the subjects and verb forms whether you are speaking English or Spanish. Imagine how strange it would sound to you if a Spanish speaker said: "I is from Cuba." Of course you would understand the meaning, and that is what anyone is striving for: to be understood. So never lose hope, you'll always be able to get your message across. The language, however, does have a much better ring to it when the subjects and verbs correspond. Verb conjugation will be explained in greater depth in Chapter 6.

Adjectives

Adjectives are words that describe nouns. Unlike English, in Spanish all adjectives agree in number and gender with the nouns they modify. So if a noun is singular (plural), then a singular (plural) adjective must be used. If the noun is feminine (masculine), then you must be sure to give the correct feminine (masculine) form of the adjective you are using. Another difference is that in English, adjectives generally precede the nouns they modify, for example: "the blue house." In Spanish, most adjectives come after the nouns they describe. For example, translated to Spanish, "the blue house" becomes "la casa azul," where "casa" is "house," and "azul" is "blue." You will find out more about adjectives in Chapter 9.

Adverbs

Adverbs are words that describe verbs, adjectives, or other adverbs. Adverbs are used about the same way in both languages. In English, most adverbs end in *ly*, for example, *slowly*. In Spanish, adverbs end in *mente*; for example, *lentamente* (slowly). Adverbs will be discussed in greater detail in Chapter 18.

I'll Just Look It Up in the Dictionary

Using a bilingual dictionary requires a little more knowledge than using an English dictionary. Unlike English dictionaries where even if you don't know how to spell a word, you'll eventually come across it if you search carefully. To use a bilingual dictionary effectively and correctly, you must know and be aware of the differences between the various parts of speech.

The ABCs of Using a Dictionary

Before you try to look up your very first word, take the time to study the abbreviations at the front of your dictionary. You will probably find a quite long, comprehensive list. Don't get discouraged. There are really only a small handful that you will find truly important and that require your attention:

➤ *adj.*   Adjective.

➤ *adv.*   Adverb.

➤ *f.*   Feminine noun. The gender of nouns will be explained further in Chapter 6.

➤ *m.*   Masculine noun.

➤ *n.*   Noun (sometimes an *s* is used.) The *n.* designation is generally used only if the noun can be either masculine or feminine.

➤ *pl.*   Plural noun. More on plural nouns in Chapter 6.

➤ *v.i.* (or *v. intr.*)   Intransitive verb. An intransitive verb can stand alone as a sentence. "I write," for instance.

➤ *v.t.* (or *v. tr.*)   Transitive verb. A transitive verb may be followed by a direct object. For example, "He puts on his coat." Unlike "write" as in the previous example, "puts on" may not stand alone. A transitive can also be used in the passive, where the subject is acted upon. For example, "I was helped."

➤ *v.r.*   Reflexive verb. When using a reflexive verb, the subject acts upon itself, as in "I comb my hair." Reflexive verbs will be discussed in Chapter 22.

Learning how to use a bilingual dictionary requires a certain amount of grammatical expertise. You must know how to use the various parts of speech. Let's take the English word *mean*. Consider the following sentences and how the meaning of the word **mean** changes:

That boy is *mean*.   (adjective)

What can that *mean*?   (verb)

What is the *mean* (average)?   (noun)

If we change *mean* to the plural, its meaning changes:
What is the *means* of transportation?   (noun)

Now look up the word *mean* in a bilingual dictionary. You might see:

mean [min] *vt* significar; *adj* (miserly) tacaño(ña), (unkind) mezquino(na), malo(a); *n* (average) promedio *m*, media *f*; see also *means*.

means [minz] *n* (method, way) medio *m*; *npl* (money) recursos.

Using the Spanish definition of *mean* just given, look at the following English sentences, figure out which part of speech *mean* occupies, and complete the translated sentence into Spanish, using the correct translation of *mean*.

➤ *That boy is mean.*

Figure out the part of speech and complete the Spanish sentence:

Ese muchacho es _____.

The correct answer is *mezquino*, an adjective.

➤ *What can that mean?*

The Spanish sentence would be:

¿Qué puede_____eso?

Did you translate *mean* to *significar*, a verb? Great!

➤ *What is the mean?*

This term refers to the average of two numbers. Because the correct word can be either masculine or feminine, you will have to use *el* in front of the masculine word and *la* in front of the feminine one. (Articles will be discussed in detail in Chapter 6.) So, the Spanish translation would be:

¿Cuál es_____?

Did you choose *el promedio* or *la media*? Both are correct.

➤ *What is the means of transportation?*

Means is plural in English but masculine, singular in Spanish. Use *el* before the noun you choose.

Your Spanish sentence should be:

¿Cuál es _____ de transporte?

The answer is *el medio.*

As a Rule
In Spanish, an inverted question mark ¿ is placed at the beginning of a sentence to prepare you for what will follow. It's really a very clever idea.

As you can see, to successfully look up the meanings of a word you want to use, you must do three things:

1. Verify the part of speech—noun, verb, adjective, or adverb—that you want to use.

2. Verify that you have chosen a word with the meaning you want, by looking up the Spanish word you have chosen and seeing if the English meaning that is given is the one you want. (Sometimes you might have to think of a synonym for the word you want to use to get the proper Spanish meaning.)

3. Check that you are using the correct form of the word: the right number (singular or plural) and the right gender (masculine or feminine).

Use your bilingual dictionary to see if you can find the correct word to complete each of the following Spanish sentences:

1. That boy dances *well.*   Ese muchacho baila _____.

2. Where is the *well*?   ¿Dónde está _____?

3. I heard the *cry* of the animal.   Oí _____ del animal.

4. The child is going *to cry*.   El niño va a _____.

5. I have *just* ten dollars.   Tengo _____ diez dólares.

The Least You Need to Know

➤ The Spanish language contains the same parts of speech as English.

➤ To use a bilingual dictionary effectively, you must know the differences between the various parts of speech.

Chapter 5

Are Idioms for Idiots?

In This Chapter

➤ What are idioms?

➤ What is slang?

➤ Idioms vs. Slang

➤ How to use idioms

➤ Expressing your feelings with gestures

A knowledge of idioms is very important for a complete and correct understanding of a language. Imagine that you are shopping in one of Madrid's finest jewelry stores. You overhear a conversation between a couple as they examine the prices of diamond necklaces. The woman selects one that she likes, but her husband replies "Este collar cuesta un ojo de la cara." You interpret this to mean that the necklace costs an eye that is taken from your face. Sounds like a pretty drastic measure, wouldn't you say? In reality, the expression "costar un ojo de la cara" means "to cost a small fortune," although you'd never figure that out from the vocabulary and grammar in the sentence.

What Is an Idiom?

In any language, an *idiom* is a particular word or expression whose meaning cannot be readily understood by analyzing its traditional grammatical construction or its component words. An idiom, however, is considered to be an acceptable component of the standard vocabulary of the language. Some common English idioms are

To look on the bright side	On the other hand
To fall head over heels	To be down and out

What Is Slang?

What's the difference between an idiom and slang? *Slang* refers to colorful, popular, informal words or phrases that are *not* part of the standard vocabulary of a language. Slang is considered unconventional and has evolved to describe particular things or situations in street language. Slang vocabulary is composed of coinages; arbitrarily changed words; and extravagant, forced, or facetious figures of speech. Some examples of English slang are

Give me a break!	Tough luck!
Get real!	Get a life!

Idioms vs. Slang

Idioms are acceptable in oral and written phrases, whereas slang, although freely used in informal conversations, is generally considered substandard in formal writing or speaking. Much slang is, at best, X-rated.

Which Is It?

Take a look at some of these popular expressions. Are they idioms or slang? I'm sure that you will immediately realize that it would be impossible to translate them into Spanish because they are too colloquial. Certainly these expressions couldn't be translated word for word. Read them carefully and decide if they are idioms (acceptable terms) or slang (street language). When you speak a foreign language, it's important to know what phrases you may use politely, and which will be offensive.

You drive me crazy!	She got angry and lost it.
Keep your shirt on!	He's on his way up.
I'm always on the go!	Did you fall for it?
He likes to play the field.	Don't jump the gun!
It's raining cats and dogs!	

Did you recognize that these items are idiomatic expressions that we use in English all the time? Now compare the sentences just seen with these:

Shucks!	Don't dis my friend.
What a cop out!	My son is a computer geek.
She just flipped out!	That's tacky!

Did you notice how the slang sentences used substandard English and were more offensive than those containing idiomatic expressions? Excellent! You probably won't use much Spanish slang, but the idioms sure will come in handy.

There are a great many idioms in Spanish. In this chapter you will look at six categories of idioms that you might find helpful: travel and transportation, time, location and direction, expressing opinions, physical conditions, and weather conditions. Other idiomatic expressions will appear in their appropriate chapters.

And You're Off

Say you are taking a trip. You might be asked, "Are you going on a plane or on a boat?" In Spanish the word for "on" is "sobre." If you said "Voy sobre el avión," that would imply that you were flying on the exterior of the plane. That would be some feat. You could probably make Guinness' Book of Records! Because we all know that this is truly impossible, it would certainly be well worth your time to learn the idiomatic expressions covered in table 5.1 to avoid this type of confusion.

Table 5.1 Travel and Transportation

Idiom	Pronunciation	Meaning
en bicicleta	ehn bee-see-kleh-tah	by bicycle
a caballo	ah kah-bah-yoh	by horseback
a pie	ah pee-eh	by foot
en automóvil	ehn ow-toh-moh-beel	by car
por avión	pohr ah-bee-ohn	by plane
en barco	ehn bahr-koh	by boat
en autobús	ehn ow-toh-boos	by bus
en metro	ehn meh-troh	by subway
en taxi	ehn tahk-see	by taxi
en tren	ehn trehn	by train
en carro	ehn kah-rroh	by car

You're Off and Running

Some people have a very quiet life and don't go very far from home, while others run here and there for business or pleasure. Express what for you would be the best means of transportation to get to the following places, if you had to get there on short notice:

Example:

the drugstore   *a pie* (by foot)

your place of business or school   the park

the movies   a tropical island

your doctor   a fishing trip

the nearest hospital   a museum

Europe   the library

What Is the Proper Time Frame?

Just how time conscious are you? Do you always wear your watch because time is of the essence? Are you up and at 'em at the crack of dawn so that you get a head start on your day? Or are you more the laid-back type who doesn't give time a second thought? Whatever your personality, the idioms in table 5.2 will serve you well whenever time is on your mind.

Table 5.2 Time Expressions

Idiom	Pronunciation	Meaning
hasta la noche	ah-stah lah noh-cheh	See you this evening
hasta mañana	ah-stah mah-nyah-nah	See you tomorrow
a tiempo	ah tee-ehm-poh	on time
hasta el sábado	ah-stah ehl sah-bah-doh	until Saturday
hasta luego	ah-stah loo-eh-goh	see you later
adiós	ah-dee-ohs	good-bye
temprano	tehm-prah-noh	early
a veces	ah beh-sehs	from time to time
tarde	tahr-deh	late
hace que	ah-seh keh	ago (+ time)
por semana, día, mes	pohr seh-mah-nah, dee-ah, mehs	by week, day, month
inmediatamente	een-meh-dee-ah-tah-mehn-teh	immediately

What Time Is It?

Every day brings new situations into your life where time counts. Imagine that you became involved in the activities in the following examples. Choose the appropriate expression for each situation.

When you leave work for the day you would say:

If your significant other wants something done right away, it must be done:

If you have a date at 8 p.m. and you arrive at 9 p.m., you arrive:

If you have a job interview at 9 a.m and you arrive at 8 a.m. you arrive:

Where Do You Want to Go?

The most useful idioms are those that tell you how to get to where you want to go. As for me, I always have to know where the nearest restrooms can be found—just in case. Is it upstairs, downstairs, next to someplace important, near, or far (heaven forbid)? Of course, if you haven't learned the proper terms expressing location, you could wind up at the baggage claim instead of the *baño*, or worse yet, at the wrong gender baño. That's why the idioms of location and direction in table 5.3 are quite important for anyone.

Table 5.3 Idioms Showing Location and Direction

Idiom	Pronunciation	Meaning
al lado de	ahl lah-doh deh	next to
a la derecha de	ah lah deh-reh-chah deh	to the right of
a la izquierda de	ah lah ees-kee-ehr-dah deh	to the left of
en casa	ehn kah-sah	at home
al otro lado (de)	ahl oh-troh lah-doh (deh)	on the other side
dar a	dahr ah	to face
enfrente de	ehn-frehn-teh deh	in front of
hacia	ah-see-ah	toward
frente a	frehn-teh ah	facing, opposite
al centro	ahl sehn-troh	downtown
por aquí	pohr ah-kee	this way
por allá	pohr ah-yah	that way

As a Rule

When receiving directions, you can count the number of blocks, *cuadras* (kwah-drahs), you have to go, or traffic lights, *semáforos* (seh-mah-foh-rohs).

What's Your Opinion?

Everyone has an opinion about something. Some people are certainly more expressive than others. Whether you're talking about your flight, the food you ate, the movie you watched, the people you met, or life in general, you will need to know how to properly express your feelings. Table 5.4 should help.

Table 5.4   Expressing Opinions with Idioms

Idiom	Pronunciation	Meaning
en mi opinión	ehn mee oh-pee-nee-ohn	in my opinion
a decir verdad	ah deh-seer behr-dahd	to tell the truth
al contrario	ahl kohn-trah-ree-oh	on the contrary
en vez de	ehn behs deh	instead of
por supuesto	pohr soo-pwehs-toh	of course
claro	klah-roh	of course
está bien	eh-stah bee-ehn	all right
no importa	noh eem-pohr-tah	it does not matter
de acuerdo	deh ah-kwehr-doh	agreed
sin duda	seen doo-dah	without a doubt
es evidente	ehs eh-bee-dehn-teh	it is evident

How Do You Feel?

If you've ever been to the Dominican Republic, you know it can get really hot, especially in the summertime. Suppose you spent some time there at a friend's house. When you try to express your discomfort you say: "Estoy calor." Your host, a very polite person, looks at you and has to refrain from laughing. Why? In English, we use adjectives to describe how we are feeling, thus you've chosen (so you think), "I am hot." However, to express your feelings correctly in Spanish, you must say, "I have hot" (which doesn't mean that you are sick and have a fever). To say, "I am hot," would literally mean to your Spanish host that you are hot to the touch of a hand. Of course this sounds very strange and silly to us, but "Tengo calor" is the expression you need. Remember, our idioms sound very offbeat to others.

You will notice that all the idioms in table 5.5 begin with the verb *tener*, which means *to have*. Of course it will be necessary to conjugate tener as the subject of the sentence changes, but that will be discussed further in Chapter 9.

As a Rule
Note that the verb tener is used to describe physical conditions, whereas in English we use *to be*.

Table 5.5 Idiomatic Physical Conditions

Idiom	Pronunciation	Meaning
tener calor	teh-nehr kah-lohr	to be hot
tener hambre	teh-nehr ahm-breh	to be hungry
tener frío	teh-nehr free-oh	to be cold
tener vergüenza	teh-nehr behr-gwehn-sah	to be ashamed
tener dolor de	teh-nehr doh-lohr deh	to have an ache in
tener miedo de	teh-nehr mee-eh-doh deh	to be afraid of
tener razón	teh-nehr rah-sohn	to be right
tener sed	teh-nehr sehd	to be thirsty
tener sueño	teh-nehr sweh-nyoh	to be sleepy
tener *xx* años	teh-nehr ah-nyohs	to be *xx* years old

Is Everything All Right?

Tell how you feel. Start by using *tengo* (I have) and then add the correct Spanish word to express that you are: sleepy, hot, hungry, thirsty, afraid, correct.

How's the Weather?

It's always a good idea to keep on top of the weather when you travel because most of your plans are probably contingent upon it. Discussing weather in Spanish requires a different verb from the one we are used to in English. So, if you said to your host, "Está frío," he or she would think that you were talking about something you had touched, and not seen. The Spanish use the verb *hacer*, to do, or to make, to describe most weather conditions. In our country, we'd be laughed at if we said: "It makes cold." While in a Spanish-speaking country, however, you must do as the Spanish speakers do, so you will want to study the common weather expressions in table 5.6.

Table 5.6   Idiomatic Weather Expressions

Idiom	Pronunciation	Meaning
hace buen tiempo	ah-seh bwehn tee-ehm-poh	to be nice weather
hace calor	ah-seh kah-lohr	to be hot
hace fresco	ah-seh frehs-koh	to be cool
hace sol	ah-seh sohl	to be sunny
hace viento	ah-seh bee-ehn-toh	to be windy
hace frío	ah-seh free-oh	to be cold
hace mal tiempo	ah-seh mahl tee-ehm-poh	to be bad weather
¿Qué tiempo hace?	keh tee-ehm-poh ah-seh	What is the weather?

Pitfall

Never use hacer when discussing snow or rain. Use *nieva* (nee-eh-bah), it's snowing, and *llueve* (yoo-eh-beh), it's raining.

What's Doing Around the World?

You're trying to decide where you would like to go on vacation. You've got many places in mind that interest you, but what concerns you the most is the weather. You want to make sure that you don't plan your trip to Puerto Rico during the hurricane season, or purchase a ski package for Argentina in December, when they have summer. Take a look at the weather for various cities and countries and express what it is today.

El tiempo en el mundo (*world*) hispano: El quince de enero

	TIEMPO	TEMPERATURA mínima	máxima
Madrid		5°	17°
Sevilla		-3°	4°
Barcelona		20°	27°
Córdoba		7°	17°
México		21°	31°
Panamá		6°	13°
Argentina		16°	26°
Colombia		25°	37°
Perú		2°	6°

En Madrid	En Córdoba	En Argentina
En Sevilla	En México	En Colombia
En Barcelona	En Panamá	En Perú

Body Language

The Spanish people, as a whole, tend to be a very demonstrative lot, using their hands, face, and body language to communicate various emotions and feelings. Many of these gestures allow the speaker to convey certain slang expressions, without having to use words. These movements, of course, play an important role in the language and culture of the people.

1. ¡Bien hecho! (bee ehn eh-choh)

   Well done!

2. ¡No lo hagas! (noh loh ah-gahs)

   Don't do it!

3. ¡Ten cuidado! (tehn kwee-dah-doh)

   Be careful!

4. ¡Qué tacaño! (keh tah-kah-nyoh)

   What a cheapskate!

5. ¡Vamos a comer algo! (bah-mohs ah koh-mehr ahl-goh)

   Let's go eat something!

6. ¡Vamos a tomar (beber) algo! (bah-mohs ah toh-mahr [beh-behr] ahl-goh)

   Let's go get something to drink!

The Least You Need to Know

➤ Every language has its own peculiar idioms that can't be translated word for word.

➤ Idioms can be used to express means of transportation, time, feelings, opinions, directions, and the weather.

➤ Idioms, not slang, will help you speak the language the way it should be spoken.

Chapter 6

Everything You Wanted to Know About Sex

In this chapter you will get a better understanding of how the Spanish view gender. Unlike English, where ladies are ladies, gentlemen are gentlemen, and everything else is neuter, every single noun (person, place, thing, or idea) in Spanish is designated as masculine or feminine, as well as singular or plural. That's right, that taco you're consuming, that ball you're throwing, and that museum you're visiting all have a specific gender. How is the determination made? Sometimes it's obvious, sometimes there are clues, and sometimes it's just downright tricky. This chapter will teach you to make the right connections.

He vs. She

Deciding which gender to use is obvious when you're speaking about a man or a woman. But what if you want to talk about a lovely store you passed the other day? Which gender do you use with *tienda* (store)? You don't know the rules yet, so do you assume that it's feminine because women like to shop more than men? In light of the women's lib movement, you could get into trouble (whether you're male or female) for that sexist presumption. Why not learn the simple tricks contained in this chapter to avoid making errors in gender?

Suppose you want to purchase a tie that you saw in that store. You might assume that *corbata* is masculine because men wear ties more than women. But you would be wrong in your assumption. In fact, *corbata* is a feminine word. How about that dress? It must be feminine, after all, dresses are not for men. Wrong again! The word for dress, *vestido*, is masculine. By now you're probably asking yourself: "How can that be? It doesn't make sense!" You're absolutely correct. For the most part, it makes no sense. Fortunately, however, there are clues to help you with these words, and others like them. And should you come across a noun whose gender is a mystery to you, you can always resort to your trusty Spanish dictionary. Just remember, even if you make a mistake in gender, as long as you have the correct vocabulary word, you'll be understood.

As a Rule
The word *tienda* ends in *a*, and most Spanish words with this ending are feminine.

Noun Markers

All nouns in Spanish have a gender: masculine (m) or feminine (f). They are also singular (sing) or plural (pl). Noun markers help determine these characteristics for any noun. The most common markers, shown in table 6.1, are definite articles expressing "the," and the indefinite articles expressing "a," "an," or "one."

Table 6.1 Singular Noun Markers

Article	Masculine	Feminine
the	el (ehl)	la (lah)
a, an, one	un (oon)	una (oo-nah)

Some nouns in Spanish like those shown in tables 6.2 and 6.3 are very easy to mark because they *obviously* refer to masculine or feminine people:

Table 6.2 Gender-Obvious Nouns

Masculine Noun	Pronunciation	English Meaning	Feminine Noun	Pronunciation	English Meaning
el padre	ehl pah-dreh	the father	la madre	lah mah-dreh	the mother
el abuelo	ehl ah-bweh-loh	the grandfather	la abuela	lah ah-bweh-lah	the grandmother
el chico	ehl chee-koh	the boy	la chica	lah chee-kah	the girl
el amigo	ehl ah-mee-goh	the friend (m)	la amiga	lah ah-mee-gah	the friend (f)
el tío	ehl tee-oh	the uncle	la tía	lah tee-ah	the aunt
el primo	ehl pree-moh	the cousin (m)	la prima	lah pree-mah	the cousin (f)
el hombre	ehl ohm-breh	the man	la mujer	lah moo-hehr	the woman

A few nouns can be either masculine or feminine. All you have to do is simply change their identifier, without changing their spelling, to refer to either gender. Table 6.3 identifies some high-frequency nouns for which this rule applies. For example:

El estudiante estudia. *(male student)*

La estudiante estudia. *(female student)*

Table 6.3 Either Gender Nouns

Noun	Pronunciation	Meaning
artista	ahr-tees-tah	artist
dentista	dehn-tees-tah	dentist
estudiante	ehs-too-dee-ahn-teh	student
joven	hoh-behn	youth
modelo	moh-deh-loh	model

Some nouns are always masculine or feminine despite the gender of the person to whom they refer. Observe the following nouns:

Always Masculine	Always Feminine
bebé *baby*	persona *person*
bombero *firefighter*	víctima *victim*

Some endings help determine the gender of the noun and make marking easier. As you may have noticed in the preceding list, the male nouns end either in *o* or an *e*, and the female nouns all end in *a* (although a feminine noun may end in *e*). If you don't know the gender of a Spanish word, you can usually make a very accurate guess by looking at the vowel with which the word ends. Table 6.5 shows you the gender-identifying endings:

Table 6.4 Gender Identifying Endings

Masculine Endings	Example	Feminine Endings	Example
o	abrigo	a	pluma
ema	tema	ión	lección
consonants (usually)	reloj	dad	ciudad
		tad	libertad
		tud	juventud
		umbre	costumbre
		ie	serie

Of course there are always some exceptions to the rule—just to make sure that you don't get lazy, sloppy, and over-confident. Keep them in mind for future use.

Masculine nouns that end in *a*:

> el clima   (ehl klee-mah)   *the climate*
>
> el día   (ehl dee-ah)   *the day*
>
> el drama   (ehl drah-mah)   *the drama*
>
> el problema   (ehl proh-bleh-mah)   *the problem*
>
> el programa   (ehl proh-grah-mah)   *the program*
>
> el telegrama   (ehl teh-leh-grah-mah)   *the telegram*

Feminine nouns that end in *o*:

> la mano   (lah mah-noh)   *the hand*
>
> la foto (short for *fotografía*)   (lah foh-toh)   *the photo*
>
> la moto   (short for *motocicleta*)   (lah moh-toh)   *the motorcycle*

Masculine nouns that end in *és, r,* or *n* add *a* at the end to form the feminine equivalent. For example:

el francés	*the Frenchman*	la francesa	*the French woman*
el autor	*the author*	la autora	*the authoress*
el alemán	*the German*	la alemana	*the German woman*

Here are two cases where none of those rules apply:

el actor	*the actor*	el emperador	*the emperor*
la actriz	*the actress*	la emperatriz	*the empress*

Note that the accent marks from the masculine nouns in the preceding examples are dropped for the feminine equivalent.

When There's More Than One Noun

When a Spanish noun refers to more than one thing, it, just like in English, must be made plural. But you will see in table 6.6 that it is not enough to simply change the noun in Spanish, the identifier must be made plural as well.

Table 6.5   Plural Noun Markers

English	Spanish	
	Masculine	Feminine
the	los	las
some	unos	unas

Plural Nouns

Forming plural nouns in Spanish is really not that difficult. Most Spanish nouns are made plural by adding an *s* to the singular form:

Singular	Plural	Meaning
el libro	los libros	the books
un libro	unos libros	some books
la mesa	las mesas	the tables
una mesa	unas mesas	some tables

For Spanish nouns that end in a consonant (including *y*), it is necessary to add *es* to the noun to form the plural:

Singular	Plural	Meaning
el mes	los meses	the months
un mes	unos meses	some months
la explicación	las explicaciones	the explanations
una explicación	unas explicaciones	some explanations

For Spanish nouns that end in *z* it is necessary to change the *z* to a *c* and then add *es* to form the plural:

Singular	Plural	Meaning
el pez	los peces	the fish
un pez	unos peces	some fish
la actriz	las actrices	the actresses
una actriz	unas actrices	some actresses

It may be necessary to add or delete an accent mark to maintain the original stress:

el joven	los jóvenes	el examen	los exámenes
el francés	los franceses	la reunión	las reuniones

Except for nouns ending in *és*, no ending is added for nouns ending in *s*:

el martes	los martes
el paréntesis	los paréntesis

In a mixed grouping of male and female people, the masculine plural form of the noun always prevails. For example, *los amigos* can refer to male friends or a group of male and female friends. If there are only females present, use *las amigas*.

Los hijos can refer to sons or children of both genders. If there are only daughters, though, then use *las hijas*.

Some nouns are always plural:

    las gafas   *eyeglasses*

las vacaciones *vacation*

las tijeras *scissors*

Practice Those Plurals

Imagine you've misplaced some things in your hotel room. You know how messy these places can get, especially when you're living out of a suitcase. You started out looking for more than one. You've found one. Now say that you are looking for just one of the items on your list.

Example: llaves *keys*
Busco la llave.
I am looking for the key.

1. lápices *pencils*

2. regalos *gifts*

3. collares *necklaces*

4. paquetes *packages*

5. revistas *magazines*

6. lociones *lotions*

What Have You Learned About Gender?

There's a strong possibility that you're reading this book to gain a knowledge of Spanish that you can use on your job. Or perhaps you'd like a position requiring the use of your new-found knowledge. Read the following employment ads and determine whether the employer is looking for a male or a female employee.

Almacenista y secretaria recepcionista con conocimientos de computadoras, necesita distribuidora textil. Escribir al Apartado Aéreo 8732, Bogotá.

Ejecutivo de cuentas para corredor de seguros. Conocimentos amplios, presentación impecable y relaciones humanas indispensables. Enviar curriculum A.A. 482019, Bogotá.

Buscamos niños modelos para un gran proyecto comercial de televisión, para compañía de gran renombre. No exp. nec. Edad entre 3 meses y 17 años. Llame al: (201) 555-1949.

The Least You Need to Know

➤ There are certain endings that are almost always masculine (*o*, *ema*, consonants) or feminine (*a*, *ión*, *dad*, *tad*, *tud*, *umbre*, *ie*).

➤ Some nouns can be changed from masculine to feminine by adding an appropriate ending.

➤ Nouns ending in a vowel can be made plural by adding *s*; those ending in a consonant require *es*; and those ending in *s* (not *és*) remain unchanged.

Chapter 7

Let's Plan a Trip

In This Chapter

➤ Subject pronouns

➤ Conjugating verb families

➤ How to ask a question

➤ Common regular verbs

In the last chapter you learned how easy it is to tell if a Spanish noun is masculine or feminine, and how simple it is to form plurals. When you want to form a sentence, use a noun or the pronoun that can be used to replace it as the subject. In this chapter you'll learn how to construct simple Spanish sentences by using verb forms (with or without their corresponding subject nouns or pronouns) to talk about a variety of activities.

An excellent way to practice speaking about things to do is to use the language in typical, everyday situations. Imagine that you're on a trip in a Spanish-speaking country. What will you do there? Why, there's something for everyone: cosmopolitan cities, ancient ruins, sandy beaches. What will you see? The choices are endless: cathedrals, museums, parks, bullfights. Whom will you meet? The Spanish-speaking community of South and Central America and Spain. You'll have countless opportunities to use your newfound skills. So, it's time to go on to the basics.

Determining the Subject

Verbs are words that express an act, occurrence, or mode of being. But just as important in a sentence, you need to know what or who is the subject of the verb. The subject may be stated (e.g., "*I* would like to go to the Prado," or "*The tour bus* has just arrived") or understood in a command (as in "Visit the Alhambra," the subject is understood to be *you*). The subject can be a noun or a pronoun that replaces the noun. For example, in the sentence "The toreador is entering the arena," *the toreador* can be replaced with the pronoun *he* to form the new sentence, "He is entering the arena."

Subject Pronouns

Just as in English, subject pronouns in Spanish, shown in table 7.1, are given a person and a number (singular or plural). In Spanish, however, subject pronouns are used far less frequently than they are in English. This is because the verb ending usually indicates the subject quite clearly. In other words, verbs have different endings, depending on who is performing the action. If you listen carefully, you will usually be able to easily determine the subject, even when it is not used in the sentence. You will see that the Spanish only use subject pronouns for:

As a Rule
Although subject pronouns are usually omitted, you will notice that Spanish speakers regularly use the pronouns *usted* and *ustedes* in conversation. In writing, usted is abbreviated as *Ud.* and ustedes as *Uds.*

Ud. es muy inteligente.
You (sing.) are very intelligent.

Uds. son amables.
You (pl.) are very nice.

➤ *Clarity*: to differentiate who is doing the action, in cases where verb forms are the same:

Él (Ella, Ud.) **habla** bien.   *He (She, You) speak(s) well.*

Él descansa mientras **Ud.** trabaja.   *He rests while you work.*

➤ *Emphasis*: to clearly underline the fact that the subject will be performing the action:

Voy a España.   *I'm going to Spain.*

Yo voy a España.   ***I'm** going to Spain.*

➤ *Politeness*: to be extremely formal and to show impeccable manners and deference to an individual:

¡Pase **Ud.**!   *Enter!*

Table 7.1 Subject Pronouns

Person	Singular	Plural
first	yo (yoh) I	nosotros (noh-soh-trohs) we
second	tú (too) you	vosotros (boh-soh-trohs) you

Person	Singular	Plural
third	él (ehl) he	ellos (eh-yohs) they
	ella (eh-yah) she	ellas (eh-yahs) they
	usted (oo-stehd) you	ustedes (oo-steh-dehs) you

As a Rule

Distinctions are made in Spanish to accommodate groups of females only. *Nosotros* becomes *nosotras*, *vosotros* becomes *vosotras* and *ellos* becomes *ellas* when groups of women only are being spoken of. But what happens when there is a mixed group to which you want to refer? Nosotros, vosotros, and ellos are used, regardless of the number of males and females in the group.

Four Ways to Say You!

If you've studied the subject pronoun chart carefully you will notice that there are two singular and two plural forms for the English *you*. *Tú* (singular) and *vosotros* (plural) are used when speaking to a friend, relative, child, or pet. *Tú* and *vosotros* are called *familiar* forms. *Ud.* (singular) and *Uds.* (plural) are used in to show respect to an older person, or when speaking to someone you don't know very well. *Ud.* and *Uds.* are referred to as *polite* forms.

As a Rule

The plural *vosotros* form is used in Spain, since the Spaniards tend to be purists about their language. In the Spanish-speaking countries of Central and South America and the Caribbean, the *ustedes* form is used.

Tú (Usted) versus Vosotros (Ustedes)

Would you use *tú* or *usted*, *vosotros* (in Spain), or *ustedes* (in other Spanish-speaking countries) when speaking to the following people? A doctor? Your cousin? Your friend? A salesman? A woman waiting in line for a bus? Two female friends? Two male friends? A policeman from whom you are asking directions? Your friends?

As a Rule

In English, the subject pronoun *I* is always capitalized, regardless of its position in the sentence. In Spanish, *yo* is only capitalized at the beginning of a sentence.

Yo soy americana.   *I'm American.*

Mi esposo es cubano, pero *yo* soy americana.   *My husband is Cuban, but I'm American.*

Pronouns are very useful because they enable you to speak fluidly without having to constantly repeat the noun. Imagine how tedious it would be to hear "Jorge is Spanish. Jorge is from Madrid. Jorge really knows his way around the country." A better version would be "Jorge is Spanish. He's from Madrid and he really knows his way around the country." Subject pronouns may be used to replace proper nouns (the name of a person or persons) as follows:

Noun	Pronoun
Ricardo	él
Marta	ella
Pedro y Carlos	ellos
Ana y Susana	ellas
Pablo y Carlota	ellos

Which pronoun would you use when speaking about the following people:

Eduardo? Anita? Sara y Beatriz? Gloria? Arturo? Juan y Miguel? Roberto y Lupita? Alba? Blanca? Cristina y Manuel? Paco? Julio y Amalia?

Moving Right Along

You routinely use verbs to express actions, motion, or a state of being. In Spanish, there are two types of verbs: regular and irregular. All regular verbs follow a set pattern of rules, particular to the category under which they fall (i.e., *ir*, *er*, or *ar* verbs). They are very easy to use after you've learned the pattern. Irregular verbs, on the other hand, do not follow a specific pattern and their conjugations must be memorized individually. Fortunately, regular verbs far outnumber those that are irregular. Because you want to get off to a fast but simple start, you will look only at regular verbs in this chapter.

Regular Verbs

The basic "to" form of the verb is referred to as the infinitive, for example: to live, to laugh, to love. In dictionaries of any language, verbs are presented in the infinitive form, that is, the form of the verb before it has been conjugated. Most people are totally unaware that they conjugate verbs in English, never giving this grammatical process a second thought. It just comes naturally, as a result of copying speech patterns when people first learn to talk. *Conjugation*, quite simply, refers to changing the ending of a regular verb or changing the entire form of an irregular verb so that it agrees with the subject. For example, here is the infinitive verb *to sing* (a regular verb in English) conjugated into three of its forms:

    I sing   You sing   He sings

The verb *to be* is an irregular verb. Here it is conjugated in the same manner as *to sing* just was:

    I am   You are   He is

In Spanish, there are three large families of regular verbs—verbs whose infinitives end in *ar*, *er*, or *ir*. All verbs within each family are conjugated in exactly the same manner, so once you've learned the pattern for that family of verbs, you know how to conjugate all regular verbs in that family. The *ar* family is, by far, the largest.

Let's start by taking a look at the *ar* verb family, since you'll be using these verbs frequently. You'll notice immediately that the endings are really quite simple and don't require much time to memorize.

The AR Verb Family

To conjugate *ar* verbs, drop *ar* from the infinitive and then add the following endings:

Pronoun	Verb Ending
yo	o
tú	as
él, ella, Ud.	a
nosotros	amos
vosotros	áis
ellos, ellas, Uds.	an

Hablar—To Speak

Yo habl**o**
I speak

Tú habl**as**
You (sing.) speak

Él, ella, Ud. habl**a**
He, she, you (sing.) speak(s)

Nosotros habl**amos**
We speak

Vosotros habl**áis**
You (pl.) speak

Ellos, Ellas, Uds. habl**an**
They, you (pl.) speak

Conjugation 101

Now you can conjugate any *ar* verb.

Imagine that you are traveling with a tour group to various countries in Central America. Practice the conjugation of *ar* verbs to express what each person is doing on vacation:

Example: mirar (to look at)   Yo **miro** el programa.

1. anunciar   Él _____ el departe del avión.

2. buscar   Ellos _____ la oficina.

3. notar   Nosotros _____ mucho.

4. andar   Yo _____ por el parque.

5. nadar   Vosotros _____ .

The ER Verb Family

Now let's take a look at a family that will also prove very useful and easy to manage. To conjugate *er* verbs, drop *er* from the infinitive and then add these endings:

Pronoun	Verb Ending
yo	o
tú	es
él, ella, Ud.	e
nosotros	emos
vosotros	éis
ellos, ellas, Uds.	en

***Leer*—To Read**

Yo le**o**	Nosotros le**emos**
I read	*We read*
Tú le**es**	Vosotros le**éis**
You (sing.) read	*You (pl.) read*
Él, ella, Ud. le**e**	Ellos, Ellas, Uds. le**en**
He, she, you (sing.) read(s)	*They, you (pl.) read*

Conjugation 102

In the summer, when there are lots of tourists, you'll see many people doing all kinds of different things. Practice *er* verb conjugation by choosing the verb that best completes the sentence and then putting it in its correct form:

comer   *to eat*

correr   *to run*

beber   *to drink*

aprender   *to learn*

deber   *to have to*

responder   *to answer*

> **As a Rule**
> Verbs whose infinitives end in *er* or *ir* have the same endings except for the *nosotros* and *vosotros* forms, where *er* verbs use *e* and *ir* verbs use *i* in their endings.

1. Tú _____ al centro.

2. Ellos _____ en restaurante.

3. Nosotros _____ soda.

4. Ud. _____ a las preguntas.

5. Él _____ frases españolas.

6. Yo _____ firmar (to sign) muchos documentos.

> **As a Rule**
> You will find that there will be times when the subject is followed by two verbs. In these instances, only conjugate the first verb. The second verb remains in the infinitive, such as in these examples:
>
> *continues*

Quiero salir. *I want to go out.*

Sabemos jugar al tenis. *We know how to play tennis.*

Deben ir al centro. *They have to go downtown.*

The IR Verb Family

If you've mastered the *er* verb family, then you will find the *ir* verb family to be a snap. When you study the chart you'll understand why. To conjugate *ir* verbs, drop *ir* from the infinitive and then add these endings:

Pronoun	Verb Ending
yo	o
tú	es
él, ella, Ud.	e
nosotros	imos
vosotros	ís
ellos, ellas, Uds.	en

Decidir—To Decide

Yo decid**o** *I decide*	Nosotros decid**imos** *We decide*
Tú decid**es** *You (sing.) decide*	Vosotros decid**ís** *You (pl.) decide*
Él, ella, Ud. decid**e** *He, she, you (sing.) decide(s)*	Ellos, Ellas, Uds. decid**en** *They, you (pl.) decide*

Conjugation 103

When traveling in a group, some people often want to break away and go off and do their own thing. It's important to them to have some space and spend their time the way they want to. It's a matter of priorities. Using *ir* verbs, express what each tourist does:

1. vivir   Vosotros _____ rápidamente.

2. aplaudir   Ella _____.

3. escribir   Ellos _____ cartas.

4. omitir   Tú _____ mucho.

5. asistir   Él _____ a la conferencia.

6. abrir   Yo _____ una cuenta de banco.

7. descubrir   Nosotros _____ cosas interesantes.

8. recibir   Ana y Linda _____ paquetes.

Ask Me Anything

If you're planning a trip then you'll surely have loads of questions to ask. This section starts with the ones that will give you quick and easy answers: those that require a simple yes or no.

As a Rule

When writing, the Spanish use two question marks: an upside down one (¿) at the beginning of the question, and a standard one (?)at the end.

¿Quieres hacer un viaje conmigo?   *Would you like to take a trip with me?*

In Spanish, there are three ways to ask a question to elicit a yes or no answer: intonation, using the ¿verdad? tag, and by inversion.

Intonation

The easiest way to signify that you're asking a question is to simply change your intonation and raise your voice at the end of the sentence, just like in English. To do this, speak with a rising inflection.

¿(Tú) quieres ir a México?   *Do you want to go to Mexico?*

Notice how your voice starts out lower and gradually keeps rising until the end of the sentence.

The Tags ¿Verdad?, ¿No?, and ¿Está Bien?

Another very simple way to ask a yes/no question is to simply add the tags *¿verdad?* (behr-dahd), *¿no?*, and *¿está bien?* which can mean "really?," "isn't that so?," "is it?," "isn't it?," "are you?," "aren't you?," "do you?," "don't you?," or "all right" at the end of the phrase, such as:

¿Tú quieres ir a México, verdad? (¿no?) (¿está bien?)

You want to go to Mexico, right? (isn't that so? no? don't you?)

Inversion

The third way to form a question is by inversion, a technique whereby the word order of the subject (noun or pronoun) and the conjugated verb form is simply reversed. Once again, you will need to raise your voice at the end of the phrase to indicate that you are, in fact, asking a question.

¿Quieres (tú) ir a México? *Do you want to go to Mexico?*

¿Son Uds. españoles? *Are you Spanish?*

¿Es Juanita de Puerto Rico? *Is Juanita from Puerto Rico?*

Remember, whether you are using intonation or inversion, you are asking for exactly the same information: a yes/sí (see) or no/no (no) answer.

Ask Away

Is it in your nature to be inquisitive about everyone and everything? If you're anything like me, there's always a question on the tip of your tongue. Practice the art of asking away by first properly conjugating the verb for which you have the infinitive and then use intonation, tags, and inversion to satisfy your curiosity.

1. nosotros/hablar demasiado

2. él/asistir a muchos conciertos

3. Uds./comprender mucho

4. María/escribir cartas en español

And the Answer Is...

To answer affirmatively (yes), use *sí* (see) and then give your statement, such as in the following question and answer example:

¿Fuma Ud.?

Sí, fumo.

To answer negatively say *no* (no), and then place *no* (no) before the conjugated verb form. Remember, if there are two verbs, only the first is conjugated:

¿Fuma Ud.?

No, no fumo.

or

No, no quiero fumar.

You can vary your negative responses by using one of these negative expressions:

nunca (noon-kah)   *never*

nada (nah-dah)   *nothing*

nadie (nah-dee-eh)   *no one*

Sentences are made negative in Spanish in one of two ways:

➤ Put the negative word before the conjugated verb:

Nunca fumo.   *I never smoke.*

Nada puedo ver.   *I can't see anything.*

Nadie llega.   *No one is arriving.*

➤ Put *no* before the conjugated verb, and place the negative expression after the entire verb phrase. Notice how this creates a double negative, which is perfectly acceptable in Spanish:

No fumo nunca.   *I never smoke.*

No puedo ver nada.   *I can't see anything.*

No llega nadie.   *No one is arriving.*

When answering a question, a triple negative may even be used:

¿Quieres comer algo?

No, **no** quiero comer **nada**.

Verb Tables

If you want to increase your vocabulary quickly, you'll need to have as many verbs as possible on the tip of your tongue. The cognates in Chapter 3 and the lists of regular verbs in tables 7.2, 7.3, and 7.4 will certainly get you off to a flying start and will help you in many everyday situations.

Table 7.2   Common AR Verbs

Verb	Pronunciation	Meaning
andar	ahn-dahr	to walk
anunciar	ah-noon-see-ahr	to announce
ayudar	ah-yoo-dahr	to help
bailar	bah-ee-lahr	to dance
buscar	boos-kahr	to look for
caminar	kah-mee-nahr	to walk
cocinar	koh-see-nahr	to cook
comprar	kohm-prahr	to buy
dejar	deh-hahr	to let, allow, leave
desear	deh-seh-ahr	to desire
enviar	ehn-bee-ahr	to send
escuchar	ehs-koo-chahr	to listen (to)
estudiar	ehs-too-dee-ahr	to study
expresar	ehks-preh-sahr	to express
firmar	feer-mahr	to sign
funcionar	foonk-see-oh-nahr	to function
ganar	gah-nahr	to win, earn
gastar	gahs-tahr	to spend (money)
hablar	ah-blahr	to speak, talk
hallar	ah-yahr	to find
lavar	lah-bahr	to wash
llegar	yeh-gahr	to arrive
mandar	mahn-dahr	to order
mirar	mee-rahr	to look at

Verb	Pronunciation	Meaning
necesitar	neh-seh-see-tahr	to need
notar	noh-tahr	to note
olvidar	ohl-bee-dar	to forget
organizar	ohr-gah-nee-sahr	to organize
pagar	pah-gahr	to pay
participar	pahr-tee-see-pahr	to participate
preguntar	preh-goon-tahr	to ask
quitar	kee-tahr	to leave, remove
regresar	reh-greh-sahr	to return
reservar	reh-sehr-bahr	to reserve
saludar	sah-loo-dahr	to greet
telefonear	teh-leh-foh-neh-ahr	to phone
tocar	toh-kahr	to touch, play (ins.)
tomar	toh-mahr	to take
viajar	bee-ah-hahr	to travel
visitar	bee-see-tahr	to visit

Table 7.3 Common ER Verbs

Verb	Pronunciation	Meaning
aprender	ah-prehn-dehr	to learn
beber	beh-behr	to drink
comer	koh-mehr	to eat
correr	koh-rrehr	to run
creer	kreh-ehr	to believe
deber	deh-behr	to have to, owe
leer	leh-ehr	to read
prometer	proh-meh-tehr	to promise

Table 7.4 Common IR Verbs

Verb	Pronunciation	Meaning
abrir	ah-breer	to open
asistir	ah-sees-teer	to attend
cubrir	koo-breer	to cover
decidir	deh-see-deer	to decide
escribir	ehs-kree-beer	to write
omitir	oh-mee-teer	to omit
partir	pahr-teer	to divide, share
subir	soo-beer	to go up, climb
vivir	bee-beer	to live

The Least You Need to Know

➤ Subject pronouns are often omitted in Spanish because the verb ending generally indicates who the subject is.

➤ Any verb that follows a subject noun or pronoun must be properly conjugated.

➤ The easiest way to ask a question is to raise your intonation.

Part 2
Travel

Chapter 8

Greetings and Salutations

In This Chapter

➤ Hellos and good-byes

➤ The difference between *ser* (to be) and *estar* (to be)

➤ The present progressive

➤ Professions

➤ Obtaining important information

Chapter 7, "Let's Plan a Trip," helped you prepare for your upcoming trip and now you're ready to test your skills. You should feel pretty confident of your ability to combine subject nouns or pronouns with regular verbs to create simple sentences and to ask basic questions in Spanish. It's time to put your knowledge to work by engaging in a short conversation.

Imagine that you're flying to Spain for that eagerly anticipated, well-deserved vacation you've always dreamed of. Chances are you are seated next to or near a Spanish-speaking person. Don't waste this golden opportunity. Introduce yourself. Get some pointers about places to visit, sites to see, and restaurants to sample. It's the perfect way to get your trip off to a great start.

Friends, Friends, Friends

When you travel, do you get those last minute jitters? Are you nervous about how you'll manage once you've arrived in a country where not everyone speaks your language? To relieve this anxiety, consult your travel agent and your friends. They'll be

As a Rule
Married women in Spanish-speaking countries are referred to and addressed as *señora* (Mrs.). Younger women are addressed as *señorita* (Miss, Ms.).

happy to share their experiences and give you tips, hints, and recommendations on where to stay, eat, and sightsee. If at all possible, speak to someone who has lived or spent considerable time in the country you plan on visiting. What luck if you find that person sitting next to you on the plane. Don't be shy. Take the initiative and strike up a conversation.

Because your fellow traveler is still a stranger to you, good manners dictate that you employ a formal approach. Use some or all of the following phrases as an opening to your conversation:

Phrase	Pronunciation	Meaning
Buenos días	bweh-nohs dee-ahs	Hello
Buenas tardes	bweh-nahs tahr-dehs	Good afternoon
Buenas noches	bweh-nahs noh-chehs	Good evening
señor	seh-nyohr	Mr., sir
señorita	seh-nyoh-ree-tah	Miss, young woman
señora	seh-nyoh-rah	Mrs., madam, woman
Me llamo . . .	meh yah-moh	My name is . . .
¿Cómo se llama?	koh-moh seh yah-mah	What is your name?
¿Cómo está Ud.?	koh-moh ehs-tah oo-stehd	How are you?
Muy bien	moo-ee bee-ehn	Very well
Regular	reh-goo-lahr	So-so

An informal opening conversation (between young people or friends) might use these phrases:

Phrase	Pronunciation	Meaning
¡Hola!	oh-lah	Hi!
Me llamo . . .	meh yah-moh	My name is . . .
¿Cómo te llamas?	koh-moh teh yah-mahs	What's your name?

Phrase	Pronunciation	Meaning
¿Cómo estás?	koh-moh ehs-tahs	How are you?
¿Cómo te va?	koh-moh teh bah	How are you?
¿Qué tal?	keh tahl	How are things?
¿Qué pasa?	keh pah-sah	What's happening?
Nada de particular	nah-dah deh pahr-tee-koo-lahr	Nothing much

To Be or to Be—Wait a Minute!

Many people respond favorably when asked questions about themselves. They like to be the center of attention and enjoy engaging in a friendly conversation. If you'd really like to get to know the person you started talking to, ask him or her a few questions about him/herself: What country or city is he from? How does she feel at the moment? You will need to use the verbs *ser* (to be) and *estar* (to be) to ask any of these questions.

No, you didn't make a mistake while reading. In Spanish, there are two ways to express the verb *to be*. Say your impetuous teenage son was born with blond hair. If someone asked about him, you'd use the verb *ser* to say: "Es rubio" ("He's blond"). But if he's anything like my son's friend, who has green hair one day and pink the next, you might be tempted to respond with the verb *estar* (even though it's not really correct): "Está rubio" to denote the impermanence of the hair color situation. The differences between the two verbs will become apparent by the end of this section. First, let's take a closer look at the conjugations of these verbs.

Just as is in English, ser and estar, to be, are irregular, and all of their forms must be memorized. Because both verbs are used so frequently, learning them should be a top priority. Compare the conjugations in table 8.1. As you will see, there are more irregular forms in Spanish than there are in English.

Table 8.1 The Verbs Ser and Estar (to Be)

SER	ESTAR
yo soy (soh-ee)	yo estoy (ehs-toh-ee)
tú eres (eh-rehs)	tú estás (ehs-tahs)
él, ella, Ud. es (ehs)	él, ella, Ud. está (ehs-tah)
nosotros somos (soh-mohs)	nosotros estamos (ehs-tah-mohs)
vosotros sois (soh-ees)	vosotros estáis (ehs-tah-ees)
ellos, ellas, Uds. son (sohn)	ellos, ellas, Uds. están (ehs-tahn)

How Do I Tell the Difference?

You should have little trouble distinguishing between the two verbs. What will happen if you inadvertently use the wrong one? Nothing much. You'll still be understood.

Use ser in the following situations:

➤ To express origin, nationality, or an inherent characteristic or quality that will not change, for example:

Ana es de Cuba.   *Ana is from Cuba.*

Es cubana.   *She's Cuban.*

Mi hijo es rubio.   *My son is blond.*

El anillo es de oro.   *It's a gold ring.*

➤ To identify the subject or describe the subject's traits that will probably remain unchanged for an extended period of time:

Ricardo es alto.   *Ricardo is tall.*

Mi madre es profesora.   *My mother is a teacher.*

El coche es nuevo.   *The car is new.*

¿Quién es? Soy yo.   *Who is it? It's me.*

➤ To express time and dates:

Son las dos.   *It's two o'clock.*

Es el once de julio.   *It's July 11.*

➤ To express possession:

Es mi libro.   *It's my book.*

Esta cartera es de Juan.   *This is Juan's wallet.*

➤ With certain impersonal expressions:

Es necesario practicar.   *It's necessary to practice.*

Es importante estudiar.   *It's important to study.*

As a Rule

The preposition *de* (of, from), because it shows origin or a descriptive material, is preceded by the verb *ser*.

Somos de México.   *We are from Mexico.*

La casa es de madera.   *The house is made of wood.*

Use estar in the following situations:

➤ To describe a temporary state or condition of the subject:

Yo estoy triste.   *I am sad.*

La casa está sucia.   *The house is dirty.*

Las puertas están cerradas.   *The doors are closed.*

➤ To express location:

El hotel está en la ciudad.   *The hotel is in the city.*

¿Dónde está el aeropuerto?   *Where's the airport?*

➤ To form the progessive tenses (explained later in this chapter).

Estoy cantando.   *I'm singing.*

Está lloviendo.   *It's raining.*

Idioms with Estar

Imagine that you are having a phone conversation with a Spanish friend who says "Estoy a punto de salir." Your Spanish is not quite up to snuff yet and you get insulted. You hear the cognate *punto* (point) and you immediately jump to the conclusion that your friend is making a point of leaving because the phone call is rather boring. In fact, your friend was simply explaining to you that he or she was just about to leave when you called. If something doesn't sound right, it's probably because an idiomatic expression is being used. Table 8.2 will show you some idioms using *estar*.

Table 8.2   Idioms with Estar

Idiomatic Expression	Pronunciation	Meaning
estar a punto de + *infinitive*	ehs-tahr ah poon-toh deh	to be just about + *infinitive*
estar por	ehs-tahr pohr	to be in favor
estar por + *infinitive*	ehs-tahr pohr	to be inclined + *infinitive*
estar de acuerdo (con)	ehs-tahr deh ah-kwehr-doh (kohn)	to agree (with)
estar de vuelta	ehs-tahr deh bwehl-tah	to be back

Now you're ready to proceed with a more extensive conversation with the person sitting next to you on the plane. Begin with one of these phrases:

> Formal: ¿De dónde es Ud.?   *Where are you from?*

> Informal: ¿De dónde eres?   *Where are you from?*

Using Ser and Estar

Imagine that you are sitting in your hotel room having an informal conversation with your traveling companion. The verb *to be* seems to be repeated over and over again.

Should you use *ser* or *estar*? Complete the sentences with the correct form of the necessary verb.

As a Rule
To express that you are from the United States say:

Soy de los Estados Unidos.

soh-ee deh lohs ehs-tah-dohs
oo-nee-dohs

1. Nosotros _____ de países diferentes.

2. Este hotel _____ muy elegante.

3. Sus maletas (suitcases) _____ en la mesa (table).

4. Los restaurantes _____ fabulosos.

5. El museo _____ en la ciudad.

What Are You Doing Right Now?

You're on a plane going to Costa Rica. What are you doing right now? Are you thinking about your jealous friends back home? Maybe you took my advice and are speaking to the person seated next to you. Are you watching a movie or listening to the music being piped through the airline headphones? Perhaps you're just relaxing and tuning out the world. To describe whatever it is that you are doing at the moment (an action in progress) you must use the present progressive tense. Here's an example of the present progressive tense, to which we can all relate, "Right now, I'm soaking in the sun on Condado Beach in Puerto Rico." Don't be scared by the grammatical jargon, the task is easy because you just studied the verb *estar*.

To form the present progressive, use the present tense form of the verb *estar* that corresponds to the subject who is acting. Estar expresses that the subject is doing something. Next choose the verb that gives the action. You will need the gerund (the *ing* form) of this verb. To form the gerund do the following:

➤ For verbs whose infinitive ends in *ar*, drop *ar* and add *ando*.

Infinitive	Present Progressive	English
cant*ar*	cant*ando*	singing

➤ For verbs whose infinitive ends in *er* or *ir*, drop *er* or *ir* and add *iendo*.

Infinitive	Present Progressive	English
com*er*	com*iendo*	eating
escrib*ir*	escrib*iendo*	writing

As a Rule

If a verb whose infinitive ends in *er* or *ir* has a stem ending in a vowel, add *yendo* instead of *iendo*.

Infinitive	Present Progressive	English
le*er*	le*yendo*	reading
o*ír*	o*yendo*	hearing

Some common irregular gerunds that you might find useful are:

Infinitive	Present Progressive	English
decir	diciendo	saying, telling
dormir	durmiendo	sleeping
ir	yendo	going
pedir	pidiendo	asking
seguir	siguiendo	following
venir	viniendo	coming

Now you can follow the simple formula for the formation of the present progressive: *estar* (conjugated) + gerund:

¿Qué estás haciendo?   Estoy escuchando música.
keh ehs-tahs ah-see-ehn-doh   ehs-toh-ee ehs-koo-chahn-doh moo-see-kah
What are you doing?   *I'm listening to music.*

What's Happening Now?

If I could see you on the plane right now, I'd want to know what you are doing. Tell me that you are reading a book, listening to music, eating, singing, speaking Spanish, watching a film, and sleeping.

What's Your Line?

If you want to ask about someone's line of work or answer about your own, you'll need the proper question and answer. In a formal situation use:

   ¿Cuál es su profesión?   *What is your profession?*

In an informal setting use:

   ¿Cuál es tu profesión?   *What is your profession?*

The response to either of these questions would be:

   Soy + your profession.   *I am + your profession.*

Use *ser* to ask about and express the professions provided in table 8.3.

As a Rule

Unless otherwise indicated, change *o* to *a*, or add *a* to a final consonant to get the female counterpart for the jobs listed.

Mi hermana es secretaria.

La señora Rueda es profesora.

Mi tía es jueza.

Table 8.3 Professions

Profession	Spanish Translation	Pronunciation
actor (actress)	actor (actriz)	ahk-tohr (ahk-trees)
cashier	cajero	kah-heh-roh
dentist	dentista (m or f)	dehn-tees-tah
doctor	doctor (m) médico (m)	dohk-tohr meh-dee-koh
electrician	electricista (m or f)	eh-lehk-tree-sees-tah
firefighter	bombero	bohm-beh-roh
hairdresser	barbero	bahr-beh-roh
jeweler	joyero	hoh-yeh-roh
lawyer	abogado	ah-boh-gah-doh
manager	gerente (m or f)	heh-rehn-teh
mechanic	mecánico	meh-kah-nee-koh
musician	músico	moo-see-koh
nurse	enfermero	ehn-fehr-meh-roh
police officer	policía (m or f)	poh-lee-see-ah
postal worker	cartero	kahr-teh-roh
secretary	secretario	seh-kreh-tah-ree-oh
student	estudiante (m or f)	ehs-too-dee-ahn-teh
waitress	camarera	kah-mah-reh-rah

Pitfall

Do not use the indefinite article *un* (*una*) when expressing someone's profession. Simply place the profession after the conjugated form of the verb *ser*, to be.

Soy sastre.   *I am a tailor.*

Ella es camarera.   *She is a waitress.*

I Am Curious

The person next to you seems rather nice. Perhaps she can give you some pointers to help you have a more interesting and enjoyable stay in the country you plan on visiting. You'll need more than simple yes/no answers. What you really want is information. Whatever the situation or problem, you will be able to see it through with the words and phrases in table 8.4.

Table 8.4 Information Questions

Word/Phrase	Pronunciation	Meaning
adónde	ah-dohn-deh	to where
a qué hora	ah keh oh-rah	at what time
a quién	ah kee-ehn	to whom
a qué	ah keh	to what
cuál	kwahl	which
de quién	deh kee-ehn	of, about, from whom
cuánto	kwahn-toh	how much, many
cómo	koh-moh	how
dónde	dohn-deh	where
de dónde	deh dohn-deh	from where
por qué	pohr keh	why
cuándo	kwahn-doh	when
quién*	kee-ehn	who, whom
qué	keh	what

* Note that Spanish does not have separate words to distinguish between who (subject) and whom (object). The word quién *serves for both.*

Obtaining Information the Easy Way

The easiest way to ask an information question is to put the question word immediately before the verbal phrase or thought. If you are using a subject pronoun or noun, you must remember to put it after the conjugated verb. Here are some questions you might want to ask a traveling companion. The familiar tú form (you) is in parentheses (in the cases where it is needed):

¿Con quién viaja Ud. (viajas)?   *With whom are you traveling?*

¿Por qué viaja Ud. (viajas)?   *Why are you traveling?*

¿Cómo viaja Ud. (viajas)?   *How are you traveling?*

¿Qué mira Ud. (miras)?   *What are you looking at?*

¿De dónde es Ud. (eres)?   *Where are you from?*

As a Rule

All *interrogatives* (words that ask questions) in Spanish have accent marks. This distinguishes them from words that are spelled the same but state, rather than ask for information:

¿Dónde vive Pablo?   *Where does Pablo live?*

Yo sé donde él vive.   *I know where he lives.*

Ask as Many as You Can

Read each of the following paragraphs. Ask as many questions as you can, based on the information given to you in each selection. In Paragraph 1, you are asking about Roberto. In Paragraph 2 you must ask Ana questions about herself:

1. Roberto es de los Estados Unidos. Viaja en automóvil con su familia en España. Pasan un mes en España. Desean visitar todas las ciudades importantes. Regresan a Syracuse en septiembre.

2. Me llamo Ana. Soy de Quito. Busco a una amiga por correspondencia americana porque deseo practicar el inglés. Hablo inglés sólamente cuando estoy en clase. El inglés es una lengua muy interesante. Soy una estudiante muy seria.

The Least You Need to Know

➤ Different greetings are used depending on your familiarity with the other person.

➤ The verb *ser* is used to express permanent traits, nationality, origin, time, and dates.

➤ The verb *estar* is used to express location and temporary conditions.

➤ Use the present progressive tense to explain what is going on right now.

Chapter 9

Getting to Know You

In This Chapter

➤ Members of the family

➤ Showing possession

➤ Presenting family and friends

➤ All about *tener* (to have)

➤ Describing people and things

Your conversation in the preceding chapter enabled you to make new friends and introduce yourself. If you're traveling with family members, it's now time to introduce them or help them jump in and join the discussion. Perhaps you will be presented to members of the family of your newfound friend. Be prepared for any and all circumstances.

There's a handsome Hispanic *caballero* (gentleman) in seat 4B or a sensuous, smiling señorita staring at you from across the aisle. You immediately wonder what this person is like. This chapter will help you meet that special someone.

Meet the Family!

While sitting on a tour bus taking us to the *Yunque* (the rain forest in Puerto Rico), I struck up a conversation with a lovely older couple carrying an adorable young child. I went on and on, asking questions about, and admiring and cootchie-cooing their grandson. In retrospect, I really didn't know when to stop. Imagine my overwhelming embarrassment when, at the end of the trip, the gentleman politely took me aside and explained that the child was their son. I learned a very important lesson that day: keep your mouth shut, give the other person an opportunity to talk and never, ever, make assumptions when you meet someone. If you want to prevent a potentially mortifying situation like this, consult table 9.1

Table 9.1 Family Members

Male	Pronunciation	Meaning	Female	Pronunciation	Meaning
abuelo	ah-bweh-loh	grandfather	abuela	ah-bweh-lah	grandmother
padrino	pah-dree-noh	godfather	padrina	pah-dree-nah	godmother
padre	pah-dreh	father	madre	mah-dreh	mother
padrastro	pah-drahs-troh	stepfather	padrastra	pah-drahs-trah	stepmother
hijo	ee-hoh	son, child	hija	ee-hah	daughter
hermano	ehr-mah-noh	brother	hermana	ehr-mah-nah	sister
hermanastro	ehr-mah-nahs-troh	stepbrother	hermanastra	ehr-mah-nahs-trah	stepsister
primo	pree-moh	cousin (male)	prima	pree-mah	cousin (female)
sobrino	soh-bree-noh	nephew	sobrina	soh-bree-nah	niece
tío	tee-oh	uncle	tía	tee-ah	aunt
nieto	nee-eh-toh	grandson	nieta	nee-eh-tah	granddaughter
suegro	sweh-groh	father-in-law	suegra	sweh-grah	mother-in-law
yerno	yehr-noh	son-in-law	yerna	yehr-nah	daughter-in-law
cuñado	koo-nyah-doh	brother-in-law	cuñada	koo-nyah-dah	sister-in-law
novio	noh-bee-oh	boyfriend	novia	noh-bee-ah	girlfriend

You Are Possessed

Don't fret, but you are probably possessed—that is you're somebody's somebody: your parents' child, your friend's friend, your brother's sister, or your sister's brother. There are two ways to show possession in Spanish: by using the preposition *de* or by using possessive adjectives.

Possession with De

As a Rule

No changes are necessary for *de + la*, *de + los*, or *de + las*.

Son los padres *de la* muchacha.

Es la abuela *de los* muchachos.

Es el tío *de las* muchachas.

In English we use *'s*, or *s'* if it is plural, after a noun to show possession. But apostrophes don't exist in Spanish. If you wanted to talk about Santiago's sister, you would have to say "la hermana de Santiago," which translates word-for-word to "the sister of Santiago." To express possession or relationship, the preposition *de* (of), is used and the word order is changed from what we are accustomed to in English.

> Es la madre de Enrique.   *She's Enrique's mother.*

If the possessor is referred to not by name, but by a common noun such as *the boy*, (e.g. "He is the boy's father") then, in Spanish, *de* contracts with the definite article *el* to become *del* (of the):

> Es el padre *del* muchacho.

Now that you understand how to use *de* to express possession, how would you say: Miguel's aunt? the boys' father? the girls' grandparents? Lupe's uncle? The family's cousins? The nephew's girlfriend?

Cultural Tidbit

When you are introduced to Spanish-speaking people, it is important to understand how they use last names. Spanish speakers usually have more than one *apellido* (ah-peh-ee-doh), last name: *el apellido paterno* (the first last name, which comes from the father's last name, and *el apellido materno* (the mother's maiden name). A person always identifies him- or herself by the paternal surname.

Let's take the example of Gabriel Cruz Rodríguez. Gabriel may also call himself Gabriel Cruz y Rodríguez (*y* means *and*). Gabriel's father's last name was Cruz and his mother's maiden name was Rodríguez.

continues

Suppose that Gabriel marries Sarita Sánchez (father) González (mother). After the wedding, Sarita would normally drop her maternal last name (González) and then add her husband's last name to that of her father. She would now be called Sarita Sánchez de (of) Cruz.

It may seem very unfair and the ultimate in *machismo*, but Spanish women remained forever linked to the men in their lives.

Let's say that some time later, Gabriel and Sarita have a child, Alfredo. Alfredo's apellidos would be as follows: Alfredo Cruz (father's first apellido, considered to be his last name) Sánchez (his mother's maiden name). He might also call himself Alfredo Cruz y Sánchez.

What's in an Apellido?

Look carefully at the following family tree. What is the apellido paterno of Ramón Vega Pérez? of Ana Fernández Rueda? What is the apellido materno of Ramón? of Ana? What will Ana's married name be? What name will she drop? If Ramón and Ana have a son named Diego what will his name be? What about their daughter María? What would your name be if you followed this tradition?

Ramón Vega Pérez   Ana Fernández Rueda

Diego   María

Possessive Adjectives

The possessive adjectives *my, your, his, her,* etc. are used to show that something belongs to someone. In Spanish, possessive adjectives agree with the nouns they describe (the person or thing that is possessed) and not with the subject (the person possessing them). See how this compares with English:

ENGLISH	SPANISH
He speaks with his parents.	Habla con sus padres.
He speaks with their parents.	Habla con sus padres.
She speaks with our uncle.	Habla con nuestro tío.

Sus padres (his or their parents) is used because *sus* agrees with the word *padres*, which is plural and can mean his, her, its, your, or their. *Nuestro tío* (our uncle) is used because *nuestro* agrees with the word *tío*, which is masculine. This difference makes Spanish somewhat tricky for English speakers. Just remember that it is important to know the gender (masculine or feminine) of the thing possessed. When in doubt, look it up! Table 9.2 summarizes the use of possessive adjectives.

Table 9.2 Possessive Adjectives

Used Before Masculine Nouns		Used Before Feminine Nouns		
Singular	**Plural**	**Singular**	**Plural**	**English**
mi	mis	mi	mis	my
tu	tus	tu	tus	your
su	sus	su	sus	his, her, your, its
nuestro	nuestros	nuestra	nuestras	our
vuestro	vuestros	vuestra	vuestras	your
su	sus	su	sus	their

What Do You Prefer?

State your preference for each of the following items. Use the first two examples to learn how to structure your responses.

Mi actor favorito es _____.   Mis actores favoritos son _____.

    actrices

    canción (song)

    restaurantes

    deporte (sport)

    color

    película (film)

Let Me Introduce You

When I travel, I like to speak to as many new and different people as I can. It's truly amazing how many great tips you can get and how much money you can save by just listening to the experiences and advice of others. If you want to introduce yourself, here's the way to start:

To introduce yourself you would say:

Buenos días. Me llamo _____.

bweh-nohs dee-ahs. meh yah-moh

Hello. My name is _____.

You might ask about a companion:

¿Ud. conoce (Tú conoces) a mi primo, Paco?

oo-stehd koh-noh-seh (too koh-noh-sehs) ah mee pree-moh pah-koh

Do you know my cousin, Paco?

If the answer to this question is *no*, then you would say:

Quiero presentarle (presentarte) a mi primo, Paco.

kee-eh-roh preh-sehn-tahr-leh (preh-sehn-tahr-teh) ah mee pree-moh pah-koh

I'd like to introduce you to my cousin, Paco.

Or you might respond:

Le (Te) presento a mi primo, Paco.

leh (teh) preh-sehn-toh ah mee pree-moh pah-koh

Let me present you to my cousin, Paco.

To express pleasure at having met someone in a formal situation, you might say:

> Mucho gusto (en conocerle [te]).
>
> moo-choh goo-stoh (ehn koh-noh-sehr-leh [teh])
>
> *It's nice to meet (know) you.*

If you are introduced to someone less formally, it would be alright to say:

> Encantado (m)/Encantada (f).
>
> ehn-kahn-tah-doh
>
> *Delighted.*

The correct reply to an introduction is:

> El gusto es mío.
>
> ehl goos-toh ehs mee-oh
>
> *The pleasure is mine.*

Can You?

You have been sitting next to a very interesting traveler for quite some time now. Unfortunately, this person has been very engrossed in reading a magazine. You've decided to make your move and strike up a conversation. You'll even try that tired old line of asking if you know someone in common. Grab the moment and see if you can do the following:

1. Introduce yourself to someone.
2. Ask someone if they know a member of your family.
3. Introduce a member of your family to someone.
4. Express pleasure at having met someone.
5. Respond to someone saying how glad they are to have met you.

Taking the Conversation a Little Further

That wasn't difficult at all. Now your curiosity has gotten the best of you and you'd really like to take the conversation a little further. Maybe you want to discuss your marital situation, your age, or just ramble on about your family and friends. If you want to strike up a friendship, you have to keep the conversation flowing. A verb that you will find most helpful is *tener*, to have. Like the verbs *ser* and *estar*, to be, tener is an irregular verb and all of its forms (as seen in table 9.3) must be memorized:

Table 9.3 Conjugating Tener (to Have)

Conjugated Form of Tener	Pronunciation	Meaning
Yo tengo	tehn-goh	I have
Tú tienes	tee-eh-nehs	You have
Él, Ella, Ud. tiene	tee-eh-neh	He, She, one has
Nosotros tenemos	teh-neh-mohs	We have
Vosotros tenéis	teh-neh-ees	You have
Ellos, Ellas, Uds. tienen	tee-eh-nehn	They have

Idioms with Tener

In Chapter 4, many idioms with *tener* that express physical conditions were presented. To refresh your memory, review Chapter 4.

You should now be prepared for some different idioms with *tener*. Imagine that you have arrived at your destination and have spent the past 45 minutes at the airport taking care of some necessary business. You're tired and hungry and all you want to do is get to your hotel and start your vacation. You want to find the exit and you want to find it now. Spanish is a very easy language, just add the letter *o* and whatever you say will sound okay—right? You approach a distinctive looking couple and decide to try out what you remember from your high school days and ask: "¿Tiene éxito?" The couple looks at you in a strange way and replies: "Sí," and walks away, somewhat confused. You just asked if they were successful and are no closer to your exit than you were a minute ago. To avoid this type of mistake, study the other tener idioms in table 9.4:

Table 9.4 Idioms with Tener

Idiom	Pronunciation	Expression
tener cuidado	teh-nehr kwee-dah-doh	to be careful
tener éxito	teh-nehr ehk-see-toh	to be successful
tener ganas de	teh-nehr gah-nahs deh	to feel like
tener lugar	teh-nehr loo-gahr	to take place
tener prisa	teh-nehr pree-sah	to be in a hurry
tener que + *inf.*	teh-nehr keh	to have to + *inf.*
tener suerte	teh-nehr swehr-teh	to be lucky

Make sure to conjugate the verb when you use it in context, such as in the following examples:

Yo siempre tengo cuidado.   *I'm always careful.*

Nosotros tenemos éxito.   *We are successful.*

¿Tú tienes ganas de salir?   *Do you feel like going out?*

Using Tener

From the following list of idioms, determine which one goes with each of the sentences that follow to appropriately complete the thought. Then conjugate tener so that the verb agrees with the subject.

tener cuidado	tener éxito
tener suerte	tener lugar
tener prisa	tener dolor de estómago

1. Nosotros _____ cuando vamos a la playa.

2. La fiesta _____ el 6 de septiembre.

3. El doctor gana mucho dinero. Él _____.

4. Mis hermanos comen demasiado. Ahora ellos _____.

5. Yo tengo un profesor de español excelente. Yo _____.

6. Ya es tarde y tú tienes una cita. Tú _____.

What's He/She Like?

Your conversation with the person sitting next to you is becoming increasingly more intimate as the flight continues. What if you were asked to describe yourself? What would you want to say? Are you a romantic? Do you consider yourself patient? Do your friends consider you to be an introvert or an extrovert? If you want to describe a person, place, thing, or idea in detail, you must use adjectives. Spanish adjectives always agree in gender (masculine or feminine) and number (singular or plural) with the nouns or pronouns they modify. In other words, all the words in a Spanish sentence must conform. Notice the difference between the adjectives in the two examples below:

Su padre está contento.   *Her father is happy.*

Su madre está contenta.   *Her mother is happy.*

Fortunately for you, adjectives follow the same, or almost the same rules for gender and plural formation as the nouns you studied in Chapter 6.

Gender of Adjectives

Most adjectives form the feminine by simply replacing the *o* ending of the masculine singular form with an *a*, as shown in table 9.5. Remember the sound changes as well, the final *o* sound (oh) of the masculine changes to the *a* sound (ah) in the feminine.

Table 9.5   Forming Feminine Adjectives

Masculine	Pronunciation	Feminine	Meaning
alto	ahl-toh	alta	tall
atractivo	ah-trahk-tee-boh	atractiva	attractive
bajo	bah-hoh	baja	short
bonito	boh-nee-toh	bonita	pretty
divertido	dee-behr-tee-doh	divertida	fun
enfermo	ehn-fehr-moh	enferma	sick
extrovertido	ehks-troh-behr-tee-doh	extrovertida	extroverted
feo	feh-oh	fea	ugly
guapo	gwah-poh	guapa	pretty
impulsivo	eem-pool-see-boh	impulsiva	impulsive
introvertido	een-troh-behr-tee-doh	introvertida	introverted
listo	lees-toh	lista	ready
malo	mah-loh	mala	bad
moreno	moh-reh-noh	morena	dark-haired, dark-skinned
nuevo	nweh-boh	nueva	new
pequeño	peh-keh-nyoh	pequeña	small
rico	ree-koh	rica	rich
rubio	roo-bee-oh	rubia	blond
simpático	seem-pah-tee-koh	simpática	nice
tímido	tee-mee-doh	tímida	shy
viejo	bee-eh-hoh	vieja	old

Refer to Chapter 3 for more adjectives.

If an adjective already ends in an *e*, *a*, or a consonant, it is not necessary to make any changes at all. Both the masculine and feminine forms are spelled and pronounced exactly the same as in table 9.6:

Table 9.6 Adjectives Ending in E, A, or a Consonant

Adjectives Ending in *E*			Adjectives Ending in *A*		
Adjective	**Pronunciation**	**Meaning**	**Adjective**	**Pronunciation**	**Meaning**
alegre	ah-leh-greh	happy	egoísta	eh-goh-ees-tah	selfish
amable	ah-mah-bleh	nice	idealista	ee-deh-ah-lees-tah	idealistic
eficiente	eh-fee-see-ehn-teh	efficient	materialista	mah-teh-ree-ah-lees-tah	materialistic
independiente	een-deh-pehn-dee-ehn-teh	independent	optimista	ohp-tee-mees-tah	optimistic
inteligente	een-teh-lee-gehn-teh	intelligent	pesimista	peh-see-mees-tah	pessimistic
paciente	pah-see-ehn-teh	patient	realista	reh-ah-lees-tah	realistic
pobre	poh-breh	poor			
responsable	rehs-pohn-sah-bleh	responsible			
triste	trees-teh	sad			
valiente	bah-lee-ehn-teh	brave			

Adjectives Ending in a *Consonant*					
Adjective	**Pronunciation**	**Meaning**	**Adjective**	**Pronunciation**	**Meaning**
cortés	kohr-tehs	courteous	joven	hoh-behn	young
cruel	kroo-ehl	cruel	normal	nohr-mahl	normal
emocional	eh-moh-see-oh-nahl	emotional	sentimental	sehn-tee-mehn-tahl	sentimental
fácil	fah-seel	easy	tropical	troh-pee-kahl	tropical

As a Rule

Adjectives of nationality, although they end in a consonant, add *a* to form the feminine:

español   *española*

francés   *francesa*

alemán   *alemana*

Adjectives that end in *or*, add *a* to form the feminine:

trabajador   *trabajadora*

hablador   *habladora*

encantador   *encantadora*

More Than One? What Are They Like?

Adjectives are also often made plural in the same way as nouns.

➤ When the singular form of the adjective ends in a vowel, simply add an *s*:

Singular	Plural
alto	altos
alta	altas
egoísta	egoístas
grande	grandes

➤ If an adjective ends in a consonant, add *es*:

Singular	Plural
fácil	fáciles
emocional	emocionales
sentimental	sentimentales
popular	populares

The Right Position

In Spanish, descriptive adjectives are generally placed after the nouns they modify. Compare this with English where the opposite is done:

un hombre interesante   *an interesting man*

Adjectives of description may be placed before the noun to emphasize the quality of the characteristic being described:

Juan tiene malos sueños.   *Juan has bad dreams.*

Anita tiene bellos ojos.   *Anita has beautiful eyes.*

When used before the noun, *bueno* becomes *buen*, *grande* becomes *gran*, and *malo* becomes *mal*.

Esteban es un buen muchacho.   *Stephen is a good boy.*

As a Rule
Y (and) becomes *e* before a word beginning with the vowel sound *i*.

Héctor es un hombre amable e interesante.

Hector is a nice, interesting man.

Complete the Descriptions

Of course you have an opinion about everything that you're not at all shy to express. Tell how you feel about all the things and people in the following list. Remember that the verb *ser* requires that you describe a typical, permanent characteristic.

1. El Prado es un museo _____.

2. Las películas españolas son _____.

3. El presidente de los Estados Unidos es un hombre _____.

4. Las tiendas de Madrid son _____.

5. Las corridas de toros son _____.

Personal Ads

Read the following personal ads taken from a few Spanish magazines and newspapers. Describe the person writing the ad and the type of person being sought.

PERSONAL ADS	
1. Abogado norte americano y director de galerías de arte, alto, atractivo, sofisticado, 47. Busca amorosa Joven, educada, 28-42, cabello largo, preferiblemente que hable algún inglés. Para romance, matrimonio y familia. Manhattan.	2. Chileno, 28, 6', 166 libras. Me gusta la música romántica, bailar, deportes y estudiar. Deseo conocer Dama, 25-35, comprensiva, buen humor, inteligente, honesta, para fines de amistad.
3. Dama De 40, trabajadora, cariñosa, simpática, desea conocer Caballero brasileño con las mismas cualidades, para una bonita amistad o fines serios.	4. Dominicana, 37, divorciada, 2 niños, busca Compañero para la vida, 35-40, 5'10" o más, trabajador, divertido, buen sentido del humor, que no fume.

The Least You Need to Know

➤ There are no apostrophes in the Spanish language.

➤ To show possession in Spanish use *de* or a possessive adjective. The adjective must agree with the person or thing possessed.

➤ *Tener* is an important irregular verb that has several idiomatic uses.

➤ Adjectives agree in number and gender with the nouns they describe and are usually placed after the noun they modify.

Finally, We're at the Airport

You've really accomplished quite a bit so far: you've planned your trip, introduced yourself and your family or friends, and struck up a conversation with someone you just met. Perhaps you've been successful in obtaining the names of some fabulous restaurants, attractions you don't want to miss, or even the phone number of someone who would be thrilled to show off his hometown.

Once you're on the ground and have deplaned, you'll find that there are many things to do before you can catch a ride to wherever you are staying. Your first stop may be the passport check. Then it's off to retrieve your bags so that you can pass uneventfully through customs. You'll certainly want to pick up some of the local currency (pesos, pesetas, bolívares, etc.) before you choose a means of transportation to your destination. You will be able to achieve all this and more by the time you finish this chapter.

Inside the Plane

The person next to you is blowing smoke rings in your face, is carrying his pet lizard in his shirt pocket, and has his headset turned up to the max (and you don't like his taste in music). You *must* change your seat. And while you have the stewardess's attention, you'd like to ask some questions about takeoff and landing. This section gives you what you need to solve any problems like this and get the information you need.

The Plain Plane

Once inside the airplane, you will hear the person making the announcements refer to many items in and around the plane. Generally, this is done to make every traveler aware of the necessary safety precautions that could save lives. If you have any questions or doubts, the words in table 10.1 will help you get information and solve any airplane problem.

Cultural Tidbit

In the airport, you'll often see a sign that says *Bienvenido*, which means *Welcome*.

Table 10.1   Inside the Plane

Aiport Term	Spanish Translation	Pronunciation
airline	la aerolínea	lah ah-eh-roh-lee-neh-ah
airline terminal	la terminal	lah tehr-mee-nahl
airplane	el avión	ehl ah-bee-ohn
airport	el aeropuerto	ehl ah-eh-roh-pwehr-toh
aisle	el pasillo	ehl pah-see-yoh
by the window	cerca de la ventana	sehr-kah deh lah behn-tah-nah
crew	el equipo	ehl eh-kee-poh
to deboard, exit	salir	sah-leer
emergency exit	la salida de emergencia	lah sah-lee-dah deh eh-mehr-hehn-see-ah
gate	la salida	lah sah-lee-dah
landing	el aterrizaje	ehl ah-teh-rree-sah-heh
life vest	el chaleco salvavidas	ehl chah-leh-koh sahl-bah-bee-dahs
(no) smokers	(no) fumadores	noh foo-mah-doh-rehs

Aiport Term	Spanish Translation	Pronunciation
on the aisle	en el pasillo	ehn ehl pah-see-yoh
row	la fila	lah fee-lah
seat	el asiento	ehl ah-see-ehn-toh
seat belt	el cinturón de seguridad	ehl seen-too-rohn deh seh-goo-ree-dahd
takeoff	el despegue	ehl dehs-peh-geh
to smoke	fumar	foo-mahr
trip	el viaje	ehl bee-ah-heh

Airline Advice

To make your flight more enjoyable and comfortable, airlines give certain advice that they would like their passengers to follow. Read some of the tips the airlines suggest. Can you tell what rules and regulations are being explained to you?

La FAA exige que todo equipaje de mano que se traiga abordo de aviones se guarde en un compartimiento alto especial para ello, debajo del asiento del pasajero, o bien en depósitos generales para guardar equipaje durante el despegue y el aterrizaje. Para su mayor conveniencia, en todos nuestros aviones hay compartimientos altos y muchos tienen también depósitos generales para guardar equipaje.

➤ **Artículos de Valor en Su Equipaje**

No incluya en su equipaje artículos de valor (dinero, joyas, etc.) ni documentos como pasaportes.

Dichos artículos no están sujetos a indemnización en caso de pérdida o extravío.

➤ **Artículos Frágiles**

No debe incluir en su equipaje artículos frágiles o de fácil deterioro. Dichos artículos no están sujetos a indemnización en caso de daños.

On the Inside

The plane has landed and everyone rushes to leave and to take care of all the necessary chores. Expect to find signs everywhere pointing you and leading you in various directions. Where should you go first (after your identity has been verified and it has been established that you're not an international jewel thief, or worse)? Because it will probably take some time for your bags to arrive, you might want to stop at a money exchange. Or, if you're anything like me, you'll probably head for the nearest *baños* (bathrooms).

Table 10.2 gives you all the words you'll need to know once you're in the airport as well as outside on the way to your first destination!

Table 10.2   Inside the Airport

Airport Term	Spanish Translation	Pronunciation
arrival	la llegada	lah yeh-gah-dah
baggage claim area	el reclamo de equipaje	ehl reh-klah-moh deh eh-kee-pah-heh
bathrooms	los baños	lohs bah-nyohs
bus stop	la parada de autobús	lah pah-rah-dah deh ow-toh-boos
car rental	el alquiler de carros	ehl ahl-kee-lehr deh kah-rrohs
carry-on luggage	el equipaje de mano	ehl eh-kee-pah-heh deh mah-noh
cart	el carrito	ehl kah-rree-toh
departure	la salida	lah sah-lee-dah
destination	la destinación	lah dehs-tee-nah-see-ohn
elevators	los ascensores	lohs ah-sehn-soh-rehs
entrance	la entrada	lah ehn-trah-dah
exit	la salida	lah sah-lee-dah
flight	el vuelo	ehl bweh-loh
gate	la puerta	lah pwehr-tah
information	las informaciones	lahs een-fohr-mah-see-oh-nehs
lost and found	la oficino de objetos perdidos	lah oh-fee-see-nah deh ohb-heh-tohs pehr-dee-dohs
to miss the flight	perder el vuelo	pehr-dehr ehl bweh-loh
money exchange	el cambio de dinero	ehl kahm-bee-oh deh dee-neh-roh
passport control	el control de pasaportes	ehl kohn-trohl deh pah-sah-pohr-tehs
porter	el portero	eh pohr-teh-roh
security check	el control de seguridad	ehl kohn-trohl deh seh-goo-ree-dahd
stop-over	la escala	lah ehs-kah-lah
suitcase	la maleta	lah mah-leh-tah
taxis	los taxis	lohs tahk-sees
ticket	el boleto	ehl boh-leh-toh

Cultural Tidbit

El Aeropuerto Internacional de México Benito Juárez, is one of the most important centers of air traffic in the world. Millions of tourists pass through this airport each year and are treated to a picturesque view of Mexico City. Because high mountains surround this capital city, pilots are given very special training to make the difficult landing. Because the airport is some distance from the city, travelers take the subway, bus, taxi, or a *colectivo* (where people going in the same direction share the price of a van or car).

Signs Everywhere

Bomb scares and terrorist threats have airline security on constant red alert. Don't even try joking about weapons with airline personnel, they'll immediately flag you for a search. There are signs all over the airport giving the traveler warnings, tips, and regulations that must be followed. It is of utmost importance that you are cognizant of what is and what is not allowed. Should you break a rule unintentionally, it can be a mighty unpleasant experience to be approached by the policía who is speaking a language in which your abilities are limited. The following text are examples of information you might see on signs in any airport servicing a large Spanish-speaking population. Read them carefully and then match each sign with the information it gives you, provided in the bulleted list that follows:

A.

CONSEJOS A LOS PASAJEROS

Postar armas en el avión está terminantemente prohibido por ley.

Las reglas en vigor imponen la inspección de los pasajeros y de su equipaje al momento de pasar por seguridad.

Esta inspección puede ser rehusada. Los pasajeros que se rehusen a pasar por esta inspección no van a ser autorizados a pasar por el control de seguridad.

B.

Los carritos para cargar el equipaje están reservados para los pasajeros; su utilización fuera del aeropuerto está prohibida.

C.

ATENCIÓN:

Para su seguridad, todos objetos abandonado puede ser destruído por la policía.

Le pedimos cordialmente a los pasajeros que conserven su equipaje consigo.

97

D.

> ATENCIÓN: No ponga su seguridad en peligro. No acepte ningún equipaje de otra persona.

E.

> Por favor presente todo su equipaje al registro, incluyendo su equipaje de mano.

F.

> *TRANSPORTE DE ARMAS DE FUEGO*
>
> Las armas de fuego transportadas dentro de su equipaje deben estar descargadas y declaradas.
>
> Los pasajeros que transporten una arma sin declarar o sin descargar son sujetos a una multa de mil dólares o su equivalente.

Which sign is telling you that

➤ If you leave something behind it might be destroyed? ___

➤ All of your baggage will be checked, even carry-ons? ___

➤ You can be searched for hidden weapons? ___

➤ You may carry a weapon if you declare it? ___

➤ You can only use the baggage cart within the airport? ___

➤ You shouldn't carry a suitcase for someone else? ___

What's the Message?

Perhaps you've chosen to travel to a Spanish-speaking country and you want to make sure that you're not bringing in anything that will be dangerous or offensive. You don't want to risk a thorough Customs inspection. Read the following restrictions and see if you can determine what will alert the authorities that you might pose a risk.

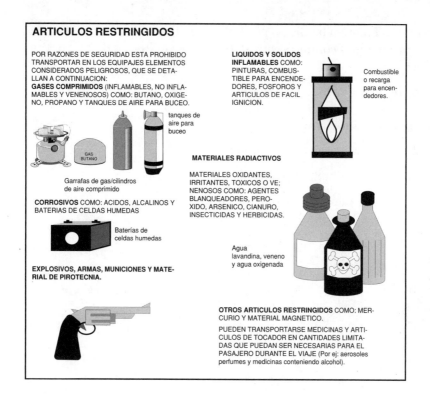

Going, Going, Gone...

The irregular verb *ir*, to go, will certainly come in handy if you need directions at the airport, or anywhere else for that matter. When you want to tell someone exactly where it is you want to go, refer to the conjugation of *ir* in table 10.3 and commit it to memory.

Table 10.3   Conjugating Ir (to Go)

Conjugated Form of Ir	Pronunciation	Meaning
yo voy	boy	I go
tú vas	bahs	you go
él, ella, Ud. va	bah	he, she, you, one goes
nosotros vamos	bah-mohs	we go
vosotros vais	ba-ees	you go
ellos, ellas, Uds. van	bahn	they go

Ir is generally followed by the preposition *a* (to). If the location to which the subject is going is masculine, *a* contracts with *el* (the) to become *al* (to the), as in the following example:

Yo voy al aeropuerto.   *I'm going to the airport.*

No changes are necessary with *a la*, *a los*, or *a las*:

Vamos a la salida.   *We're going to the gate.*

Van a los ascensores.   *They are going to the elevators.*

¿Vas a las ventanas?   *Are you going to the windows?*

As a Rule

Use *ir + a* to express going to a city, state, or country:

Voy a Nueva York.   *I'm going to New York.*

Ana va a Florida.   *Anna is going to Florida.*

¿Van a México?   *Are they going to México?*

As a Rule

Use *ir + en* to express the many different ways to go someplace:

Yo voy a España en avión.   *I'm going to Spain by plane.*

The only exception is:

ir a pie   to go by foot

Vamos a casa a pie.   *We walk home.*

Can You Tell Me How to Get...?

It's so easy to become disoriented in a large, bustling airport after a tiring journey. No doubt you will find it necessary to ask for directions at some point. Here are some easy ways of asking:

¿Dónde está la salida?
dohn-deh ehs-tah lah sah-lee-dah
Where is the exit?

La salida, por favor.
lah sah-lee-dah pohr fah-bohr
The exit, please.

¿Dónde están los taxis?
dohn-deh ehs-tahn lohs tahk-sees
Where are the taxis?

Los taxis, por favor.
los tahk-sees pohr fah-bohr
The taxis, please.

If you're not sure if the airport has the facilities you are looking for, or if you just want to know if they are nearby, use the word *hay* (Is there, Are there, There is, There are...). *Hay* is probably one of the most useful words in the Spanish language. This is how it works to both ask and answer questions:

¿Hay baños por aquí?
ah-ee bah-nyohs pohr ah-kee
Are there bathrooms nearby?

Hay baños al lado de la entrada.
ah-ee bah-nyohs ahl lah-doh deh lah ehn-trah-dah
There are bathrooms next to the entrance.

Giving and Receiving More Complicated Directions

Suppose the place you are looking for is out of pointing distance and is not nearby. In this case you'll need more specific directions. The verbs in table 10.4 will be very helpful in getting you where you want to go, or perhaps, in letting you help someone else who is lost.

Table 10.4 Verbs Giving Directions

Verb	Pronunciation	Meaning
bajar	bah-hahr	to go down
caminar	kah-mee-nahr	to walk
continuar	kohn-tee-noo-ahr	to continue

continues

Table 10.4 Continued

Verb	Pronunciation	Meaning
cruzar	kroo-sahr	to cross
doblar	doh-blahr	to turn
ir	eer	to go
pasar	pah-sahr	to pass
seguir	seh-geer	to follow, continue
subir	soo-beer	to go up
tomar	toh-mahr	to take

In order to give you proper directions, a person in the know has to give you a command. Because you are being told where to go or what to do, the subject of the command is *you*. In English, the subject *you* is understood and is not used. In Spanish, although often omitted, the subject pronoun for *you* may be used in the command. You have already learned that there are four ways to say *you* in Spanish: (the familiar *tú* and *vosotros* forms, and the polite *Ud.* and *Uds.* forms. It is highly unlikely that you will be commanding a family member or friend, so let's concentrate on the formal commands.

To form commands of regular verbs using Ud.:

1. Drop the *o* ending from the yo form of the present tense of the verb you're using.

2. If the verb is an *ar* infinitive verb, add an *e*.

    If the verb is an *er* or *ir* infinitive verb, add an *a*.

If you want to use Uds. as your subject, just add an *n* to the *Ud.* form. Here's how it's done:

Infinitive	Present Tense Yo Form	Formal Commands Singular (Ud.)	Plural (Uds.)	Meanings
tomar	tomo	tome	tomen	take
leer	leo	lea	lean	read
abrir	abro	abra	abran	open

Here are some examples:

¡Tome el autobús!   *Take the bus.*

¡Lea este folleto!   *Read this brochure.*

¡Abran sus maletas!   *Open your suitcases.*

As a Rule
Spanish requires an upside down exclamation mark (¡) at the beginning of an emphasized command, as well as at the end.

Some Spanish verbs have an irregular yo form. You have already seen this with tener. You will come across others in later chapters. These verbs will follow the same rules for the formation of commands. Look for these verbs in the future: *decir* (to say), *hacer* (to do), *poner* (to put), *salir* (to go out), and *venir* (to come). Here is how it works with tener:

| | **Present Tense** | **Formal Commands** | |
Infinitive	Yo Form	Singular (Ud.)	Plural (Uds.)
tener	tengo	tenga	tengan

And here is an example of it being used in a command:

¡Tengan cuidado!   *Be careful.*

Three important verbs that you will find extremely useful and that are irregular in the command form are:

| | **Formal Commands** | |
Verb (Meaning)	Singular (Ud.)	Plural (Uds.)
dar (to give)	Dé	Den
ir (to go)	Vaya	Vayan
ser (to be)	Sea	Sean

Here is an example of ir being used in a command:

¡Vaya al aeropuerto ahora!   *Go to the airport now.*

Using Commands

Before you will be able to readily receive or give commands, you'll need a little practice. This will certainly make your life a lot easier should you ever need directions. Complete the following exercise by filling in the missing command forms as well as their meanings:

Verb	Ud.	Uds.	Meaning
ir	_____	_____	_____
continuar	_____	_____	_____
seguir*	¡Siga!	_____	_____
bajar	_____	_____	_____
caminar	_____	_____	_____
subir	_____	_____	_____
pasar	_____	_____	_____
tomar	_____	_____	_____
doblar	_____	_____	_____
cruzar*	¡Cruce!	_____	_____

* These verbs, and others ending in car, gar, zar, *and* guir, *have special spelling changes that will be explained in Chapter 11. Once you have learned the Ud. form, however, Uds. should be a snap for you.*

Prepositions

Prepositions are used to show the relation of a noun to another word in a sentence. Refresh your memory with the idiomatic expressions for direction and location in Chapter 4, which are, in fact, prepositional phrases. Then add these simple prepositions in table 10.5, which might also be useful for giving or receiving directions:

Table 10.5   Prepositions

Preposition	Pronunciation	Meaning
a	ah	to, at
alrededor (de)	ahl-reh-deh-dohr (deh)	around
antes (de)	ahn-tehs (deh)	before
cerca (de)	sehr-kah (deh)	near
contra	kohn-trah	against
de	deh	of, from, about
debajo (de)	deh-bah-hoh (deh)	under
delante (de)	deh-lahn-teh (deh)	in front (of)
después (de)	dehs-pwehs (deh)	after

Preposition	Pronunciation	Meaning
detrás (de)	deh-trahs (deh)	behind, in back (of)
en	ehn	in
encima (de)	ehn-see-mah (deh)	above
entre	ehn-treh	between, among
frente a	frehn-teh ah	opposite, facing
hacia	ah-see-ah	toward
lejos (de)	leh-hohs (deh)	far (from)
para	pah-rah	for, in order to
por	pohr	by, through
sin	seen	without
sobre	soh-breh	on, upon

Contractions

In certain cases, contractions form with the prepositions *a* and *de*, whether they are used alone or as part of a longer expression. *A + el* becomes *al* and *de + el* becomes *del*. For example:

> Hablo al hombre.   *I speak to the man.*

> Hablo del hombre.   *I speak about the man.*

As a Rule

There are no contractions with *la*, *los*, and *las*.

Hablo a la muchacha, a los hombres, y a las mujeres.
I speak to the girl, the men, and the women.

Por vs. Para

Since both *por* and *para* can mean for, there is often much confusion about when to use each. Keep in mind that even if you use the wrong word, you'll still be understood because your meaning will be, more or less, clear. Besides, Spanish speakers are probably used to us gringos who make this mistake fairly often. Still, the main differences that you should keep in mind are the following:

Por Indicates	Para Indicates
motion Paso **por** el aeropuerto. *I pass by the airport.*	**destination to a place** El avión sale **para** Madrid. *The airplane leaves for Madrid.*
means, manner Viajo **por** tren. *I travel by train.*	**destination to a recipient** Este regalo es **para** mi esposo. *This gift is for my husband.*
a period of time Trabajo **por** la noche. *I work at night*	**a time limit** La cita es **para** el lunes. *The appointment is for Monday.*
frequency; in exchange for Salgo una vez **por** semana. *I go out once a week.* Son dos libros **por** $20. *They are two books for $20.*	**purpose** Es un billete **para** entrar. *It's an admission ticket.*

Are You Dazed and Confused?

Did you ever get directions from someone and shake your head as if you understood where to go. The only trouble was that there were so many rights and lefts and so much pointing, that you lost track in the middle and then just pretended to know what to do. You'll find the phrases in table 10.6 to be an invaluable aid if you need to have something repeated, or if you need more information.

Table 10.6   Expressing Lack of Understanding and Confusion

Expression	Pronunciation	Meaning
Con permiso	kohn pehr-mee-soh	Excuse me
Yo no comprendo	yoh noh kohm-prehn-doh	I don't understand
Yo no te oígo	yoh noh teh oy-goh	I don't hear you
Repita por favor	reh-pee-tah pohr fah-bohr	Please repeat it
Hable más despacio	hah-bleh mahs dehs-pah-see-oh	Speak more slowly
¿Qué dijó?	keh dee-hoh	What did you say?

Tip

Always be polite. After getting directions from a Spanish-speaking person you should say: "Muchas gracias" (moo-chahs grah-see-ahs), "Thank you." The answer you will probably receive is "De nada" (deh nah-dah), "You're welcome."

The Least You Need to Know

➤ The irregular verb *ir* is used to give directions.

➤ To form commands of regular verbs, start with the present tense yo form, drop the *o* and add *e* for *ar* verbs and *a* for *er* and *ir* verbs.

➤ Leaving out the subject (tú, Ud., vosotros, or Uds.) when you give a command is optional.

➤ If you don't understand what is being said to you, don't be afraid to say "Yo no comprendo. Repita por favor."

Chapter 11

Let's Get to the Hotel

In This Chapter

➤ Getting around town

➤ Renting an affordable car

➤ Cardinal numbers

➤ How to tell time

Maneuvering your way through passport control, baggage claim,, and customs may take a bit of time. Although you're probably quite tired and travel-worn, be patient. Despite your honest face and harried look, the people in charge have a job to do and are just trying to be efficient.

Hopefully your travel agent has provided you with transfers (transportation to your final destination) as part of your travel package. If so, expect a bus, car, or taxi to be waiting to whisk you away. Look for the driver carrying a sign bearing your name or the name of your hotel. If not, then it's up to you to find your own way. The choices available to you will be presented in this chapter.

The Way to Go

Buses, subways, trains, taxis, and cars will usually be available to get you where you want to go. Before making a choice, consider what is of foremost importance to you. If money is tight and you're traveling light, you might opt for a bus, subway, or train. If you're in a big hurry and the cost is no object, take a cab. If it's comfort you want and you're an experienced international driver, you might want to rent a car. Weigh all the pros and cons and make the decision that's best for you.

Method of Transportation	Pronunciation	Meaning
el coche	ehl koh-cheh	car
el automóvil	ehl ow-toh-moh-beel	car
el carro	ehl kah-rroh	car
el taxi	ehl tahk-see	taxi
el autobús	ehl ow-toh-boos	bus
el tren	ehl trehn	train
el metro	ehl meh-troh	subway

Cultural Tidbit

If you opt for public transportation in Madrid, you will be pleased to find that it is inexpensive, efficient, and runs frequently. Numbers are used to clearly mark bus stops (*la parada de autobús*—lah pah-rah-dah deh ow-toh-boos). You must hail for the bus to stop; buses don't stop automatically at every stop on the route. There are no free transfers, but the fare is so cheap that you won't mind this minor inconvenience. If you need a free bus map (*Plano de la Red*—plah-noh deh lah rehd), they are available at designated kiosks in front of major tourist attractions and hotels. Most buses run from 6 a.m. until midnight. Some, however, do provide 24-hour service.

There are subway systems in Madrid and Barcelona that can be proud of their cleanliness (no graffiti), comfort, safety, and economy. In fact, the eleven metro lines in Madrid, with interchangeable points, are a popular means of transportation. Maps (*el plan del Metro*— ehl plahn dehl meh-troh) indicate by numbers and different colors the various subway routes. They are available without charge at metro stops, hotels, department stores, tourist offices, and other convenient spots. Transfers from one subway line to another are free, and connections are indicated by *correspondencia* (koh-rrehs-pohn-dehn-see-ah) signs. You may transfer as often as you like on one ticket, provided that you do not exit to the street. To navigate the *metro*, find the *línea* (lee-neh-ah) you need. Look in the direction you want to go and find the name of the last station. Follow the signs indicating that station. The metro is open seven days a week from 6:00 a.m. until 1:30 a.m.

You can buy single metro tickets (*un billete sencillo*—oon bee-yeh-teh sehn-see-yoh) or in a pack of ten (*un billete de diez viajes*—oon bee-yeh-teh deh dee-ehs bee-ah-hehs). Tourist tickets (*un metrotour de tres días* or *de cinco días*—oon meh-troh-toor deh trehs *or* seen-koh dee-ahs), available through travel agencies, tourist offices, and subway stations, enable you to choose unlimited bus, subway, and train travel for three or five consecutive days. A monthly commuter pass (*una tarjeta de abono transportes*—oo-nah tahr-heh-tah deh ah-boh-noh trahns-pohr-tehs) is another option.

Choosing the Best Means of Transportation

If you're going to Madrid or Mexico City, from the airport, public transportation is very convenient. You might decide, however, to take a taxi. Those with meters impose surcharges for luggage, night fares, and holiday fares. You might also opt for the public service taxis, known as a *gran turismos* (grahn too-rees-mohs), that are unmetered and have higher rates than those for regular taxis. Should this be your choice, it would be wise to ask in advance for the fare to your destination.

In Mexico City, orange colored taxis have the number of their taxi stand painted on their doors and can be called by phone. Yellow cabs, as they do here in the United States, simply cruise for passengers. Due to the rapid rise in inflation, taxis don't have set prices. It is best to fix the rate with the *chofér* (choh-fehr) before the trip.

Don't forget that you can also travel very economically by taking *un colectivo* (oon koh-lehk-tee-boh), a car or van that you share with others who have the same destination or who are going in your general direction.

Spanish train fare is a best-buy in Europe because it is the most inexpensive train fare in Europe. *Una Tarjeta Turística* (oo-nah tahr-heh-tah too-rees-tee-kah—Tourist Card), available only to non-residents, permits unrestricted travel, without kilometer limitation on any line, and without having to pay supplements. The card can be for first- or second- class travel and its price varies depending on the duration of travel time requested: 8, 15, or 22 days. A Eurail Pass can be purchased in the United States and provides unlimited travel rights. Its price varies depending upon whether you choose 15, 25, 40, 60, or 90 days of travel.

Go-Go Verbs and Others with Spelling Changes

You might decide to *hacer una excursión* (ah-sehr oo-nah ehks-koor-see-ohn), go on an outing by subway, bus, train, or car. Whatever means of transportation you choose (*escoger*—ehs-koh-hehr), it's sure to be the right one for you. If you would like to use the verbs given in this paragraph (and others similar to them) while planning a trip, you will have to learn their idiosyncrasies and irregularities.

Go-Go verbs are regular or irregular verbs whose yo form ends in *go* instead of *o*. Because these are all high-frequency verbs, it would be best to spend a little time familiarizing yourself with the correct yo forms.

Let's start with verbs that are regular in all forms except yo:

Verb	Meaning	Yo Form	Remaining Conjugations
hacer	to make, do	yo ha*go*	haces, hace, hacemos, hacéis, hacen
poner	to put	yo pon*go*	pones, pone, ponemos, ponéis, ponen
salir	to leave, go out	yo sal*go*	sales, sale, salimos, salís, salen
traer	to bring	yo trai*go*	trae, traes, traemos, traéis, traen
valer	to be worth	yo val*go*	vales, vale, valemos, valéis, valen

As a Rule

Use hacer to express the following:

Phrase	Pronunciation	Meaning
hacer la maleta	ah-sehr lah mah-leh-tah	to pack
hacer una pregunta	ah-sehr oo-nah preh-goon-tah	to ask a question
hacer un viaje	ah-sehr oon bee-ah-heh	to take a trip
hacer una visita	ah-sehr oo-nah bee-see-tah	to pay a visit

For the irregular go-go verbs, just concentrate on the yo form for the time being. You will see the complete conjugations of these verbs in later chapters.

Verb	Meaning	Yo Form
decir	to tell, say	yo di*go*
oír	to hear	yo oi*go*
tener	to have	yo ten*go*
venir	to come	yo ven*go*

Other spelling changes occur in regular verbs in order to preserve the original sound of the verb. These changes occur before an *o* or an *a* and enable the consonant to be pronounced correctly. Since all of the verbs you will be looking at end in *er, ir,* or *uir,* the only subject that will be affected in the present tense is *yo.* Why is that? Quite simply because only *ar* infinitives have verbs forms that end in *a.* All yo forms end in *o* and so, therefore, all yo forms will be affected. Verbs that end in *er, ir,* and *uir* will have an *a* ending in the command form, because opposite letters are used to form commands.

Pitfall
Remember to drop the accent from the yo form of oír before adding *go.*

¿Oyes algo?
Do you hear something?

Yo no oigo nada.
I don't hear anything.

Now take a closer look at some of these verbs that you might want to use with regularity:

Verbs ending in *cer* and *cir* change *c* to *z* before *o* or *a*:

Verb	Meaning	Affected Conjugation	Unaffected Conjugations	Command
convencer	to convince	yo conven*z*o	convences convence convencemos convencéis convencen	Conven*za* Ud. Conven*zan* Uds.

Verbs ending in *ger* and *gir* change *g* to *j* before *o* or *a*:

Verb	Meaning	Affected Conjugation	Unaffected Conjugations	Command
escoger	to choose	yo esco*j*o	escoges escoge escogemos escogéis escogen	Esco*ja* Ud. Esco*jan* Uds.

continues

113

continued

Verb	Meaning	Affected Conjugation	Unaffected Conjugations	Command
recoger	to pick up	yo reco*jo*	recoges recoge recogemos recogéis recogen	Reco*ja* Ud. Reco*jan* Uds.
dirigir	to direct	yo diri*jo*	diriges dirige dirigimos dirigís dirigen	Diri*ja* Ud. Diri*jan* Uds.

Verbs ending in *guir* change *gu* to *g* before *o* or *a*:

Verb	Meaning	Affected Conjugation	Unaffected Conjugations	Command
seguir	to follow, continue	yo si*go*	sigues sigue seguimos seguís siguen	Si*ga* Ud. Si*gan* Uds.

Which or What Do You Prefer?

When you're on a trip and meet someone new, there are many questions you'll want to ask them: "What's your name? address? profession? What activities do you like?" The list is endless. In Spanish there are two words that can mean either *which* or *what*: *cuál* or *qué*. So how do you know when to use each?

As a Rule

The verb *seguir*, as you may have noticed, undergoes another spelling change, as well. This change will be explained in greater detail in Chapter 12.

➤ *¿Qué?* asks what? when referring to a description, definition, or explanation and asks which? when used before a noun.

¿Qué es esto?   *What's that?*

¿Qué estás haciendo?   *What are you doing?*

¿Qué libro lee Ud.?   *Which book are you reading?*

➤ *¿Cuál? ¿Cuáles?* asks what? before the verb *ser* (to be) (except when asking for the definition of a word) and means which (one)? before the preposition *de*.

¿Cuál es su nombre? *What's your name?*

¿Cuáles deseas? *Which (ones) do you want?*

So if you want to go off on your own, expect to ask questions using ¿qué? and ¿cuál? to get you where you want to go. Do you feel confident to ask what bus you need to take and what its number is? These are the sentences you would need:

¿Qué autobús tomo? ¿Cuál es su número?
keh ow-toh-boos toh-moh kwahl ehs soo noo-meh-roh
Which bus do I take? *What is its number?*

As a Rule
¿Cuál? becomes *¿cuáles?* when the noun to which you are referring is plural.

¿Cuál es la fecha?
What is the date?

¿Cuáles son los meses del año?
What are the months of the year.

Using ¿Qué? and ¿Cuál?

Now that you've learned about ¿qué? and ¿cuál? you can ask all those nosy questions that you didn't know how to express before. Imagine that you are speaking to the passenger next to you on the plane. Ask him/her for the following information: name, address, what he/she is reading, what his/her nationality is, and which subway line to take to Mexico City.

Fill'er Up

Do you feel daring enough to rent a car at *un alquiler de coches*? Make sure to compare the rates and models available at several rental agencies before making a final decision. Bear in mind that the cost of fuel in other countries is generally more than double the price back home. The following phrases will prove very useful when renting a car:

Quiero alquilar un *make of car*
kee-eh-roh ahl-kee-lahr oon
I'd like to rent a…

Prefiero el cambio automático.
preh-fee-eh-roh ehl kahm-bee-oh ow-toh-mah-tee-koh
I prefer automatic transmission.

¿Cuánto cuesta por día (por semana) (por kilómetro)?
kwahn-toh kwehs-tah pohr dee-ah (pohr seh-mah-nah) (por kee-loh-meh-troh)
How much does it cost per day (per week) (per kilometer)?

¿Cuánto es el seguro?
kwahn-toh ehs ehl seh-goo-roh
How much is the insurance?

¿Está incluída la gasolina?
ehs-tah een-kloo-ee-dah lah gahs-oh-lee-nah
Is the gas included?

¿Acepta Ud. tarjetas de crédito? ¿Cuáles?
ah-sehp-tah oo-stehd tahr-heh-tahs deh kreh-dee-toh kwah-lehs
Do you accept credit cards? Which ones?

You've decided to rent a car, that's great, but take a tip from me: carefully inspect the car, inside and out, because you never know what might go wrong once you're on the road. Make sure there is *un gato* (oon gah-toh)—a jack, and *una goma de repuesto* (oo-nah goh-mah deh reh-pwehs-toh)—a spare tire in the trunk. It's no fun to get stuck on a road in the middle of nowhere.

Table 11.1 Exterior Car Parts

Car Part	Spanish Translation	Pronunciation
battery	la batería	lah bah-teh-ree-ah
bumper	el parachoques	ehl pah-rah-choh-kehs
carburetor	el carburador	ehl kahr-boo-rah-dohr
door handle	el tirador de puerta	ehl tee-rah-dohr deh pwehr-tah
fan	el ventilador	ehl behn-tee-lah-dohr
fender	el guardafango	ehl gwahr-dah-fahn-goh
gas tank	el tanque	ehl tahn-keh
headlight	el faro delantero	ehl fah-roh deh-lahn-teh-roh
hood	la capota	lah kah-poh-tah
license plate	la placa de matrícula	lah plah-kah deh mah-tree-koo-lah
motor	el motor	ehl moh-tohr
radiator	el radiador	ehl rah-dee-ah-dohr
tail light	el faro trasero	ehl fah-roh trah-seh-roh
tire	la goma, la llanta	lah goh-mah, lah yahn-tah
transmission	la transmisión	lah trahns-mee-see-ohn
trunk	el baúl	ehl bah-ool
wheel	la rueda	lah roo-eh-dah
winshield wiper	el limpia parabrisas	ehl leem-pee-ah pah-rah-bree-sahs

Table 11.2 Interior Car Parts

Car Part	Spanish Translation	Pronunciation
accelerator	el acelerador	ehl ah-seh-leh-rah-dohr
directional signal	el direccional	ehl dee-rehk-see-oh-nahl
gear shift	el cambio de velocidades	ehl kahm-bee-oh deh beh-loh-see-dah-dehs
horn	la bocina	lah boh-see-nah
ignition	el contacto	ehl kohn-tahk-toh
radio	la radio	lah rah-dee-oh
steering wheel	el volante	ehl boh-lahn-teh
brakes	los frenos	lohs freh-nohs
clutch pedal	el embrague	ehl ehm-brah-geh
glove compartment	la guantera	lah gwahn-teh-rah
hand brake	el freno de mano	ehl freh-noh deh mah-noh
air bag	la bolsa de aire	lah bohl-sah deh ah-ee-reh
anti-lock brakes	los frenos anti-bloqueantes	lohs freh-nohs ahn-tee bloh-keh-ahn-tehs

In Europe, distance is measured by kilometers. Look at table 11.3 for the approximate equivalents:

Table 11.3 Distance Measures (Approximate)

Miles	Kilometers
.62	1
3	5
6	10
12	20
31	50
62	100

Point Me in the Right Direction

Imagine that you've rented a car but have ignored learning the road signs. Your vacation would certainly be somewhat spoiled if you received a traffic ticket while visiting a

As a Rule
Use the word *el semáforo* (*una luz de tráfico*) to refer to a traffic light. Don't forget to stop *al semáforo rojo* (at the red light) and to go *al semáforo verde* (at the green light).

foreign country. Take a moment to read these road signs. You might find that some of them are tricky and not at all as obvious as they first seem.

My husband and I, with kids in tow, were traveling from the city of Santo Domingo to the lovely Casa de Campo resort at the other side of the island. When we got to a fork in the road, which just sort of crept up on us a little too quickly, I screamed, "Go this way!" He went that way. How much easier life would have been had I just said: "Go north." Don't be like me, know your compass directions.

Guarded railroad crossing	Yield	Stop	No U-turn	No passing	Border crossing
Right of way	Dangerous intersection ahead	Gasoline (petrol) ahead	Traffic signal ahead	Speed limit	Traffic circle (roundabout) ahead
Parking	No vehicles allowed	Dangerous curve	Minimum speed limit	All traffic turns left	End of no passing zone
Pedestrian crossing	Oncoming traffic has right of way	No bicycles allowed	One-way street	Detour	
No parking allowed	No entry	No left turn	Danger ahead / Entrance to expressway	Expressway ends	

Direction	Pronunciation	Meaning
al norte	ahl nohr-teh	to the North
al este	ahl ehs-teh	to the East
al sur	ahl soor	to the South
al oeste	ahl oh-ehs-teh	to the West

As a Rule

Remember, if one thing on your car doesn't work, you'd have to say something like:

El motor no funciona.   *The motor doesn't work.*

El motor is the singular subject of your sentence and the verb must agree with it.

In the event that more than one thing is malfunctioning, you must remember to make the verb plural, to agree with the plural subject, for example:

Los frenos no funcionan.   *The brakes don't work.*

How Much Is It?

If you want to be able to express what bus, subway, or flight you are taking, or to find out just how big a dent that rent-a-car is going to make in your pocket, you must learn the Spanish numbers in table 11.4. They will also come in handy when you want to tell time.

Table 11.4   Cardinal Numbers

Number	Spanish Translation	Pronunciation
0	cero	seh-roh
1	uno	oo-noh
2	dos	dohs
3	tres	trehs
4	cuatro	kwah-troh
5	cinco	seen-koh
6	seis	seh-ees

continues

Table 11.4   Continued

Number	Spanish Translation	Pronunciation
7	siete	see-eh-teh
8	ocho	oh-choh
9	nueve	noo-eh-beh
10	diez	dee-ehs
11	once	ohn-seh
12	doce	doh-seh
13	trece	treh-seh
14	catorce	kah-tohr-seh
15	quince	keen-seh
16	dieciséis	dee-ehs-ee-seh-ees
17	diecisiete	dee-ehs-ee-see-eh-teh
18	dieciocho	dee-ehs-ee-oh-choh
19	diecinueve	dee-ehs-ee-noo-eh-beh
20	veinte	behn-teh
21	veintiuno	behn-tee-oo-noh
22	veintidós	behn-tee-dohs
30	treinta	treh-een-tah
40	cuarenta	kwah-rehn-tah
50	cincuenta	seen-kwehn-tah
60	sesenta	seh-sehn-tah
70	setenta	seh-tehn-tah
80	ochenta	oh-chen-tah
90	noventa	noh-behn-tah
100	ciento	see-ehn-toh
101	ciento uno	see-ehn-toh oo-noh
200	dos cientos	dohs see-ehn-tohs
500	quinientos	kee-nee-ehn-tohs
1,000	mil	meel
2,000	dos mil	dohs meel
100,000	cien mil	see-ehn meel
1,000,000	un millón	oon mee-yohn
2,000,000	dos milliones	dohs mee-yoh-nehs

Cultural Tidbit

The Spanish, like many other European cultures, write the number one with a little hook on top: 1. In order to distinguish a 1 from the number 7, they put a line through the 7 when they write it: 7̶.

In numerals and decimals, where we use commas, the Spanish use periods, and vice versa:

ENGLISH	SPANISH
1,000	1.000
.25	0,25
$9.95	$9,95

(To avoid confusion, the English style of writing numbers will be used throughout this book.)

Spanish numbers are not too tricky. But look carefully at table 11.5, and then be aware of these rules:

➤ The conjunction *y* (and) is used only for compound numbers between 30 and 99. Use of y with numbers between 16 and 29 is very rare.

diez y seis libros	16 books
veinte y un días	21 days
veinte y nueve dólares	$29

➤ *Uno* (one) is used only when counting and becomes *un* before a masculine noun and *una* before a feminine noun:

uno, dos, tres…	*one, two, three…*
un hombre y una mujer	*a man and a woman*
treinta y un muchachos	*thirty-one boys*
veintiuna muchachas	*twenty-one girls*

➤ When written as one word, the numbers 16, 22, 23, and 26 have accents:

17 diecisiete and 21 veintiuno

but

16 dieciséis, 26 veintiséis

➤ In compounds of cien (doscientos, trescientos) there must be agreement with a feminine noun:

doscientos hombres *two hundred men*

trescientas mujeres *three hundred women*

➤ *Ciento* becomes *cien* before nouns and before the numbers *mil* and *millones*. Before all other numbers, ciento is used:

cien libros *one hundred books*

ciento veinte carros *one hundred and twenty cars*

cien mil personas *one hundred thousand people*

cien millones de dólares *one billion dollars*

➤ *Un*, although not used before ciento or mil, is used before millón. If a noun follows millón, put *de* between millón and the noun.

cien pesetas *one hundred pesetas*

mil quinientos años *fifteen hundred years*

un millón de habitantes *a million inhabitants*

What's Your Number?

Phone numbers in Madrid consist of seven numbers grouped in one group of three and two pairs. The regional code for Madrid is (1). This number must be dialed before the phone number when calling from outside the city. In South American, Central American, and Caribbean countries the phone numbers are grouped in three pairs. How would you ask the operator for these numbers: 325 11 72; and 45 67 89?

What Time Is It?

Learning Spanish numbers makes it relatively easy to learn how to tell time, as explained in table 11.5. A question that you will probably ask or hear very often is:

¿Qué hora es?
keh oh-rah ehs
What time is it?

Table 11.5 Telling Time

The Time	Spanish Translation	Pronunciation
It is 1:00.	Es la una.	ehs lah oo-nah
It is 2:05.	Son las dos y cinco.	sohn lahs dohs ee seen-koh
It is 3:10.	Son las tres y diez.	sohn lahs trehs y dee-ehs
It is 4:15.	Son las cuatro y cuarto.	sohn lahs kwah-troh ee kwahr-toh
It is 5:20.	Son las cinco y veinte.	sohn lahs seen-koh ee behn-teh
It is 6:25.	Son las seis y veinticinco.	sohn lahs seh-ees ee behn-tee-seen-koh
It is 7:30.	Son las siete y media.	sohn lahs see-eh-teh ee meh-dee-ah
It is 7:35. (25 min. to 8)	Son las ocho menos veinticinco.	sohn lahs oh-choh meh-nohs behn-tee-seen-koh
It is 8:40. (20 min. to 9)	Son las nueve menos veinte.	sohn lahs noo-eh-beh meh-nohs behn-teh
It is 9:45. (15 min. to 10)	Son las diez menos cuarto.	sohn lahs dee-ehs meh-nohs kwahr-toh
It is 10:50. (10 min. to 11)	Son las once menos diez.	sohn lahs ohn-seh meh-nohs dee-ehs
It is 11:55. (5 min. to noon)	Son las doce menos cinco.	sohn lahs doh-seh meh-nohs seen-koh
It is noon.	Es mediodía.	ehs meh-dee-oh-dee-ah
It is midnight.	Es medianoche.	ehs meh-dee-ah-noh-cheh

➤ Use *es* for *it is* when it is one o'clock. For the other numbers, because they are plural, use *son*.

➤ To express the time after the hour, use *y* and the number of minutes past the hour.

➤ To express time before the next hour (after half past), use *menos + the number of the following hour*:

Son las tres menos cuarto.   *It's 2:45.*

It is not unusual to hear the time expressed as follows:

Son las dos y cuarenta y cinco.   *It's 2:45.*

Knowing how to ask for and give the time is not enough if you want to schedule activities. You might want to know *at what time* something is planned. Imagine that you asked someone at what time a sporting event was taking place and the person responded: "Hace dos horas." You might mistake this as meaning "at two o'clock" or "there are two hours before the match." You might think that means you have two hours before the play begins. In fact, you've missed the match because it started two hours ago. The expressions in table 11.6 will help you to deal with time.

Table 11.6 Time Expressions

Time Expressions	Spanish Translation	Pronunciation
a second	un segundo	oon seh-goon-doh
a minute	un minuto	oon mee-noo-toh
an hour	una hora	oo-nah oh-rah
in the morning	de la mañana	deh lah mah-nyah-nah
in the afternoon (p.m.)	de la tarde	deh lah tahr-deh
in the evening	de la noche	deh lah noh-cheh
at what time?	¿a qué hora?	ah keh oh-rah
at exactly...	a la...en punto	ah lah... ehn poon-toh
at about 2:00	a eso de las dos	ah eh-soh deh lahs dohs
a quarter of an hour	un cuarto de hora	oon kwahr-toh deh oh-rah
a half hour	una media hora	oo-nah meh-dee-ah oh-rah
in an hour	en una hora	ehn oo-nah oh-rah
in a couple of hours	en un par de horas	ehn oon pahr deh oh-rahs
in a second (flash)	en un abrir y cerrar de ojos	ehn oon ah-breer ee seh-rrahr deh oh-hohs
in a while	dentro de un rato	dehn-troh deh oon rah-toh
often	a menudo	ah meh-noo-doh
until 2:00	hasta las dos	ahs-tah lahs dohs
before 3:00	antes de las tres	ahn-tehs deh lahs trehs
after 3:00	después de las tres	dehs-pwehs deh lahs trehs
since what time?	¿desde qué hora?	dehs-deh keh oh-rah
since 6:00	desde las seis	dehs-deh lahs seh-ees

Time Expressions	Spanish Translation	Pronunciation
an hour ago	hace una hora	ah-seh oo-nah oh-rah
per hour	por hora	pohr oh-rah
late (in arriving)	en retraso	ehn reh-trah-soh
on time	a tiempo	ah tee-ehm-poh
good-bye	adiós	ah-dee-ohs

The Least You Need to Know

➤ The verbs *hacer, poner, salir, traer,* and *valer* are regular in all forms except yo, where they end in *go*.

➤ The verbs *decir, oír, tener,* and *venir* are irregular verbs whose yo form also ends in *go*.

➤ *¿Qué?* and *¿cuál? (¿cuáles?)* are used to ask what? and which? *¿Qué?* is used before nouns and *¿cuál? (¿cuáles?)* is used before the preposition *de* and before the verb *ser*, except when giving a definition.

➤ Tell time easily by giving the hour and the number of minutes past the hour.

Hooray We're at the Hotel

To get to your hotel, you've found a mode of travel that caters to your pocketbook and your needs. No matter how you've chosen to travel, remember to look out the window as you ride along. Taking in your surroundings right from the start will give you the lay of the land and help you get your bearings. Before you know it, your hotel will suddenly appear, off in the distance. As you approach, you just feel that you've made a wise choice.

For some, the bare necessities are acceptable when it comes to travel accommodations. After all, why pay for luxurious décor when you plan on spending most of your time outside your room? The money saved would be better spent on entertainment and souvenirs. For others, everyday comforts represent the bare minimum they'd accept. They expect downright opulence. It's what they feel they've earned and deserve. Vacation means being treated like royalty. Whatever your personal preferences may be, this chapter will teach you how to get the room and services you desire.

This Hotel Is Great! Is There...?

Before reserving a room anywhere, even here in the United States, make sure to verify with your travel agent or the hotel management that the facilities you want and need will be at your disposal. When you arrive, you want to be assured that your expectations will be met. Ask all important questions before you send a deposit. Consult table 12.1 to find out what hotel facilities are available.

Table 12.1 Hotel Facilities

Facilities	Spanish Translation	Pronunciation
bar	el bar	ehl bahr
business center	el centro de negocios	ehl sehn-troh deh neh-goh-see-ohs
cashier	el cajero	ehl kah-heh-roh
concierge (caretaker)	el conserje	ehl kohn-sehr-heh
doorman	el portero	ehl pohr-teh-roh
elevator	el ascensor	ehl ah-sehn-sohr
fitness center	el gimnasio	ehl heem-nah-see-oh
gift shop	la tienda de regalos	lah tee-ehn-dah deh reh-gah-lohs
laundry and dry cleaning service	la lavandería	lah lah-bahn-deh-ree-ah
maid service	la gobernanta	lah goh-behr-nahn-tah
restaurant	el restaurante	ehl rehs-tow-rahn-teh
swimming pool	la piscina	lah pee-see-nah
valet parking	la atendencia del garaje	lah ah-tehn-dehn-see-ah dehl gah-rah-heh

Cultural Tidbit

In Spanish buildings, the word *piso* refers to floors above the ground level. The ground floor is called *la planta baja* (lah plahn-tah bah-hah), which literally means: *the lower floor*. On an elevator button, you can expect to see this abbreviated as PB or B. The basement is called *el sótano*. The "first floor" is really on the second story of any building. A typical Spanish elevator pad might look like this:

4	3
2	1
PB	Sót

Do you want a great view when you book a hotel room? I never thought I did until I went to Dorado Beach in Puerto Rico. We booked a room facing the pool. What a mistake! Night and day all we heard were kids screaming and yelling—and here we were, trying to get away from ours. Next time I go, you can be sure that I'll ask for *una habitación con vista al mar*. And I'll also expect a lot of other amenities, too. Table 12.2 will help you get exactly what you want.

Table 12.2 Getting What You Want Nicely Furnished

Amenities	Spanish Translation	Pronunciation
a single room	una habitación con una sola cama	oo-nah ah-bee-tah-see-ohn kohn oo-nah soh-lah kah-mah
a double room	una habitación con dos camas	oo-nah ah-bee-tah-see-ohn kohn dohs kah-mahs
air conditioning	el aire acondicionado	ehl ah-ee-reh ah-kohn-dee-see-oh-nah-doh
alarm clock	el despertador	ehl dehs-pehr-tah-dohr
balcony	el balcón	ehl bahl-kohn
bathroom (private)	el baño privado	ehl bah-nyoh pree-bah-doh
on the courtyard	con vista al patio	kohn bees-tah ahl pah-tee-oh
on the garden	con vista al jardín	kohn bees-tah ahl har-deen
on the sea	con vista al mar	kohn bees-tah ahl mahr
safe (deposit box)	la caja fuerte	lah kah-hah fwehr-teh
shower	la ducha	lah doo-chah
telephone (dial-direct)	el teléfono (directo)	ehl teh-leh-foh-noh (dee-rehk-toh)
television (color)	la televisión (en color)	lah teh-leh-bee-see-ohn (ehn koh-lohr)
toilet facilities	el W.C.	ehl doh-bleh-beh

Cultural Tidbit

In older establishments in some Spanish-speaking countries, toilet facilities are located in separate rooms: a sink and bathtub (or shower) are located in what is called *el baño* (ehl bah-nyoh), the bathroom, while the toilet and bidet are in the W.C. (water closet). Showers may be the handheld type and are not affixed to the wall, which sometimes makes them rather difficult to use. Most bathrooms today, however, are just like ours.

Expressing Need

What if you need something for your room to make your stay more enjoyable? Any of the following phrases will help you:

As a Rule
Remember that the verb *faltar* agrees with the number of things needed:

Me falta una toalla. *I need a towel.*

Me falta*n* seis perchas. *I need six hangers.*

Phrase	Pronunciation	Meaning
Quisiera	kee-see-eh-rah	I would like
Me falta(n)	meh fahl-tah(n)	I need
Necesito	neh-seh-see-toh	I need

I have to have enough towels. That's one of my pet peeves. Unfortunately, hotels never seem to give you enough. If something you need or want is missing from your room, don't be shy. Ask for it! Remember, the management wants to please you and make your stay enjoyable. Table 12.3 lists a few things you might need.

Table 12.3 Necessities

Necessity	Spanish Translation	Pronunciation
an ashtray	un cenicero	oon seh-nee-seh-roh
a bar of soap	una barra de jabón	oo-nah bah-rrah deh hah-bohn
a beach towel	una toalla de baño	oo-nah toh-ah-yah deh bah-nyoh
a blanket	una manta	oo-nah mahn-tah
hangers	unas perchas	oo-nahs pehr-chahs
ice cubes	cubitos de hielo	koo-bee-tohs deh yeh-loh
mineral water	agua mineral	ah-gwah mee-neh-rahl
a pillow	una almohada	oo-nah ahl-moh-ah-dah
a roll of toilet paper	un rollo de papel higiénico	oon roh-yoh deh pah-pehl ee-hee-eh-nee-koh
tissues	pañuelos de papel	pah-nyoo-weh-lohs deh pah-pehl
a towel	una toalla	oo-nah toh-ah-yah
a transformer electric adaptor)	un transformador	oon trahns-fohr-mah-dohr (an

Just in Case

You've just walked into your room for the first time. If you're like me, you open every drawer to see if there's anything of interest inside and you read all the notices and papers they leave on the dresser. You notice this sign that appears on the back of your door. What information is it giving you?

CONDUCTA EN CASO DE INCENDIO

En caso de incendio en su habitación, si Ud. no puede controlar el fuego:

☞ Consiga la salida y cierre bien la puerta de su habitación al salir. Siga las luces en el piso.

☞ Avise a la recepción.

En caso de que Ud. oiga la alarma de fuego:

☞ Consiga la salida y cierre otra vez la puerta de su habitación al salir. Siga las luces en el piso.

☞ Si el humo bloquea el pasillo o la escalera:

Quédese en su habitación:

☞ Asómese a la ventana mientras espera la llegada de los bomberos.

Going to the Top

When you get on an elevator in a Spanish-speaking country, someone will probably ask you: "¿Qué piso, por favor (keh pee-soh pohr fah-bohr)?" In that situation you will be happy that you studied the ordinal numbers in table 12.4. That way you can give the correct answer: "El tercer piso, por favor (ehl tehr-sehr pee-soh pohr fah-bohr)."

Table 12.4 Ordinal Numbers

Ordinal Number	Spanish Translation	Pronunciation
1st	primero	pree-meh-roh
2nd	segundo	seh-goon-doh
3rd	tercero	tehr-seh-roh
4th	cuarto	kwahr-toh
5th	quinto	keen-toh
6th	sexto	sehks-toh

continues

Table 12.4 Continued

Ordinal Number	Spanish Translation	Pronunciation
7th	séptimo	sehp-tee-moh
8th	octavo	ohk-tah-boh
9th	noveno	noh-beh-noh
10th	décimo	deh-see-moh

As a Rule

The Spanish ordinal numbers are abbreviated as follows. You will note that a superscript ° or ^{er} is used to denote a masculine first, second, third, etc. item in a sequence, while a superscript ^{a} is used for the feminine:

Stands Alone (Masculine)	Stands Alone (Feminine)	Used Before a Masculine Noun	Used Before a Feminine Noun
primero 1°	primera 1^{a}	*primer 1er*	primera 1^{a}
segundo 2°	segunda 2^{a}	segundo 2°	segunda 2^{a}
tercero 3°	tercera 3^{a}	*tercer 3er*	tercera 3^{a}
cuarto 4°	cuarta 4^{a}	cuarto 4°	cuarta 4^{a}

Es el 1°. *It's the first.*

Es la 4ª vez. *It's the fourth time.*

Es el 3er día. *It's the third day.*

➤ *Primero* and *tercero* drop their final *o* before a masculine singular noun:

el primer día *the first day*   el tercer hombre *the third man*

la primera semana *the first week*   la tercera mujer *the third woman*

but

el siglo tercero *the third century*

➤ Ordinal numbers are made feminine by changing the final *o* of the masculine form to *a*, for example:

el segundo acto   *the second act*   la segunda escena   *the second scene*

➤ The Spanish usually use ordinal numbers through the tenth. After that, cardinal numbers are used:

la tercera cuadra   *the fourth block*

la Sexta Avenida   *Sixth Avenue*

la página veinte   *page 20*

➤ A cardinal number that replaces an ordinal number is always masculine, since *número*, a masculine word, is understood.

Using Ordinal Numbers

Imagine that you are in El Corte Inglés, a large department store in Madrid. Look at the directory that shows what can be found on each floor. Where would you expect to be able to buy tobacco? flowers? records? toys? travel items? Where can you park? Where can you get the following services: an interpreter? photos? a travel agency? keys made?

I'm Afraid There'll Have to Be a Change

Verbs are perhaps the most useful tool in any language because they help you express actions. You couldn't have a conversation without them. There are a few categories of regular *ar*, *er*, and *ir* verbs in Spanish that require spelling changes within the stem of the verb. Only the beginning of the verb is affected. The regular endings remain the same. It is really quite necessary that you become acquainted with some of the verbs in each group because they are in frequent use.

I like to call these verbs "shoe verbs" because the rules for the spelling changes work as if we put the subject pronouns that follow one set of rules within the shoe, and the others, outside the shoe. To make that more clear, let's look at the pronouns that go in and out of the shoe:

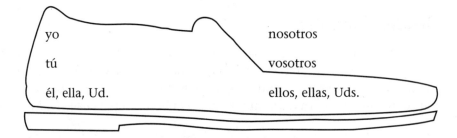

In other words, all verb forms in these categories—yo, tú, él, ella, Ud., ellos, ellas, Uds.—will follow one set of rules, while nosotros and vosotros will follow a different set of rules. Now let's look at the different categories.

Verbs Ending in AR and ER

For verbs ending in *ar* or *er*, the stem vowel change takes place in the present tense as follows: *e* to *ie* and *o* changes to *ue* in all forms of the shoe except nosotros and vosotros.

pensar—to think

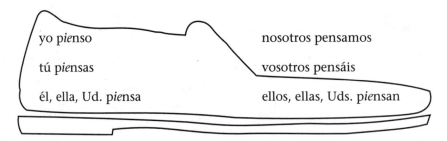

Other verbs that are conjugated just like *pensar* that you will find useful are

Verb	Pronunciation	Meaning
atravesar	ah-trah-beh-sahr	to cross
cerrar	seh-rrahr	to close
comenzar	koh-mehn-sahr	to begin
empezar	ehm-peh-sahr	to begin
quebrar	keh-brahr	to break

querer—to want

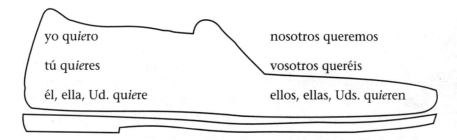

yo qu*i*ero	nosotros queremos
tú qu*i*eres	vosotros queréis
él, ella, Ud. qu*i*ere	ellos, ellas, Uds. qu*i*eren

Other verbs that are conjugated just like querer that you will find useful are

Verb	Pronunciation	Meaning
descender	deh-sehn-dehr	to descend
entender	ehn-tehn-dehr	to understand
perder	pehr-dehr	to lose

mostrar—to show

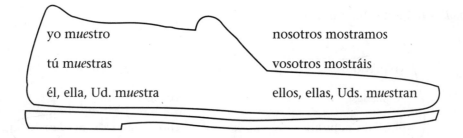

yo m*u*estro	nosotros mostramos
tú m*u*estras	vosotros mostráis
él, ella, Ud. m*u*estra	ellos, ellas, Uds. m*u*estran

Other verbs that are conjugated just like mostrar that you will find useful are

Verb	Pronunciation	Meaning
almorzar	ahl-mohr-sahr	to eat lunch
contar	kohn-tahr	to tell
costar	kohs-tahr	to cost
encontrar	ehn-kohn-trahr	to meet, find
jugar (u to ue)	hoo-gahr	to play games, sports
recordar	reh-kohr-dahr	to remember

As a Rule

As you've noticed from the preceding list of verbs, the *o* in the stem changes to *ue* in all of the verbs except for one: *jugar*, to play. There is no *o* in jugar; instead the *u* changes to *ue*. It is a very high-frequency verb, so it may be helpful to pay special attention to this distinction.

The verb *jugar* changes *u* to *ue* as follows:

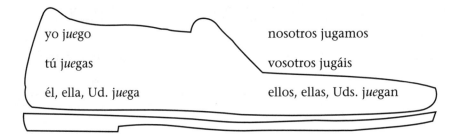

yo j*ue*go   nosotros jugamos

tú j*ue*gas   vosotros jugáis

él, ella, Ud. j*ue*ga   ellos, ellas, Uds. j*ue*gan

poder—to be able to, can

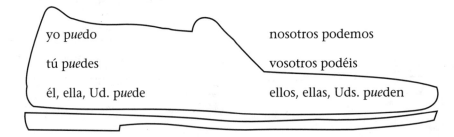

yo p*ue*do   nosotros podemos

tú p*ue*des   vosotros podéis

él, ella, Ud. p*ue*de   ellos, ellas, Uds. p*ue*den

Other verbs that are conjugated just like poder that you will find useful are

Verb	Pronunciation	Meaning
doler	doh-lehr	to ache, pain
resolver	reh-sohl-behr	to resolve
volver	bohl-behr	to return

Using AR and ER Verbs

You've finally settled into your hotel and are dozing off by the side of the pool. You hear bits and pieces of the conversations of the other guests. Complete each of their sentences with the correct form of the appropriate verb from the following list:

almorzar

entender

cerrar

pensar

costar

poder

descender

volver

1. ¿Qué _____ tú de esta idea?

2. Nosotros _____ al mediodía.

3. Yo _____ toda la conversación.

4. ¿A qué hora _____ Uds.?

5. Vosotros _____ jugar al parque.

6. ¿Cuánto _____ la blusa?

7. Nosotros _____ del autobús.

8. Vosotros siempre _____ las ventanas.

Verbs Ending in IR

For verbs ending in *ir*, the stem vowel change takes place in the present as follows: *e* changes to *ie*, *o* changes to *ue*, and *e* changes to *i* in all forms of the shoe except nosotros and vosotros. For example:

preferir—to prefer

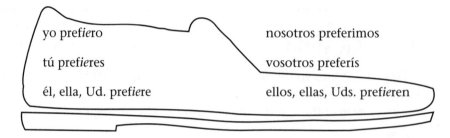

yo pref*ie*ro   nosotros preferimos

tú pref*ie*res   vosotros preferís

él, ella, Ud. pref*ie*re   ellos, ellas, Uds. pref*ie*ren

Other verbs that are conjugated just like preferir that you will find useful are

Verb	Pronunciation	Meaning
advertir	ahd-behr-teer	to notify, warn
consentir	kohn-sehn-teer	to consent
mentir	mehn-teer	to lie
referir	reh-feh-reer	to refer
sentir	sehn-teer	to regret

dormir—to sleep

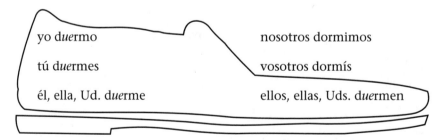

yo d*ue*rmo   nosotros dormimos

tú d*ue*rmes   vosotros dormís

él, ella, Ud. d*ue*rme   ellos, ellas, Uds. d*ue*rmen

Another verb that is conjugated just like dormir that you will find useful is

Verb	Pronunciation	Meaning
morir	moh-reer	to die

repetir—to repeat

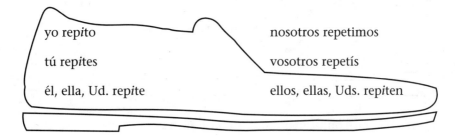

yo repito	nosotros repetimos
tú repites	vosotros repetís
él, ella, Ud. repite	ellos, ellas, Uds. repiten

Other verbs that are conjugated just like repetir that you will find useful are

Verb	Pronunciation	Meaning
impedir	eem-peh-deer	to prevent
medir	meh-deer	to measure
pedir	peh-deer	to ask
reír*	reh-eer	to laugh
servir	sehr-beer	to serve

* reír keeps the accent over the i in all forms.

Using IR Verbs

You are sitting in the lobby and you hear the people all around you giving their opinions. Complete their sentences by giving the correct form of the verb in parentheses:

1. Yo (preferir) _____ ver el museo.

2. Nosotros no (dormir) _____ bastante.

3. Ellas (repetir) _____ muchas frases.

4. Vosotros (mentir) _____ todo el tiempo.

5. Él no (morir)_____.

6. Tú (reír) _____ mucho.

Verbs Ending in UIR

For verbs ending in *uir* (except *guir*, see Chapter 11), insert a *y* after the *u* in all forms except nosotros and vosotros:

concluir—to conclude, end

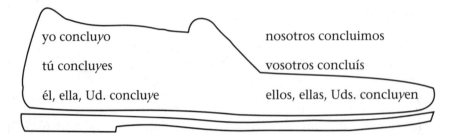

yo concluyo	nosotros concluimos
tú concluyes	vosotros concluís
él, ella, Ud. concluye	ellos, ellas, Uds. concluyen

Other verbs that are conjugated just like concluir that you will find useful are

Verb	Pronunciation	Meaning
construir	kohn-stroo-eer	to build
contribuir	kohn-tree-boo-eer	to contribute
destruir	dehs-troo-eer	to destroy
incluir	een-kloo-eer	to include
sustituir	soos-tee-too-eer	to substitute

As a Rule
In the vosotros form, put the accent on the a.

Vosotros confiáis en vuestros amigos.

You confide in your friends.

Vosotros continuáis.

You continue.

Verbs Ending in IAR and UAR

Some verbs ending in *iar* and *uar* require an accent in all forms except nosotros.

guiar—to guide

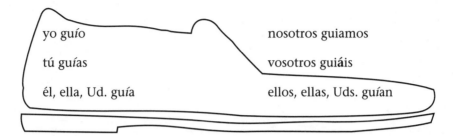

yo guío	nosotros guiamos
tú guías	vosotros guiáis
él, ella, Ud. guía	ellos, ellas, Uds. guían

Other verbs that are conjugated just like guiar that you will find useful are

Verb	Pronunciation	Meaning
confiar (en)	kohn-fee-ahr (ehn)	to confide (in), rely (on)
enviar	ehn-bee-ahr	to send
variar	bah-ree-ahr	to vary

continuar—to continue

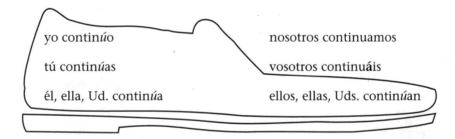

yo continúo	nosotros continuamos
tú continúas	vosotros continuáis
él, ella, Ud. continúa	ellos, ellas, Uds. continúan

Another verb that is conjugated just like continuar that you will find useful is

Verb	Pronunciation	Meaning
actuar	ahk-too-ahr	to act

Some verbs in Spanish have both spelling changes and stem changes. The most common verb of this type that you will want to use on a frequent basis is the verb *seguir*. The *e* in the stem of seguir changes to *i* except in the nosotros and vosotros forms, and the *gu* changes to *g* in the yo form. Here is what the verb looks like when it is conjugated:

seguir—to continue, follow

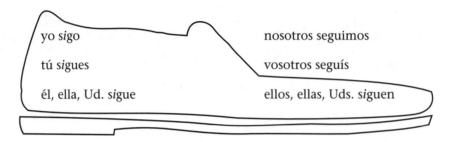

yo s*i*go	nosotros seguimos
tú s*i*gues	vosotros seguís
él, ella, Ud. s*i*gue	ellos, ellas, Uds. s*i*guen

Using UIR, IAR, and UAR Verbs

You really wish you could take a little *siesta* on the beach, but you are prevented from doing so by the people merrily chatting away as they pass by your chair. Complete what they say by giving the correct form of the verb that is provided in English:

1. Yo (send) _____ una carta a mi familia.

2. Nosotras (include) _____ a todo el mundo.

3. Ud. (continue) _____ leyendo cuando yo hablo.

4. Ellos (contribute) _____ a esta conversación interesante.

5. Tú (act) _____ rápidamente.

6. Vosotros (guide) _____ a los otros al teatro.

7. Ella (continues) _____ hablando todo el tiempo.

The Least You Need to Know

➤ Ordinal numbers are used until the tenth. After that, use cardinal numbers.

➤ *Shoe verbs* follow a pattern of conjugation that resembles the outline of a shoe. Remember the shoe and you'll remember how to conjugate the verb.

➤ *Ar* and *er* verbs change *e* to *ie* and *o* to *ue* in all forms except nosotros and vosotros.

➤ *Ir* verbs change *e* to *ie*, *o* to *ue*, and *e* to *i* in all forms except nosotros and vosotros.

➤ *Uir* verbs (except *guir*) add *y* before *u* in all forms except nosotros and vosotros.

➤ Some *iar* and *uar* verbs stress *í* and *ú* in all forms except nosotros and vosotros.

Part 3
Fun and Games

Chapter 13

How's the Weather Today?

In This Chapter

➤ Weather conditions

➤ Days of the week

➤ Months of the year

➤ The four seasons

➤ Keeping an appointment

➤ All about *dar* (to give)

Your hotel room is exactly what you'd hoped for and you're feeling great. Everything is in working condition and there are even plenty of towels. You've unpacked and now you're eager to go out on the town and have a wonderful time. You're up early and you've had breakfast. However, when you look outside, you see clouds looming overhead. There's no sun in sight. What should you plan for the day?

Your first impulse will probably be to turn on the radio or T.V. to get the latest weather report. Suddenly you realize, however, that all the forecasters are babbling away in rapid-fire Spanish and your knowledge of cognates isn't helping you very much. You've got to find something to do, so you pick up some brochures depicting indoor activities. Lo and behold, they're all written in Spanish, so you can't tell what's open or closed. This chapter will provide you with all the vocabulary you need so that you can understand the forecast and determine on what days you can do certain things.

It's 20 Degrees and They're Wearing String Bikinis!

You've opened your Spanish newspaper to the weather page. The weather forecaster has predicted a temperature of 20 degrees. You open your hotel window and you're greeted with a balmy sea breeze and a view of a beach studded with bikini-clad bathers. Something must be amiss. Could *el pronóstico* (the forecast) be wrong? It's time to consult with someone in the know at *la recepción*. Phrases that will enable you to discuss the weather are listed in table 13.1.

Table 13.1   Weather Expressions

Expression	Pronunciation	Meaning
¿Qué tiempo hace?	keh tee-ehm-poh ah-seh	What's the weather?
Hace buen tiempo	ah-seh bwehn tee-ehm-poh	It's beautiful
Hace calor	ah-seh kah-lohr	It's hot
Hace sol	ah-seh sohl	It's sunny
Hace mal tiempo	ah-seh mahl tee-ehm-poh	It's nasty (bad)
Hace frío	ah-seh free-oh	It's cold
Hace fresco	ah-seh frehs-koh	It's cool
Hace viento	ah-seh bee-ehn-toh	It's windy
Hay relámpagos	ah-ee reh-lahm-pah-gohs	It's lightning
Truena	troo-eh-nah	It's thundering
Hay niebla (neblina)	ah-ee nee-eh-blah (neh-blee-nah)	It's foggy
Hay humedad	ah-ee oo-meh-dahd	It's humid
Hay nubes/ Está nublado	ah-ee noo-behs/ ehs-tah noo-blah-doh	It's cloudy
Está cubierto	ehs-tah koo-bee-ehr-toh	It's overcast
Llueve/ Está lloviendo	yoo-eh-beh/ ehs-tah yoh-bee-ehn-doh	It's raining
Hay llovias torrenciales	ah-ee yoh-bee-ahs toh-rrehn-see-ahl-ehs	It's pouring

Expression	Pronunciation	Meaning
Nieva/ Está nevando	nee-eh-bah/ ehs-tah neh-bahn-doh	It's snowing
Hay un vendaval	ah-ee oon behn-dah-bahl	There's a windstorm
Hay granizo	ah-ee grah-nee-soh	There's hail
Hay lloviznas	ah-ee yoh-bees-nahs	There are showers

As a Rule

The verbs *llover* (ue), *tronar* (ue), and *nevar* (ie) are stem-changing according to the indications in parentheses. Remember to make the necessary changes when conjugating these verbs:

Llueve   *It's raining*

Truena   *It's thundering*

Nieva   *It's snowing*

If you want to use the present progressive (as discussed in Chapter 8) to stress that the weather condition is in existence at the moment, conjugate the verb *estar* (está—*It is*). Drop the *ar* or *er* infinitive ending from the verb and add *ando* or *iendo* respectively: *Está lloviendo, Está nevando*. The present progressive doesn't work with tronar.

So, why *is* everyone wearing shorts and bikinis when it's 20 degrees out? The answer is really quite simple. The Spanish-speaking world uses Celsius (centigrade) rather than Fahrenheit to tell the temperature: 0°C = 32°F. Use these thermometers to help you:

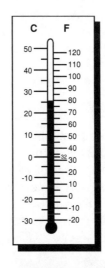

What's the Temperature?

Should you bring along a sweater? Will you need a winter coat? How about your new bathing suit? If you want to dress appropriately and be comfortable, you'll want to know what the temperature is. To find out, you would ask:

¿Cuál es la temperatura?
kwahl ehs lah tehm-peh-rah-too-rah
What's the temperature?

The way to answer the question "What's the temperature?" is to simply give the number of degrees followed by the word *grados* (grah-dohs, degrees). To be more formal, you could say: "Hay una temperatura de *xx* grados" (ah-ee oo-nah tehm-peh-rah-too-rah deh *xx* grah-dohs). If it's below zero, you'll need to add *menos* (minus) before the number. If the temperature is one degree, make sure that grado is used in the singular: *Un grado*. For example:

Menos cinco grados.
meh-nohs seen-koh grah-dohs
It's five below.

Hay una temperatura de cuarenta grados.
ah-ee oo-nah tehm-peh-rah-too-rah deh kwah-rehn-tah grah-dohs
It's forty degrees.

As a Rule
To change Fahrenheit to Centigrade: subtract 32 from the Fahrenheit temperature and multiply the remaining number by 5/9. To change Centigrade to Fahrenheit: multiply the Centigrade temperature by 9/5 and add 32 to the remaining number.

Cultural Tidbit
In Spain, the weather is much like it is in the northeastern United States where it is temperate for much of the year and the seasons change every three months. Autumn is probably the best time of the year to visit Spain because the climate is generally excellent and you can expect to have sunny days with blue skies most of the time.

In the Paper It Says...

You are reading the complimentary newspaper available at the hotel you are staying at in Uruguay. You're curious about the weather and turn to that section. Study the symbols in the following table that will help you interpret the symbols on a weather map. Learn what each smybol means. If you ever want to know the weather in the countries you visit (and you will), you're going to love knowing this vocabulary.

Symbol	Weather Expression	Pronunciation	Meaning
	cielo claro	see-eh-loh klah-roh	clear sky
	algo nubloso	ahl-goh noo-bloh-soh	slightly cloudy
	nubloso	noo-bloh-soh	cloudy
	inestable	een-ehs-tah-bleh	changeable
	lluvioso	yoo-bee-oh-soh	rainy
	tormenta eléctrica	tohr-mehn-tah eh-lehk-tree-kah	electrical storm
	frente frío	frehn-teh free-oh	cold front
	frente cálido	frehn-teh kah-lee-doh	warm front
	frente estacionario	frehn-teh ehs-tah-see-oh-nah-ree-oh	stationary front
	temperatura máxima	tehm-peh-rah-too-rah mahk-see-mah	maximum temperature

Cultural Tidbit

In tropical climes it is customary to take an afternoon nap, *una siesta* (oo-nah see-ehs-tah), to avoid the intense heat that occurs in the middle of the day. Indoors is the place to be when the scorching sun is at its peak. And so in some countries, small businesses close for the hottest part of the day, and stay open extra hours into the evening. The word *siesta* evolved from *la sexta hora* (lah sehk-stah oh-rah), high noon.

What Day Is It?

In the midst of a glorious vacation, did you ever have to pause for a moment to remember what day it was? It happens to me all the time. That's probably because I absolutely refuse to wear a watch once I've left work. For me, the best part of vacation, besides the rest and relaxation, is that time is not of the essence and I don't have to scurry to get things done. I become totally caught up in having fun and every day seems like a Satur-

Cultural Tidbit
Unlike our calendars, Spanish calendars start with Monday.

day. Occasionally, because I don't want to miss my flight home, I ask, "What day is it, anyway?" When sightseeing, however, it is somewhat important to keep track of the day so that you don't wind up at the attraction you were dying to see on the day that it's closed. That can happen very easily, as we all know. Study the days of the week in table 13.2 to ensure that you get to do everything you want.

Table 13.2 Days of the Week

Day of the Week	Spanish Translation	Pronunciation
Monday	lunes	loo-nehs
Tuesday	martes	mahr-tehs
Wednesday	miércoles	mee-ehr-koh-lehs
Thursday	jueves	hoo-eh-behs
Friday	viernes	bee-ehr-nehs
Saturday	sábado	sah-bah-doh
Sunday	domingo	doh-meen-goh

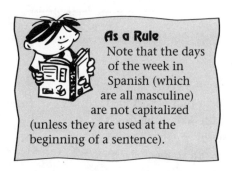

As a Rule
Note that the days of the week in Spanish (which are all masculine) are not capitalized (unless they are used at the beginning of a sentence).

To express *on* a certain day, the Spanish use the indefinite article *el*, such as:

El martes yo voy al centro.
ehl mahr-tehs yoh boy ahl sehn-troh
On Tuesday(s) I go downtown.

On what days do you go to the movies? go to the super-market? do laundry? go out with friends? eat out? work hard?

This Is the Best Time of the Month

If your travels or business take you to Latin America, you can certainly see why it's important to know the names of the months. You wouldn't want to sit by a pool in Argentina in July and you couldn't expect to indulge in winter sports in Peru in December. You want to make sure that you plan your trip wisely. A slip of the tongue and you could wind up being in the wrong place at the wrong time. Table 13.3 will help you identify the months so that when you read brochures in Spanish, you will be able to choose the best time for a visit.

Table 13.3   Months of the Year

Month of the Year	Spanish Translation	Pronunciation
January	enero	eh-neh-roh
February	febrero	feh-breh-roh
March	marzo	mahr-soh
April	abril	ah-breel
May	mayo	mah-yoh
June	junio	hoo-nee-oh
July	julio	hoo-lee-oh
August	agosto	ah-gohs-toh
September	septiembre	sehp-tee-ehm-breh
October	octubre	ohk-too-breh
November	noviembre	noh-bee-ehm-breh
December	diciembre	dee-see-ehm-breh

Cultural Tidbit

Translated literally, the phrase, "Febrero es loco y marzo no poco" means "February is crazy and March is not a little (crazy)." Why is this commonly heard in Spain? The weather in these two months is very unpredictable and can be very hot one day, and very cold the next.

To express *in* a certain month, the Spanish use the preposition *en*:

Vamos a España en julio.
bah-mohs ah ehs-pah-nyah ehn hoo-lee-oh
We are going to Spain in July.

In which month(s) do you celebrate your birthday? take your vacation? participate in a favorite sport? watch the most television? feel the laziest?

As a Rule

Like the days of the week, all months in Spanish are masculine and are not capitalized (unless they are used at the beginning of a sentence).

The Four Seasons

Some like it hot. They go to Spain in the summer or Chile in the winter. Some like it cold. They go to Argentina in the summer and Costa Rica in the winter. Whatever you like, just make sure you plan your trip when the weather will be perfect, so you don't have to worry about hurricanes, storms, or other adverse weather conditions. Table 13.4 gives you the names of the seasons.

Table 13.4   The Seasons of the Year

Season of the Year	Spanish Translation	Pronunciation
winter	el invierno	ehl een-bee-ehr-noh
spring	la primavera	lah pree-mah-beh-rah
summer	el verano	ehl beh-rah-noh
autumn, fall	el otoño	ehl oh-toh-nyoh

To express *in* with the seasons, the Spanish use the preposition *en* + the definite article for all the seasons. Here's some wishful thinking to show you how it's done:

Voy a Puerto Rico en el invierno, en la primavera, en el verano y en el otoño.

boy ah pwehr-toh ree-koh ehn ehl een-bee-ehr-noh, ehn lah pree-mah-beh-rah, ehn ehl beh-rah-noh ee ehn ehl oh-toh-nyoh

I go to Puerto Rico in the winter, in the spring, in the summer, and in the fall.

In which season do you go to the beach? watch a football game? go on outdoor picnics? watch the leaves turn colors?

You Have a Date for What Date?

It's common when we have a lot on our mind to lose track of the date. I guess that's why so many of us have watches designed to help us remember. If you're traveling for pleasure, one day seems to run into the next and somewhere along the line the date does get lost. When you're in a Spanish-speaking country, the dates are expressed as follows:

➤ day of week + el +(cardinal) number + de + month + de + year

For example, "lunes el once de julio de 1996."

➤ The first day of each month is expressed by primero. Cardinal numbers are used for all other days:

el primero de enero   *January 1st*

el dos de febrero   *February 2nd*

➤ In Spanish the date is expressed in thousands and hundreds, not in hundreds, as we do in English. For example, in Spanish, *1996* is expressed as "mil novecientos noventa y seis."

➤ To express *on* with dates, use the definite article el:

Salgo *el* tres de mayo.   *I'm leaving on May 3.*

Cultural Tidbit

When the Spanish write the date in numbers, the sequence is *day + month + year*. This is the reverse of the *month + day + year* sequence that we use. Notice how different this looks:

SPANISH	ENGLISH
el 22 de abril 1977	April 22, 1977
22.4.77	4/22/77
el cinco de febrero 1995	February 5, 1995
5.2.95	2/5/95

In order to get information about the date you need to ask the following questions:

¿Cuál es la fecha de hoy?
kwahl ehs lah feh-chah deh oh-ee
What is today's date?

¿A cuántos estamos hoy?
ah kwahn-tohs ehs-tah-mohs oh-ee
What's today's date?

¿Qué día es hoy?
keh dee-ah ehs oh-ee
What day is today?

The answer to your question would be one of the following:

Hoy es lunes el primero de abril.
oh-ee ehs loo-nehs ehl pree-meh-roh deh ah-breel
Today is Monday, April 1.

Estamos a lunes el primero de abril.
ehs-tah-mohs ah loo-nehs ehl pree-meh-roh deh ah-breel
Today is Monday, April 1.

The new year has just begun and you are starting to fill out your date book. Of course you have some dates that are especially important to you. Give the day and dates for these important events of the year: your birthday, a friend's birthday, Thanksgiving, New Year's, Mother's Day, Valentine's Day, Father's Day, Memorial Day.

There are words and expressions commonly used with days, weeks, and months that will help you schedule your time for maximum benefit. Keep the expressions in table 13.5 in mind when you make your plans.

Table 13.5 Time Expressions

Expression	Pronunciation	Meaning
en	ehn	in
hace	ah-seh	ago
por	pohr	per
durante	doo-rahn-teh	during
próximo(a)	prohk-see-moh(mah)	next
último(a)	ool-tee-moh(mah)	last
pasado(a)	pah-sah-doh(dah)	last
la vispera	lah bees-peh-rah	eve

As a Rule

The adjectives *próximo*, *último*, and *pasado* must be used in their feminine form to describe a feminine noun:

Masculine Example	Meaning	Feminine Example	Meaning
el próximo día	the next day	la próxima noche	the next night
el último año	the last year	la última hora	the last hour
el mes pasado	the past month	la semana pasada	the past week

anteayer	ahn-teh-ah-yehr	day before yesterday
ayer	ah-yehr	yesterday
hoy	oh-ee	today
mañana	mah-nyah-nah	tomorrow
pasado mañana	pah-sah-doh mah-nyah-nah	day after tomorrow
el día siguiente	ehl dee-ah see-gee-ehn-teh	next day
desde	dehs-deh	from
una semana de hoy	oo-nah seh-mah-nah deh oh-ee	a week from today
dos semanas de mañana	dohs seh-mah-nahs deh mah-nyah-nah	two weeks from tomorrow

Cultural Tidbit

Perhaps you've noticed by now that the word *mañana* can mean morning or tomorrow. It is a very common practice for people from Spanish-speaking cultures to use *mañana* to refer to an indefinite time in the future, not necessarily the next morning or day. Spanish speakers have a more relaxed attitude towards time than we do in the United States, and so, being on time is a relative thing. Being late, or doing something mañana, is not considered rude, but rather allowing oneself a certain amount of luxury time.

155

What's the Date?

Imagine that you are at an important business meeting where you must use your Spanish to refer to certain past and future dates. If today were *el siete de agosto*, give the date for the following:

anteayer	dos semanas de mañana	la vispera
mañana	una semana de mañana	hace siete días

Give Me Good Weather

Don't you always pray that when you travel you will have good weather? Once when my husband and I were traveling, we found that we were heading right into a potential hurricane. Luckily we didn't give up and turn around, because the storm passed. We went for it and gave it our best shot. Study table 13.6 to learn how to use the verb *dar* (dahr), to give, which has an irregular yo form only.

Table 13.6   The Verb Dar—To Give

The Conjugation of Dar	Pronunciation	Translation
yo doy	yoh doh-ee	I give
tú das	too dahs	you give
él, ella, Ud. da	ehl, eh-yah, oo-stehd dah	he, she, you give(s)
nosotros damos	noh-soh-trohs dah-mohs	we give
vosotros dáis	boh-soh-trohs dah-ees	you give
ellos, ellas, Uds. dan	eh-yohs, eh-yahs, oo-stehd-ehs dahn	they, you give

Expressions with Dar

Imagine that you are walking along the Paseo del Prado in Madrid. A young man approaches and says, "Quiero dar un paseo con Ud." Is this guy trying to make a pass at you? Before you give him *una bofetada* (oo-nah boh-feh-tah-dah), a slap, familiarize yourself with the following idioms with dar:

Table 13.7 Idioms with Dar

Idiom	Pronunciation	Meaning
dar a	dahr ah	to face
dar un abrazo	dahr oon ah-brah-soh	to hug
dar con	dahr kohn	to run into
dar de beber (comer)	dahr deh beh-behr (koh-mehr)	to give a drink (feed)
dar las gracias a	dahr lahs grah-see-ahs ah	to thank
dar un paseo	dahr oon pah-seh-oh	to take a walk, go for a ride
dar recuerdos (a)	dahr reh-kwehr-dohs (ah)	to give regards (to)
dar una vuelta	dahr oo-nah bwehl-tah	to take a stroll

Cultural Tidbit

Spain has a relatively mild climate, so outdoor life is important year-round. Part of the daily routine of Spanish life is the *paseo*, the stroll or walk, which usually takes place between the hours of 7 p.m. and 10 p.m. From tots, to teenagers, to young couples, to senior citizens, the *paseo* represents an opportunity to socialize with one's family, friends, and peers.

During the paseo, it is common to stop at one's favorite cafeteria or bar to enjoy some *tapas* (tah-pahs), hors-d'oeuvres. The snack is a necessity because work ends around 7:30 p.m. and dinner isn't served until 10 p.m.

Using Dar

Different people are doing different things right now. Use the correct form of the verb *dar* to express what is going on with each of the following subjects:

1. (to take a stroll) Ellos _____.

2. (to give regards) Vosotros _____ a Ana.

3. (to thank) Nosotros _____ al hombre.

4. (to hug) Yo _____ a mi novio.

5. (to run into) Tú _____ con Julio en el parque.

The Least You Need to Know

➤ The days and months, in dates, are written in reverse order from what we are accustomed to.

➤ The verb *dar*, to give, has an irregular yo form and is used in many different idiomatic expressions.

Let's See the Sights

You've looked out the window and listened to the weather report for the day. You've consulted your guide book and some brochures to ascertain what activities you'd like to have fun doing. The next step is to take out a bus or subway map of the city and check out the location of some important tourist attractions. This way, you can plan a logical itinerary of interesting sights to see, which are grouped in a common area. You don't want to run back and forth across town, wasting time, when you can have a good game plan instead.

This chapter presents you with interesting places to visit and a wide variety of things to do in Spanish-speaking countries. In no time flat you'll develop the proficiency you'll need to make suggestions and plans and to give your impressions and opinions. Because there are so many countries you might choose to visit within and outside the Spanish-speaking community, you'll be given the names of the most popular ones in Spanish.

What Would You Like to See?

Do you have a Type-A personality? Are you a super-active person who loves to rapidly fly from one activity to another, always afraid that you'll miss this museum or that church? Or are you the laid-back, mellow, Type B, who just feels like relaxing and soaking up the sun? All of the Spanish-speaking countries offer a broad variety of things to do and see. Travel brochures available at hotels and tourist offices propose countless suggestions. When you're ready to make a decision, consult table 14.1, which lists common activities and sites.

Table 14.1   Where to Go and What to Do

El Lugar	The Place	La Actividad	The Activity
el acuario	the aquarium	ver los peces	see the fish
la arena	the ring	ver la corrida de toros	see the bullfights
el estadio	the stadium	ver la corrida de toros	see the bullfights
el carnival	the carnival	mirar el desfile, las carrozas	look at the parade, floats
el castillo	the castle	ver los cuartos	see the rooms
la catedral	the cathedral	ver las vidrieras	see the stained glass windows
el circo	the circus	ver los espectáculos	see the shows
el club	the nightclub	ver un espectáculo	see a show
la feria	the fair	mirar las exposiciones	look at the exhibits
la fuente	the fountain	mirar el chorro de agua	look at the spray of water
la iglesia	the church	ver la arquitectura	see the architecture
el museo	the museum	ver las pinturas, las esculturas	see the paintings, sculptures
el parque de atracciones	amusement park	montar en los tiovivos	go on the rides

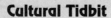

Cultural Tidbit

Bullfighting is a colorful event that usually takes place in large Spanish cities on Sunday afternoons (from 5 p.m. to 7 p.m.) and on important holidays from March to October.

Before the festivities begin, all of the participants parade around the arena while *pasadoble* music blares and the crowd roars in eager anticipation. The bullfight consists of three parts, or chances, called *suertes* (soo-ehr-tehs). In the first suerte, *picadores* (pee-kah-doh-rehs), mounted bullfighters carrying a long, large needlelike instrument called a *pica* (pee-kah), stick the bull in the nape of the neck. In the second suerte, *banderilleros* (bahn-deh-ree-yeh-rohs) appear on foot and thrust barbed darts called *banderillas* (bahn-deh-ree-yahs) into the neck and shoulders of the bull. Finally, in the third chance, the *matador* (mah-tah-dohr) or *torero* (toh-reh-roh) (the bullfighter who kills the bull), enters the arena with a red cape. This cape, which is attached to a staff so it is easier to hold and display, that is used to anger the bull. The matador also carries a fine steel sword, with which he kills the animal after several dramatic passes of the flag. Of course the matador must wait for the most opportune moment. In the meantime, the public lauds the art and bravery of the bullfighter.

If seeing a bullfight interests you, you can purchase tickets through your hotel, at the *plaza de toros*, or, in Madrid, at the official city box office.

If you have never witnessed a bullfight before, it would be best to avoid a *Novillada*, a *corrida* (fight) with inexperienced matadores and bulls that are either very young or old. You might feel uncomfortable with what you see.

Keep in mind, that in South America and Mexico, it is not always customary to kill the bull.

What Do You Want to See?

Are you off to the Prado to see the famous artwork, or are you really curious to observe a bullfight? Perhaps you want to admire the stained glass windows of a famous church or statues in a public square. To express what you would like to see or are going to see, you will need the irregular verb *ver* (to see) that is presented in table 14.2. Ver is a very easy verb to learn because it is only irregular in the yo form, where an extra *e* is added. All other forms follow the rules for regular *er* verbs.

Table 14.2   The Verb Ver—To See

Conjugated Form of Ver	Pronunciation	Meaning
yo veo	yoh beh-oh	I see
tú ves	too behs	you see
él, ella, Ud. ve	ehl, eh-yah, oo-stehd beh	he, she, you see(s)
nosotros vemos	nohs-oh-trohs beh-mohs	we see
vosotros véis	bohs-oh-trohs beh-ees	you see
ellos, ellas, Uds. ven	eh-yohs, eh-yahs, oo-stehd-ehs behn	they see

Cultural Tidbit

In Madrid there are many interesting attractions for tourists to see. The Prado museum, which houses over 6,000 works of art by such renowned Spanish artists as Goya, Velázquez, El Greco, Murillo, and Zurbarán, and is considered one of the most important art museums in the world, is a must see. Its annex, El Casón del Buen Retiro, is an archaeological museum that contains collections from practically all the different cultures that have flourished in Spain.

(If you want to see Picasso's "Guérnica", you'll have to stop at the Reina Sofía Art Center.)

You can visit beautiful botanical gardens in el Parque del Retiro, just two blocks away from the Prado. In the park, there is a small lake where rowboats may be rented and two buildings where art shows take place.

More Than One Way to Make a Suggestion

Have you always had your heart set on a romantic (second) honeymoon in Cancún. The seductive brochures, the enticing ads, and the pictures your friends have shown you have convinced you that this is a vacation spot you'd really enjoy. How will your spouse feel about this? Will your enthusiasm be shared? There's only one way to find out. You'll just have to drop a few hints and make some coy suggestions.

One way to make a suggestion in Spanish is to ask this simple question:

¿Por qué no + *the verb in the nosotros form*?

For example:

¿Por qué no vamos a Cancún?
pohr keh noh bah-mohs ah kahn-koon?
Why don't we go to Cancún?

¿Por qué no partimos mañana?
pohr keh noh pahr-tee-mohs mah-nyah-nah
Why don't we leave tomorrow?

As a Rule
When using the command form that expresses "Let's," the subject pronoun *nosotros* is never used.

You can also tell someone what you'd like to do and then ask how he/she feels about the idea. Of course, they may think you're trying to be a little pushy. But what the heck. Go for it!

Quiero ir a Cancún.
kee-eh-roh eer ah kahn-koon
I want to go to Cancún.

¿Qué piensa(s)?
keh pee-ehn-sah(s)
What do you think?

¿Qué cree(s)?
keh kreh-eh(s)
What do you think?

To express the English "Let's," use the nosotros form of the irregular verb *ir + a + the infinitive of the thing you are suggesting*. For example:

Vamos a viajar a Cancún.
bah-mohs ah bee-ah-hahr ah kahn-koon
Let's travel to Cancún.

Vamos a partir mañana.
bah-mohs ah pahr-teer mah-nyah-nah
Let's leave tomorrow.

The last way to make a polite suggestion is to use the nosotros form of the present subjunctive tense. Although this sounds complicated, it is really quite simple. Just insert the opposite letter of the infinitive ending, just like you did with commands using Ud.: for regular *ar* verbs, change the *a* ending to *e* and for regular *er* and *ir* verbs, change the *e* or *i* ending to *a*.

Viajemos a Cancún.
bee-ah-heh-mohs ah kahn-koon
Let's travel to Cancun.

Partamos mañana.
pahr-tah-mohs mah-nyah-nah
Let's leave tomorrow.

Making Suggestions

The weather is simply beautiful and you're itching to go out and have a great time. Suggest five things that you and I can do together.

Example: ¿Por qué no vamos al parque?
Quiero nadar en el mar.
¿Qué piensas?

Other Useful Phrases

I bet that you're feeling that this is quite easy. If you're feeling rather good about your progress right now, you might want to attempt a more colloquial approach. There are a number of phrases you can use. The following minitable gives you these phrases. All you have to do to complete your thought is tack on the infinitive of the verb of what you want to do and, in most cases, the activity in which you will be engaging. (The familiar forms [tú] are in parentheses.) Note the use of the polite pronoun *le* (to you) and the familiar pronoun *te* (to you) in some of the following expressions. These pronouns are used to ask about "you" and are placed before the verb. A more detailed explanation of the use of these pronouns appears in Chapter 15.

Phrase	Pronunciation	Meaning
¿Que le (te) parece + *inf. verb?*	keh leh (teh) pah-reh-seh	Do you want...?
¿Le (te) gustaría + *inf. verb?*	leh (teh) goos-tah-ree-ah	Would you like...?
¿Tiene(s) ganas de + *inf. verb?*	tee-eh-neh(s) gah-nahs deh	Do you feel like...?
¿Quiere(s)? + *inf. verb?*	kee-eh-reh(s)	Do you want...?

For example:

¿Le (te) parece...	salir?
¿Le (te) gustaría...	ir al cine?
¿Tiene(s) ganas de...	ver una corrida de toros?
¿Quiere(s)...	mirar las exposiciones?

All of the phrases in the preceding list can be made negative by using *no*:

¿No le (te) parece...?	(Don't you want...?)	nadar?
¿No le (te) gustaría...?	(Wouldn't you like...?)	ir al cine?
¿No quiere(s)...?	(Don't you want...?)	mirar las exposiciones?
¿No tiene(s) ganas de...?	(Don't you feel like...?)	ver una corrida de toros?

Are you acquainted with any grouchy-from-lack-of-sleep teenagers who give abrupt yes or no answers to questions? For the rest of us, we usually say "yes, but..." or "no, because...." In Spanish, if you'd like to elaborate on your answer, here's what you'll have to do: If you see the pronoun *le* or *te* (to you) in the question, simply use *me* (to me) before the verb in your answer to express how *you* feel:

Sí, me parece nadar.   No, no me parece nadar.

Sí, me gustaría ir al cine.   No, no me gustaría ir al cine.

For the others sentences, give the yo form of the verb in the present.

Sí, tengo ganas de ver una corrida de toros.   No, no tengo ganas de ver una corrida de toros.

Sí, quiero mirar las exposiciones.   No, no quiero mirar las exposiciones.

What's Your Opinion?

Someone suggested an activity to you. How do you feel about it? Are you interested in pursuing it further? Does it have appeal? If the answer is yes, then you might say:

Me gusta la música clásica.   Me encanta la ópera.

meh goos-tah lah moo-see-kah klah-see-kah   meh ehn-kahn-tah lah oh-peh-rah

I like classical music.   *I adore the opera.*

Soy aficionado(a) al arte.

soh-ee ah-fee-see-oh-nah-doh(ah) ahl ahr-teh

I'm an art fan.

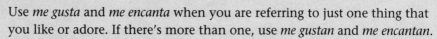

As a Rule

Use *me gusta* and *me encanta* when you are referring to just one thing that you like or adore. If there's more than one, use *me gustan* and *me encantan*.

Me gusta la música.   Me encanta la ópera.

Me gustan la música y el arte.   Me encantan las óperas.

Suppose you've gone out and tried something totally out of character for you. Chances are you're going to want to express what you think of the activity. Was it fun? Did you really enjoy it? You can give a positive opinion by saying *es* (ehs), followed by an adjective, such as "Es excelente," or "It's excellent." The following minitable provides you with a list of adjectives that will help you describe the fun you can have in Spanish-speaking countries:

As a Rule
Remember that when you use the phrase: *Soy aficionado(a) a, a* contracts with *el* to become *al*: Soy aficionada al ballet.

Adjective	Pronunciation	Meaning
estupendo	ehs-too-pehn-doh	stupendous
fenomenal	feh-noh-meh-nahl	phenomenal
excelente	ehk-seh-lehn-teh	excellent
magnífico	mag-nee-fee-koh	magnificent
fantástico	fahn-tahs-tee-koh	fantastic
terrífico	teh-rree-fee-koh	terrific
sensacional	sehn-sah-see-oh-nahl	sensational
maravilloso	mah-rah-bee-yoh-soh	marvelous
divertido	dee-behr-tee-doh	fun
regio	reh-hee-oh	great
fabuloso	fah-boo-loh-soh	fabulous
de película	deh peh-lee-koo-lah	out of this world
bárbaro	bahr-bah-roh	awesome
extraordinario	ehks-trah-ohr-dee-nah-ree-oh	extraordinary

Maybe the suggestion of how to spend your day is totally unappealing to you. Perhaps you find it boring. Use these phrases to express your dislikes:

Phrase	Pronunciation	Meaning
No me gusta	noh meh goos-tah	I don't like
Odio, detesto	oh-dee-oh, deh-tehs-toh	I hate
No soy aficionado(a)	noh soh-ee ah-fee-see-oh-nah-doh(ah)	I'm not a fan of

Here are some example sentences that describe a few activities that some people may not enjoy:

No me gusta la música clásica.

Odio (Detesto) la ópera.

No soy aficionado(a) al arte.

Are you the type of person who is a good sport and will try anything once and you don't want to be labeled contrary? O.K. You tried it but you were right, it just wasn't your cup of tea. If you want to give a negative opinion about an activity you might say, "Es aburrido," or "It's boring." Here is a list of adjectives you could use to describe something you don't like:

Adjective	Pronunciation	Meaning
aburrido	ah-boo-rree-doh	boring
asqueroso	ahs-keh-roh-soh	loathsome
feo	feh-oh	ugly
un horror	oon oh-rrohr	a horror
un desastre	oon dehs-ahs-treh	a disaster
desagradable	dehs-ah-grah-dah-bleh	disgusting
terrible	teh-rree-bleh	terrible
tonto	tohn-toh	silly
horrible	oh-rree-bleh	horrible
ridículo	ree-dee-koo-loh	ridiculous

Beyond the Blue Horizon

You might be having a wonderful time in Spain and then, all of a sudden, decide that you'd like to see other parts of Europe. Or maybe you'd like to take a trip from Spain to another continent. If this is the case, you'll most likely need to know the names of the countries you want to visit in order to make appropriate travel plans and wind up in the right place. If you can't distinguish Suiza (Switzerland) from Suecia (Sweden), you could wind up eating a smorgasbord in Stockholm instead of that chocolate fondue you craved. Making travel plans might prove to be easier if you learn the Spanish names of the countries listed in table 14.3 and the continents in table 14.4.

Table 14.3   Countries

Country	Spanish Translation	Pronunciation
Argentina	Argentina	ahr-hehn-tee-nah
Austria	Austria	ow-stree-ah
Belgium	Bélgica	behl-hee-kah
Belize	Bélice	beh-lee-seh

continues

Table 14.3   Continued

Country	Spanish Translation	Pronunciation
Bolivia	Bolivia	boh-lee-bee-ah
Brazil	Brasil	brah-seel
Canada	Canadá	kah-nah-dah
Chile	Chile	chee-leh
China	China	chee-nah
Colombia	Colombia	koh-lohm-bee-ah
Costa Rica	Costa Rica	kohs-tah rree-kah
Cuba	Cuba	koo-bah
Dominican Republic	la República Dominicana	lah reh-poo-blee-kah doh-mee-nee-kah-nah
Ecuador	Ecuador	eh-kwah-dohr
El Salvador	El Salvador	ehl sahl-bah-dohr
England	Inglaterra	een-glah-teh-rrah
France	Francia	frahn-see-ah
Germany	Alemania	ah-leh-mah-nee-ah
Greece	Grecia	greh-see-ah
Guatemala	Guatemala	gwah-teh-mah-lah
Haiti	Haití	ah-ee-tee
Honduras	Honduras	ohn-doo-rahs
Italy	Italia	ee-tahl-ee-ah
Japan	Japón	hah-pohn
Mexico	México (Méjico)	meh-hee-koh
Netherlands	los Países Bajos	lohs pah-ee-sehs bah-hohs
Nicaragua	Nicaragua	nee-kah-rah-gwah
Panama	Panamá	pah-nah-mah
Paraguay	Paraguay	pah-rah-gwah-ee
Peru	Perú	peh-roo
Portugal	Portugal	pohr-too-gahl
Puerto Rico	Puerto Rico	pwehr-toh rree-koh
Russia	Rusia	roo-see-ah

Country	Spanish Translation	Pronunciation
Spain	España	ehs-pah-nyah
Sweden	Suecia	soo-eh-see-ah
Switzerland	Suiza	soo-ee-sah
United States	los Estados Unidos	lohs ehs-tah-dohs oo-nee-dohs
Uruguay	Uruguay	oo-roo-gwah-ee
Venezuela	Venezuela	beh-neh-sweh-lah

As a Rule

Countries in Spanish are not preceded by the definite article (el, la, los, or las), except El Salvador and La Républica Dominicana, because *El* and *La* are part of the countries' names. There is no contraction of *a + el* when speaking about El Salvador. For example:

Voy a Argentina.

Voy a El Salvador.

Table 14.4 The Continents

Continent	Spanish Translation	Pronunciation
Africa	África	ah-free-kah
Antarctica	Antártica	ahn-tahr-tee-kah
Asia	Asia	ah-see-ah
Australia	Australia	ow-strah-lee-ah
Europe	Europa	eh-oo-roh-pah
North America	Norte América América del Norte	nohr-teh ah-meh-ree-kah ah-meh-ree-kah dehl nohr-teh
South America	Sud América América del Sur	sood ah-meh-ree-kah ah-meh-ree-kah dehl soor

As a Rule

Use the definite article with geographical names that are modified:

Vivo en *la* América del Norte.

but

Vivo en Norte América.

Going, Going, Gone

Do you plan on going to Puerto Rico for your next vacation? Will you be staying with relatives who have a beach house in the Condado area? To express that you are going *to* or staying *in* another country or city, use the preposition *a.*

Voy a Puerto Rico.
boh-ee ah pwehr-toh rree-koh
I am going to Puerto Rico.

Where Are You From? Where Are You Coming From?

Can you tell if a person comes from the Northeast or the South of the United States? Of course you can. The different regional accents are a dead give away. Sometimes, people who speak the same language have difficulty understanding each other because of the way the words are pronounced and rapidly strung together. Was my face red when I asked someone to translate what a fellow traveler was saying, only to find out that he was speaking to me in English, my native tongue! Always play it safe and avoid embarrassing moments by asking from where a person hails. Use the preposition *de* to express *from*:

Soy de Nueva York.
soh-ee deh noo-eh-bah yohrk
I'm from New York.

Where Are You Going?

Start your sentence with *Voy* (I'm going) and tell what country you are going to if you plan to see: a bullfight, the Great Wall, Mexican jumping beans, the Moscow circus, the leaning Tower of Pisa, Big Ben, the Eiffel Tower, home.

The Least You Need to Know

➤ To suggest an activity use any one of the following:

¿Por qué no + nosotros form of verb

Your thought and then the question: *¿Qué piensa(s)?* or *¿Qué cree(s)?*

ir a + *infinitive of the verb*

the subjunctive form of nosotros

➤ Simple phrases can express your likes (¡Es fantástico!) and dislikes (¡Es horrible!).

➤ The definite article is not generally used with the names of geographical locations.

Chapter 15

Shop Till You Drop

In This Chapter

➤ Stores and their wares

➤ Clothing, colors, sizes, and materials

➤ All about *gustar* (to like)

➤ Direct and indirect objects

➤ This, that, these, and those (a.k.a. demonstrative adjectives)

You've finally placed a check mark next to every tourist attraction on your "Don't Miss" list. You've even found a few places of your own to suggest to future travelers. It's time for a change. Why not concentrate on picking up some souvenirs and gifts for friends and relatives back home?

When I visit a foreign country, I try to bring back crafts that will remind me of my vacation for years to come. T-shirts, scarves, ashtrays, and wallets hold no appeal to me. Give me, instead, a wide-brimmed Mexican sombrero and a multi-colored serape, a set of ornate Spanish maracas, a painted mask from Puerto Rico, a carved stone statue from the Dominican Republic, or just a simple doll made from hemp. No matter what your preference, this chapter will help you purchase items that will make you and your loved ones happy.

Stores for Everyone

It's been decided. Today you're going shopping. Will you join the crowds in the open markets, browse in the small shops of local artisans, rub shoulders with the rich and famous in small boutiques, or search out a large mall (*un centro commercial* oon sehn-troh koh-mehr-see-ahl) where you can purchase anything and everything? Table 15.1 will help you find your way to the stores that carry the merchandise you're looking for.

Table 15.1 Stores (Las Tiendas—lahs tee-ehn-dahs)

La Tienda	The Store	Las Mercancías	The Merchandise
la juguetería	toy store	los juguetes	toys
la librería	bookstore	los libros	books
la florería	florist	las flores	flowers
la tienda de ropa	clothing store	la ropa	clothing
el almacén	department store	por todo	almost everything
la tabaquería	tobacco store	el tabaco	tobacco
		los cigarillos	cigarettes
		los cigarros	cigars
		las pipas	pipes
		los fósforos	matches
		los encendedores	lighters
el quiosco de periódicos	newsstand	los periódicos	newspapers
		las revistas	magazines
la tienda de discos	record store	los discos	records
		los casetes	cassette tapes
		los CDs	compact discs
la joyería	jewelry store	las joyas	jewels
		los relojes	watches
		los collares	necklaces
		un anillo, una sortija	ring
		la pulsera	bracelet
		los aretes	earrings
la marroquinería	leather goods store	las carteras	wallets
		las bolsas	pocketbooks
		las maletas	suitcases
		las carteras	briefcases

La Tienda	The Store	Las Mercancías	The Merchandise
la tienda de recuerdos	souvenir shop	las camisetas los carteles	T-shirts posters
		los monumentos en miniatura las máscaras las pinturas	miniature monuments masks paintings

Know Your Jewels

It is commonly believed that a very good bargain can be had on jewelry purchased in certain foreign countries. The rumor is true because there are taxes and duties that can be avoided. On our last trip to Puerto Rico, my husband purchased a beautiful gold necklace for me for my birthday. Before making our purchase we went to several different stores seeing how much we would have to pay for gold by the ounce. Once we found the best price, we had the opportunity to bargain with the sales clerk. It was, overall, a very friendly and amusing experience. Of course, the necklace was weighed before our eyes and a receipt was issued. Imagine how lucky I felt when I got home and saw a comparable piece in a discount store for almost twice the price. If you know your prices and are a good shopper, or if you're simply in the mood to buy some jewelry, you can use table 15.2 to get exactly what you want.

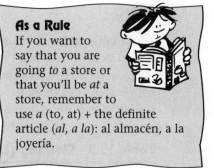

As a Rule
If you want to say that you are going *to* a store or that you'll be *at* a store, remember to use *a* (to, at) + the definite article (*al*, *a la*): al almacén, a la joyería.

Table 15.2 Jewels (Las Joyas—lahs hoh-yahs)

Jewel	Spanish Translation	Pronunciation
amethyst	la amatista	lah ah-mah-tees-tah
aquamarine	el aguamarina	ehl ah-gwah-mah-ree-nah
diamond	el diamante	ehl dee-ah-mahn-teh
emerald	la esmeralda	lah ehs-meh-rahl-dah
ivory	el marfíl	ehl mahr-feel
jade	el jade	ehl hah-deh
onyx	el ónix	ehl oh-neeks

continues

Table 15.2 Continued

Jewel	Spanish Translation	Pronunciation
pearls	las perlas	lahs pehr-lahs
ruby	el rubí	ehl roo-bee
sapphire	el zafiro	ehl sah-fee-roh
topaz	el topacio	ehl toh-pah-see-oh
turquoise	la turquesa	lah toor-keh-sah

If you are buying jewelry you might want to ask:

¿Es macizo oro?	ehs mah-see-soh oh-roh	*Is it solid gold?*
¿Es plata?	ehs plah-tah	*Is it silver?*

Clothing

You're curious about Spanish fashions and have decided to try your luck at buying a typical item of clothing. Perhaps you'll choose a T-shirt or maybe you've always craved a big sombrero to protect you from the sun. Whatever you decide to buy, table 15.3 will help you in your quest for something *a la última moda* (ah lah ool-tee-mah moh-dah), in the latest style or *tradicional* (trah-dee-see-oh-nahl).

Table 15.3 Clothing (La Ropa—lah roh-pah)

For One and All

Piece of Clothing	Spanish Translation	Pronunciation
bathing suit	el traje de baño	ehl trah-heh deh bah-nyoh
bikini	el bikini	ehl bee-kee-nee
string bikini	la tanga	lah tahn-gah
belt	el cinturón	ehl seen-too-rohn
bikini briefs	los calzoncillos	lohs kahl-sohn-see-yohs
boots	las botas	lahs boh-tahs
gloves	los guantes	lohs gwahn-tehs
handkerchief	el pañuelo	ehl pah-nyoo-weh-loh

For One and All

Piece of Clothing	Spanish Translation	Pronunciation
hat	el sombrero	ehl sohm-breh-roh
jacket	la chaqueta, el saco	lah chah-keh-tah, ehl sah-koh
jeans	los jeans, los vaqueros	lohs geens, lohs bah-keh-rohs
jogging suit	el traje de trotar, la sudadera	ehl trah-heh deh troh-tahr lah soo-dah-deh-rah
overcoat	el abrigo	ehl ah-bree-goh
pants	los pantalones	lohs pahn-tah-loh-nehs
pullover	el jersey	ehl hehr-see
pyjamas	las pijamas	lahs pee-hah-mahs
raincoat	el impermeable	ehl eem-pehr-meh-ah-bleh
robe	la bata	lah bah-tah
sandals	las sandalias	lahs sahn-dah-lee-ahs
scarf	la bufanda	lah boo-fahn-dah
shoes	los zapatos	lohs sah-pah-tohs
shorts	los pantalones cortos	lohs pahn-tah-loh-nehs kohr-tohs
sneakers	los tenis	lohs teh-nees
socks	los calcetines	lohs kahl-seh-tee-nehs
sweater	el suéter	ehl soo-eh-tehr
T-shirt	la camiseta, la playera	lah kah-mee-seh-tah, lah plah-yeh-rah
umbrella	el paraguas	ehl pah-rah-gwahs
underwear	la ropa interior	lah roh-pah een-teh-ree-ohr
vest	el chaleco	ehl chah-leh-koh

Cultural Tidbit

Because most countries use the metric system, their sizes are different from ours. Look at the following conversion chart to determine the sizes you would wear:

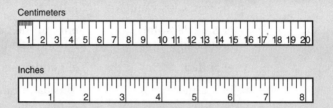

To convert centimeters into inches, multiply by .39.
To convert inches into centimeters, multiply by 2.54.

CONVERSION TABLES FOR CLOTHING SIZES

WOMEN

SHOES

American	4	$4\frac{1}{2}$	5	$5\frac{1}{2}$	6	$6\frac{1}{2}$	7	$7\frac{1}{2}$	8	$8\frac{1}{2}$	9	$9\frac{1}{2}$	10
Continental	35	35	36	36	37	37	38	38	39	39	40	40	41

DRESSES, SUITS

American	8	10	12	14	16	18
Continental	36	38	40	42	44	46

BLOUSES, SWEATERS

American	32	34	36	38	40	42
Continental	40	42	44	46	48	50

MEN

SHOES

American	7	$7\frac{1}{2}$	8	$8\frac{1}{2}$	9	$9\frac{1}{2}$	10	$10\frac{1}{2}$	11	$11\frac{1}{2}$
Continental	39	40	41	42	43	43	44	44	45	45

SUITS, COATS

American	34	36	38	40	42	44	46	48
Continental	44	46	48	50	52	54	56	58

SHIRTS

American	14	$14\frac{1}{2}$	15	$15\frac{1}{2}$	16	$16\frac{1}{2}$	17	$17\frac{1}{2}$
Continental	36	37	38	39	40	41	42	43

Cultural Tidbit

While European formality has become more and more prevalent in fashion trends, some traditional clothing can still be found.

A colorful wool or cotton *sarape*, that looks like a blanket, can still be seen on the shoulders of Mexican men.

Ponchos (as they are called in most of South and Central America), or *ruanas* (roo-ah-nahs) as they are called in the northern South American countries (Colombia, Venezuela, etc.), are capes that have an opening in the middle for the wearer's head. They are used as jackets.

In South America, Central America, and Mexico women wear white blouses and wide, colorful skirts with belts around their waists, along with sandals. In Mexico, *el huarache* (ehl hwah-rah-cheh) is a popular type of sandal.

The typical dress of *gauchos* (gow-chohs), the Argentinian cowboys, is a long woolen poncho; long, baggy pants that are gathered at the ankles and resemble bloomers, *bombachas* (bohm-bah-chahs); knee-high leather boots; and a flat-brimmed hat. They carry a *facón* (fah-kohn), a large knife, which is often worn in the back of a black silver-studded belt called a *rastra* (rahs-trah).

The Mexican sombrero is a wide-brimmed hat made out of straw or felt that can be as wide as two feet! The hat is big so that it can protect you from the strong sun by providing *sombra* (sohm-brah), shade.

The *torero* (bullfighter) is outfitted in a short waist-length jacket and knee-length skin-tight pants made of silk or satin, both richly embroidered in gold, silver, and silk. He also wears heavy silk stockings and flat black shoes resembling slippers.

You want to make sure that you get your right size. Be aware that in Spanish-speaking countries there is a much more formal relationship between a sales person and a customer than the relationships we are accustomed to in the United States. Sales people are always courteous, respectful, and attentive, but more reserved. Of course, in smaller, neighborhood stores, the atmosphere is far more friendly. If you were shopping and wanted to make sure you got the right size for shoes or clothing, you would tell the salesperson one of the following phrases:

Llevo el tamaño…   yeh-boh ehl tah-mah-nyoh   *I wear…*
  pequeño   peh-keh-nyoh   *small*
  mediano   meh-dee-ah-noh   *medium*
  grande   grahn-deh   *large*

Mi talla es... mee tah-yah ehs *My size is...*
   pequeña peh-keh-nyah *small*
   mediana meh-dee-ah-nah *medium*
   grande grahn-deh *large*

Pitfall

Upon making purchases in a foreign country remember to save your receipts. Some countries return the sales or value-added tax (VAT) that is charged to foreign visitors when they are abroad. In Spain, for example, there is a seven percent VAT added to the rates for all restaurants and hotel rooms. Special customer windows in large stores and tax rebate windows at the airport of departure will help you find out about any money due to you. If you buy something very costly, you may be assessed a tax by the state in which you live.

Colors

When I look at the world I usually describe things as red, yellow, green, blue, etc. My friend Vivian, on the other hand, *una artista*, talks about tangerine, burnt sienna, aubergine, and turquoise, and I rarely understand the shade or color she means. Whether you prefer the exotic or the ordinary, table 15.4 will help you with the basic colors you'll need in everyday situations.

Table 15.4 Colors (Los Colores—los koh-lohr-ehs)

Color	Spanish Translation	Pronunciation
beige	beige	beh-geh
black	negro	neh-groh
blue	azul	ah-sool
brown	marrón, pardo	mah-rrohn, pahr-doh
gray	gris	grees
green	verde	behr-deh
orange	anaranjado	ah-nah-rahn-hah-doh
pink	rosado	roh-sah-doh
purple	púrpura, morado	poor-poo-rah, moh-rah-doh
red	rojo	roh-hoh
white	blanco	blahn-koh
yellow	amarillo	ah-mah-ree-yoh

As a Rule

To describe a color as *light*, add the word *claro* (klah-roh) after the color.

To describe a color as *dark*, add the word *oscuro* (oh-skoo-roh) after the color.

light blue   *azul claro*

dark green   *verde oscuro*

As a Rule

Colors are adjectives and must agree with the noun they are describing. Remember that to change from masculine to feminine only if the adjective ends in *o*. No change is necessary when the adjective ends in an *e* or a consonant. All adjectives are made plural by adding an *s*, unless they already end in *s*. If an adjective ends in a consonant, add *es* to get the plural.

Materials

Did you ever wish you brought along a travel iron, or do you hang your travel-wrinkled clothes in a steamy bathroom hoping for the best? Do you insist on permanent press, or do you prefer more exotic materials that give you a more sophisticated, sexy look. If you plan on making a clothing purchase while on vacation, table 15.5 will help you pick the material you prefer for your special wants and needs.

Table 15.5 Materials (Las Telas—lahs teh-lahs)

Material	Spanish Translation	Pronunciation
cashmere	casimir	kah-see-meer
chiffon	gasa	gah-sah
corduroy	pana	pah-nah
cotton	algodón	ahl-goh-dohn
denim	tela tejana	teh-lah teh-hah-nah
flannel	franela	frah-neh-lah
gabardine	gabardina	gah-bahr-dee-nah

continues

Table 15.5   Continued

Material	Spanish Translation	Pronunciation
knit	tejido de punto	teh-hee-doh deh poon-toh
lace	encaje	ehn-kah-heh
leather	cuero	kweh-roh
linen	hilo	ee-loh
satin	raso	rah-soh
silk	seda	seh-dah
suede	gamuza	gah-moo-sah
taffeta	tafétan	tah-feh-tahn
velvet	terciopelo	tehr-see-oh-peh-loh
wool	lana	lah-nah

Look at Labels

Look carefully at all labels for the following information:

incontractable   een-kohn-trahk-tah-bleh   *non-shrinkable*

lavable   lah-bah-bleh   *washable*

inarrugable   een-ah-rroo-gah-bleh   *permanent press*

What Do You Put On?

Are you a clotheshorse, always making sure that you appear only in the latest styles? Or is comfort of the utmost importance and you tend to stick to jeans and T-shirts? Imagine that you've found yourself in the following situations. Describe in detail (including jewelry) what you wear to go to: work, the beach, a formal dinner party, your friend's house, skiing.

What's the Object?

I have an absolutely fabulous black dress. Imagine that I was telling you about it and said: "I wear *my black dress* often. I put on *my black dress* to go to parties. I love *my black dress*." How tedious and boring! It would be much easier to say: "I wear *my black dress* often. I put *it* on to go to parties. I love *it*."

What did I do to improve my conversation? I stopped repeating *my black dress* (a direct object noun) and replaced it with *it* (a direct object pronoun). Just what exactly are direct objects? Let's take a closer look:

Direct objects (which can be nouns or pronouns) answer the question "*whom* or *what* is the subject acting upon?" and may refer to people, places, things, or ideas:

> I see *the boy*.   I see *him*.

> I like *the dress*.   I like *it*.

> He pays *Jane, Mike, and me*.   He pays *us*.

Indirect objects can be replaced by indirect object pronouns. Take the story of my friend Georgette, who is crazy about her new boyfriend, Paul. This is what she told me: "I write *to Paul*. Then I read my loveletters *to Paul*. I buy presents *for Paul*. I bake cookies *for Paul*. I cook dinners *for Paul*." To get to the point more efficiently, all she had to say was: "I write to Paul and then I read *him (to him)* my loveletters. I buy *him (for him)* presents. I bake *him* cookies *(for him)* and I cook *him* dinners *(for him)*."

How do indirect objects differ from direct objects? Take a closer look:

Indirect objects answer the question "*to whom* is the subject doing something" or "*for whom* is the subject acting?"

> I speak to the boys.   I speak *to them*.

> I buy a gift for Mary.   I buy a gift *for her*. (I buy *her* a gift.)

> He gives (to) *me* a tie every Christmas.

We use direct and indirect pronouns automatically in English all the time to prevent the constant, monotonous repetition of a word and to allow our conversation to flow naturally. Direct and indirect object nouns in Spanish may be replaced by the pronouns in table 15.6.

As a Rule

Look at the following two English sentences from the earlier examples:

I write (to) him loveletters.

I buy (for) him presents.

Notice that the *to* or *for* is often understood, but not used in English. So be careful in Spanish when choosing a direct or indirect object pronoun. If the words *to* or *for* make sense in the sentence, even though they do not actually appear, use an indirect object pronoun.

Table 15.6 Object Pronouns

Direct Object Pronouns		Indirect Object Pronouns	
Pronoun	**Meaning**	**Pronoun**	**Meaning**
me (meh)	me	me (meh)	(to) me
te (teh)	you (familiar)	te (teh)	(to) you (familiar)
le (leh)	you, him	le (leh)	(to) him, her, you, it
lo (loh)	you, him, it		
la (lah)	her, it		
nos (nohs)	us	nos (nohs)	(to) us
os (ohs)	you (familiar)	os (ohs)	(to) you
los (lohs)	them, you	les (lehs)	
las (lahs)	them, you		(to) them

The Personal A

The clue to the correct usage of an indirect object is the Spanish preposition *a* (*al, a la, a los, a las*) followed by the name of or reference to a person. The verb telefonear (*a*) is always followed by *a* + *person* and will, therefore, always take an indirect object pronoun.

> ¿Telefonea a Paco?   *Are you calling Paco?*

Pitfall
Never use the personal a with *ser* (to be) or *tener* (to have).

Ella es mi amiga.
She is my friend.

Tengo dos hijos.
I have two sons.

The rule just given can be somewhat tricky because of the personal *a*. What is the personal *a*? It's the preposition *a* that is used before the direct object of the verb, if the direct object is a person, pet, or pronoun referring to a person.

Visito a mis amigos.   *I visit my friends.*

Queremos al perro.   *We love the dog.*

¿Ves a alguien?   *Do you see someone?*

In order to correctly choose between the use of a direct or indirect pronoun you must remember to see if adding the word *to* or *for* makes sense in your sentence. If it does, then choose an indirect object pronoun. If not, you must use the direct object pronoun.

As you can see, you should have little problem using the direct or indirect object pronouns for me, to me (*me*); you, to you (*te, nos*); or us, to us (*nos*) because these pronouns are all exactly the same. You must be careful, however, when differentiating between *him* (her, it, you, them) or *to (for) him* (her, it, you, them) because there are now two sets of pronouns:

> him (it, you)—lo, le
> her (it, you)—la
> them—los, las
>
> to him (it, you)—le
> to her (it, you)—le
> to them—les

Sometimes this does get a bit tricky. Remember to choose the pronoun that reflects the number and gender of the noun to which you are referring:

> Ella lleva el vestido rojo.   *Ella lo lleva.*
>
> Él lleva la camisa blanca.   *Él la lleva.*
>
> Llevo mis zapatos negros.   *Los llevo.*
>
> Ellas llevan sandalias amarillas.   *Las llevan.*
>
> Él habla a Ana.   *Él le habla.*
>
> Él habla a Pablo.   *Él le habla.*
>
> Él habla a Ana y Pablo.   *Él les habla.*

Pitfall
Be careful! Some verbs like escuchar (to listen to), buscar (to look for), pagar (to pay for), and mirar (to look at) take direct objects in Spanish because the English prepositions are built directly into the meaning of the Spanish verbs.

As a Rule
In Spanish America, *lo* is generally used instead of *le* as the direct object to express *him* and *you*.

Lo veo.   *I see him (it).*

The Position of Object Pronouns

Although we can automatically place object pronouns in their proper place in English, correct placement in Spanish does not follow English rules and requires some practice. Let's take a closer look:

➤ Object pronouns are normally placed before the verb.

> Yo lo llevo.
>
> Yo le hablo.
>
> Yo no lo llevo.
>
> Yo no le hablo.
>
> ¡No lo lleve!
>
> ¡No le hable!

➤ When direct and indirect object pronouns are used with an infinitive or a gerund (estar + -ando, -iendo endings), they may be placed before or after the verb. When the gerund is followed by the object pronoun, count back three vowels and add an accent to obtain the proper stress.

As a Rule

A gerund is a word derived from a verb but used as a noun. It may be used as a subject or object. The gerund always ends in -ing.

Example: Swimming is fun. (subject)   I enjoy jogging. (object)

Quiero llevarla.   La quiero llevar.   Estoy llevándola.   La estoy llevando.

➤ In an affirmative command, the object pronoun follows the verb form and is attached to it. Again, count back three vowels and add an accent for proper stress. Note in the preceding example that in a negative command, the object pronoun precedes the verb:

¡No lo (la) lleve!   ¡Llévela!

That's the Way I Like It

When you go on vacation there are bound to be loads of things you like, from the food you eat, to your living accommodations, to the places you visit. In order to express that something is pleasing to you, you will want to use the verb *gustar*.

Translated literally, *gustar* means *to be pleasing to*. You can't simply say: "I like" in Spanish. What you must say is: "_____ is (are) pleasing *to* me." The word *to* is very important. It instructs you to use an indirect object pronoun to get your point across. The verb *gustar* will agree with the noun in the blank, since that word is the subject of the sentence. For our purposes, and in general, the noun in the blank will be either in the third person singular (él, ella, Ud.) or plural (ellos, ellas, Uds.) form.

The hat is pleasing to them.
They like the hat.   *Les gusta el sombrero.*
Here, *gusta* agrees with *sombrero*, the subject of the sentence.

The shirts are pleasing to him.
He likes the shirts.   *Le gustan las camisas.*
Gustan agrees with camisas, the subject of the sentence.

Let's say you've gone shopping and you've picked out some shirts that you really love. Here is how you would express your likes:

Me gust*a la camisa.*
I like the shirt.
(*The shirt* is pleasing to me.)

Me gust*an las camisas.*
I like the shirts.
(*The shirts* are pleasing to me.)

Don't let the reverse word order trick you. Pick the indirect object that expresses the person to whom the noun is pleasing. Then if you remember that the subject follows the verb with gustar, you'll have little trouble. Let's take a look at a few more sentences to see how gustar works:

¿Te gusta el sombrero?   *Do you like the hat?*

Le gustan los zapatos.   *He (She, You) likes the shoes.*

Nos gusta la falda.   *We like the skirt.*

No os gusta el traje.   *You don't like the suit.*

Les gusta la blusa.   *They like the blouse.*

Three other verbs that work in exactly the same way as gustar are: encantar (ehn-kahn-tahr), to like very much; faltar (fahl-tahr), to lack, need; and disgustar, (dees-goos-tahr), to dislike.

Les encanta el abrigo.   *They love the coat.*

Me falta un vestido.   *I need a dress.*

Nos disgusta la bufanda.   *We dislike the scarf.*

As a Rule

If you want to specify who likes what, use the preposition *a* + the person's name (pronouns that may be used will be discussed in Chapter 19) before the gustar construction.

A Marta le gustan las casetas.   *Marta likes the cassettes.*

A Roberto y a Juan no les gusta la música.   *Roberto and Juan don't like the music.*

Putting Gustar to Work

Imagine that your traveling companion has spent the day alone shopping. Upon arriving home he/she unwraps all of his/her purchases in order to get your opinion, because if you don't like it, it's going back. Tell if you like or dislike: the red hat, the small shirt, the big T-shirt, and the green shoes.

Using Direct Object Pronouns

Imagine that you are on a shopping spree in the Galerías Preciados department store in Spain and your arms are loaded with all your "finds." Your friend joins you and questions your choices. Answer all of his questions efficiently by using a direct object pronoun:

1. ¿Compras el pantalón azul?
2. ¿Quieres los guantes negros?
3. ¿Escoges la corbata roja?
4. ¿Tomas las camisas blancas?
5. ¿Consideras el traje de baño verde?
6. ¿Detestas los zapatos amarillos?

Using Indirect Object Pronouns

Your friend doesn't know what to buy her friends and family members as gifts. Offer suggestions of what to buy and what not to buy.

For example:

Pablo/un radio/un libro
Cómprele un radio.
No le compre un libro.

sus hijos/camisas/corbatas
Cómpreles una camisa.
No les compre corbatas.

Roberto/abrigo/chaqueta

sus hermanas/vestidos/faldas

sus padres/sombreros/guantes

su amiga/una camiseta/una bolsa

sus amigos/casetas/discos

su abuela/una pulsera/un reloj

Asking for What You Want

Do you get annoyed when a sales clerk hovers over your shoulder constantly watching you as you examine the merchandise? Or are you a total clod at picking out something that fits well, looks nice, and is appropriate, and so you crave the assistance of someone "in the know?" Here are some phrases to help you deal with most common situations:

Upon entering a store an employee might ask you:

¿En qué puedo servirle?
ehn keh pweh-doh sehr-beer-leh
How may I help you?

¿Los están atendiendo?
lohs ehs-tahn ah-tehn-dee-ehn-doh
Is someone helping you?

¿Qué desea?
keh deh-seh-ah
What would you like?

If you are just browsing, you would answer:

No, gracias. Simplemente estoy buscando.
noh grah-see-ahs seem-pleh-mehn-teh ehs-toh-ee boos-kahn-doh
No, thank you, I am (just) looking.

If you want to see or buy something, you would answer:

Sí, estoy buscando un (una) xxx por favor
see ehs-toh-ee boos-kahn-doh oon (oo-nah) xxx pohr fah-bohr
Yes, I 'm looking for a xxx please.

And of course, if you're a shopper like me, you'd want to know:

¿Hay ventas (gangas)?
ah-ee behn-tahs (gahn-gahs)
Are there any sales?

¿Hay rebajas (descuentos)?
ah-ee reh-bah-hahs (dehs-kwehn-tohs)
Are there any discounts?

As a Rule

To ask which item a person prefers, use *¿qué?* before the noun.

¿Qué camiseta prefiere(s)?

To ask which of many someone prefers use *¿cuál?*

¿Cuál de los dos (pantalones) prefiere(s)?

¿Cuál quiere?

¿Cuáles te gustan?

You may answer by using the appropriate definite article and an adjective:

El azul.   *The blue one.*

Las pequeñas.   *The small ones.*

Expressing Opinions

That shirt is you. You just love those pants. What a perfect jacket! If you are happy with an item you will want to express your pleasure by saying one of the following phrases:

Phrase	Pronunciation	Meaning
Me gusta(n) (mucho).	meh goos-tah(n) (moo-choh)	I like it (a lot).
Me queda muy bien.	meh keh-dah moo-ee bee-ehn	It suits (fits) me very well.
Me queda perfectamente.	meh keh-dah pehr-fehk-tah-mehn-teh	It suits (fits) me perfectly.
Está(n) bien.	ehs-tah(n) bee-ehn	It's nice.
Es elegante.	ehs eh-leh-gahn-teh	It's elegant.
Es práctico(a).	ehs prahk-tee-koh(kah)	It's practical.
Siempre es bonito(a).	see-ehm-preh ehs boh-nee-toh(tah)	It's always attractive.

Face it! The cookies you ate all winter are showing on your hips and your stomach hangs over your pants in an embarrassing fashion. You like a tight fit but this is simply out of the question. If you are disappointed with the way you look, you might make use of one of the following comments:

Phrase	Pronunciation	Meaning
No me gusta(n).	noh meh goos-tah(n)	I don't like it.
No me queda bien.	noh meh keh-dah bee-ehn	It doesn't suit (fit) me.
Es horrible.	ehs oh-rree-bleh	It's horrible.
Es pequeño.	ehs peh-keh-nyoh	It's too small.
Es apretado.	ehs ah-preh-tah-doh	It's too tight.
Es corto.	ehs kohr-toh	It's too short.
Es largo.	ehs lahr-goh	It's too long.
Es chillón(ona).	ehs chee-yohn(yoh-nah)	It's too loud.
Es estrecho.	ehs ehs-treh-choh	It's too narrow.

As a Rule

Remember to change verbs and adjectives to accomodate plural subjects. There is no agreements of adverbs in Spanish, therefore, the adverb *demasiado*, too, does not change.

Los pantalones son demasiado cortos.

La blusa es demasiado apretada.

If you're not satisfied and want something else:

Estoy buscando algo más (menos) + *adjective*
ehs-toh-ee boos-kahn-doh ahl-goh mahs (meh-nohs)
I'm looking for something more (less) …

I'll Take This, That, One of These, and Some of Those

When I go shopping I want a consultant. So I either bring along a friend or rely on the opinion of a well-put-together sales person. It's a common practice to ask how *this* shirt, *that* blouse, *these* pants, or *those* skirts look on the person buying them. A demonstrative adjective points out someone or something being referred to and allows you to be specific by expressing *this, that, these,* and *those,* as shown in table 15.7.

Table 15.7 Demonstrative Adjectives

Demonstrative Adjective	Masculine	Feminine
this	este	esta
these	estos	estas
that (near speaker)	ese	esa
those (near speaker)	esos	esas
that (away from speaker)	aquel	aquella
those (away from speaker)	aquellos	aquellas

Notice that the demonstrative adjective you choose depends upon the physical proximity of the noun to the subject.

➤ Este (esta, etc.) refers to what is near or directly concerns the speaker.

Este vestido es bonito.   *This dress is pretty.*

Estos relojes son caros.   *These watches are expensive.*

As a Rule
The tags *aquí* (here), *ahí, allí* (there), and *allá* ([over] there) are used respectively with *este, ese,* and *aquel.*

Me gusta esta falda aquí.
I like this skirt here.

No le encantan esos zapatos allí.
I don't love those shoes there.

Nos falta aquel libro allá.
We need that book (over) there.

➤ Ese (esa, etc.) refers to someone (thing) not particularly near or not directly concerning the person being addressed.

Ese hombre es guapo.   *That man is handsome.*

Esas bufandas son baratas. *Those scarves are inexpensive.*

➤ Aquel (aquella, etc.) refers to someone (thing) that is quite remote from the speaker and the person being addressed and that concerns neither of them directly.

Aquel país es grande.   *That country is big.*

Aquella ciudad es bella.   *That city is beautiful.*

What Do You Think?

Look at the gifts your friends bought. Using the demonstrative adjectives and tags that you've just learned, express how you feel about them in more detail. Give as much detail as possible:

192

The Least You Need to Know

➤ To shop successfully in a Spanish-speaking country you must use the metric system for sizing and measuring.

➤ Use object pronouns to replace object nouns. Object pronouns are usually placed before the conjugated verb, except in an affirmative command when they come after the verb.

➤ Use an indirect object pronoun with gustar to express who is doing the liking. The object that pleases is the subject of the sentence, and gustar must agree with it.

➤ Demonstrative adjectives (este, ese, aquel) agree in number and gender with the nouns they describe. Use *este* for nouns that are closest, *ese* for nouns that are farther, and *aquel* for nouns that are the farthest from the speaker and person being addressed.

Chapter 16

Creative Cooking

In This Chapter

➤ Specialty food stores

➤ Expressing quantity

➤ Using demonstrative pronouns

➤ A special dish

You've learned to shop for souvenirs, gifts, and some basic daily necessities in Chapter 15. Armed with a metric conversion chart for clothing and shoes, you were even able to select some fabulous native fashions and footwear in the correct sizes. Shopping till you drop really works up a voracious appetite. Dinner's not until after 7 p.m. and it's only 4:30. How should you proceed to ease that rumbling in your stomach?

A great idea would be to drop into a local grocery store or specialty food store and grab something yummy to tide you over to your next meal. Why not try *un taco* filled with meat, *una tortilla* topped with *salsa verde*, or a pastry. Many different food choices are presented in this chapter. You'll also learn how to get the quantity you desire, which is important because the Spanish system of weights differs from ours. There's something special, too, at the end of the chapter.

Shopping Here and There

When I travel, the height of luxury is having a refrigerator (well-stocked with drinks and snacks) in my room. No matter where I'm traveling, once I've reached my destination and unpacked, the first thing I do is scout out the nearest food supply, and stock up. If you get the midnight munchies, come to my room. I'm always well supplied with native drinks and delicacies. If there's a stove or oven in my room, however, I usually ignore it. I don't cook on vacation, but perhaps this is something you enjoy doing. Purchase the culinary delights of your choosing from the shops listed in table 16.1.

Table 16.1 Food Shops

The Store	La Tienda	Pronunciation
bakery	la panadería	lah pah-nah-deh-ree-ah
butcher shop	la carnicería	lah kahr-nee-seh-ree-ah
candy store	la confitería	lah kohn-fee-teh-ree-ah
dairy store	la lechería	lah leh-cheh-ree-ah
delicatessen	la salchichonería	lah sahl-chee-choh-neh-ree-ah
fish store	la pescadería	lah pehs-kah-deh-ree-ah
fruit store	la frutería	lah froo-teh-ree-ah
grocery store	la abacería	lah ah-bah-seh-ree-ah
liquor store	la tienda de licores	lah tee-ehn-dah deh lee-koh-rehs
pastry shop	la pastelería	lah pahs-teh-leh-ree-ah
supermarket	el supermercado	ehl soo-pehr-mehr-kah-doh

Cultural Tidbit

If it's bread and rolls you're looking for, go to a panadería. There you will be able to purchase bread that is baked fresh two to three times a day. This bread, *pan* (pahn), available in several different sizes, is soft on the inside and crusty on the outside. *Pan dulce* (pahn dool-seh), comparable to any kind of sweet roll, cinnamon roll, or danish, is another popular item. You can even get *un croissant* (oon kroh-ee-sahnt) (borrowed from the French)—that's right, a crescent roll. This type of roll is known as *una medialuna* (oo-nah meh-dee-ah-loo-nah), literally translated as a half moon, in countries such as Argentina, Uruguay, and Chile. And finally, if you're like me and suffer from a permanent sweet tooth, head right over to a pastelería where you can purchase fancy pastries.

Where Are You Going?

You've decided to purchase some goodies for your room. Dinner is served rather late and you just want to spend some quiet time in your room snacking and relaxing. It's off you go to the local stores. To tell someone where you're going, use the verb *ir* and the preposition *a* + the appropriate definite article (*al*, *a la*) to give the correct information:

Voy a la pastelería.   *I'm going to the pastry shop.*

Voy a la salchichonería.   *I'm going to the deli.*

Try it. Tell your traveling companion where you are going to buy: vegetables, pastries, meat, fruits, fish, wine, candy, milk.

Cultural Tidbit

Although *supermercados* (soo-pehr-mehr-kah-dohs), and even *hipermercados* (ee-pehr-mehr-kah-dohs) (large specialty stores that sell food and other items) exist in Spain and Latin America, many shoppers still prefer to buy their fresh produce in smaller, specialty stores. They feel that the quality is superior. Staples, such as rice and cooking oil are purchased at supermarkets because prices there tend to be lower.

Be careful. Depending on the country you are in, the word for grocery store may vary. Don't be surprised to see any of the following: *una tienda de comestibles*, *una tienda de abarrotes*, *una aborrotería*, *una pulpería*, *una tienda de ultramarinos*, or *una bodega*. In Spain, a *bodega* is a store that sells only wine from barrels, so you won't be able to purchase any food there. When in doubt, go to the local supermercado!

Aren't you just a bit curious to try something new? It's always interesting to taste a specialty that's new to the palate instead of settling for the same old thing time after time. If you wanted to savor a typical food, would you try a fruit? a vegetable? a dessert? Do you prefer meat? fish? poultry? game? What foods (*alimientos*) tempt you? Tables 16.2 through 16.9 will help you select something your palate will enjoy.

Table 16.2 At the Grocery Store

Vegetables	Las Legumbres	Pronunciation
asparagus	los espárragos	lohs ehs-pah-rrah-gohs
broccoli	el brécol	ehl breh-kohl
carrot	la zanahoría	lah sah-nah-oh-ree-ah
corn	el maíz	ehl mah-ees
eggplant	la berenjena	lah beh-rehn-heh-nah
lettuce	le lechuga	lah leh-choo-gah
mushroom	el champiñon	ehl chahm-pee-nyohn
onion	la cebolla	lah seh-boh-yah
pepper	la pimienta	lah pee-mee-ehn-tah
potato	la papa, la patata	lah pah-pah, lah pah-tah-tah
rice	el arroz	ehl ah-rrohs
spinach	la espinaca	lah ehs-pee-nah-kah
sweet potato	la papa dulce	lah pah-pah dool-seh
tomato	el tomate	ehl toh-mah-teh

Table 16.3 At the Fruit Store

Fruits	Las Frutas	Pronunciation
apple	la manzana	lah mahn-sah-nah
apricot	el albaricoque	ehl ahl-bah-ree-koh-keh
banana	la banana	lah bah-nah-nah
blueberry	el mirtilo	ehl meer-tee-loh
cherry	la cereza	lah seh-reh-sah
date	el dátil	ehl dah-teel
fig	el higo	ehl ee-goh
grape	la uva	lah oo-bah
grapefruit	la toronja	lah toh-rohn-hah
guava	la guayaba	lah gwah-yah-bah
lemon	el limón	ehl lee-mohn
mango	el mango	ehl mahn-goh

Fruits	Las Frutas	Pronunciation
melon	el melón	ehl meh-lohn
orange	la naranja	lah nah-rahn-hah
peach	el melocotón	ehl meh-loh-koh-tohn
pear	la pera	lah peh-rah
pineapple	la piña	lah pee-nyah
raisin	la pasa	lah pah-sah
raspberry	la frambuesa, la mora	lah frahm-boo-eh-sah, lah moh-rah
strawberry	la fresa	lah freh-sah

Nuts	Las Nueces	Pronunciation
almond	la almendra	lah ahl-mehn-drah
chestnut	la castaña	lah kahs-tah-nyah
hazelnut	la avellana	lah ah-beh-yah-nah
walnut	la nuez	lah noo-ehs

Table 16.4 At the Butcher or Delicatessen

Meats	Las Carnes	Pronunciation
bacon	el tocino	ehl toh-see-noh
beef	la carne de vaca (res)	lah kahr-neh deh bah-kah (rehs)
ham	el jamón	ehl hah-mohn
lamb	la carne de cordero	lah kahr-neh deh kohr-deh-roh
liver	el hígado	ehl ee-gah-doh
pork	la carne de cerdo	lah kahr-neh deh sehr-doh
roast beef	el rosbíf	ehl rohs-beef
sausage	las salchichas	lahs sahl-chee-chahs
sweetbreads	las criadillas	lahs kree-ah-dee-yahs
veal	la carne de ternera	lah kahr-neh deh tehr-neh-rah

Fowl and Game	La Carne de Ave y de Caza	Pronunciation
chicken	el pollo	ehl poh-yoh
duck	el pato	ehl pah-toh
goose	el ganso	ehl gahn-soh
pigeon	la paloma	lah pah-loh-mah
quail	la codorniz	lah koh-dohr-nees
rabbit	el conejo	ehl koh-neh-hoh
turkey	el pavo	ehl pah-boh

Table 16.5 At the Fish Store

Fish and Seafood	El Pescado y los Mariscos	Pronunciation
clam	la almeja	lah ahl-meh-hah
crab	el cangrejo	ehl kahn-greh-hoh
crawfish	la cigala	lah see-gah-lah
flounder	el lenguado	ehl lehn-gwah-doh
halibut	el halibut	ehl ah-lee-boot
herring	el arenque	ehl ah-rehn-keh
lobster	la langosta	lah lahn-gohs-tah
mussel	el mejillón	lah meh-hee-yohn
oyster	la ostra	lah ohs-trah
red snapper	el pargo colorado	ehl pahr-goh koh-loh-rah-doh
salmon	el salmón	ehl sahl-mohn
sardine	la sardina	lah sahr-dee-nah
scallops	las conchas de peregrino	lahs kohn-chahs deh peh-reh-gree-noh
shrimp	los camarones, las gambas	lohs kah-mah-roh-nehs, lahs gahm-bahs
sole	el lenguado	ehl lehn-gwah-doh
squid	el calamar	ehl kah-lah-mahr
swordfish	el pez espada	ehl pehs ehs-pah-dah
trout	la trucha	lah troo-chah
tuna	el atún	ehl ah-toon

Table 16.6   At the Dairy

Dairy Products	Productos Lácteos	Pronunciation
butter	la mantequilla	lah mahn-teh-kee-yah
cheese	el queso	ehl keh-soh
cream	la crema	lah kreh-mah
eggs	los huevos	lohs hoo-eh-bohs
yogurt	el yogur	ehl yoh-goor

Table 16.7   At the Bakery and Pastry Shop

Breads and Desserts	Pan y Postres	Pronunciation
biscuit	el bizcocho	ehl bees-koh-choh
bread	el pan	ehl pahn
cake	el pastel	ehl pahs-tehl
cookie	la galletita	lah gah-yeh-tee-tah
custard (caramel)	la crema catalana (el flan)	lah kreh-mah kah-tah-lah-nah (ehl flahn)
marzipan	el marzapán	ehl mahr-sah-pahn
meringue	el merengue	ehl meh-rehn-geh
pie	el pastel	ehl pahs-tehl
pudding (cream)	la natilla	lah nah-tee-yah
rice pudding	el arroz con leche	ehl ah-rrohs kohn leh-cheh
rolls (sweet)	los panecillos (dulces)	lohs pah-neh-see-yohs (dool-sehs)
tart	la torta	lah tohr-tah

Table 16.8   At the Candy Store

Sweets	Los Dulces	Pronunciation
candy	los dulces	lohs dool-sehs
chocolate	el chocolate	ehl choh-koh-lah-teh
gum	el chicle	ehl chee-kleh

201

Cultural Tidbit

If you're like me, you're a chocoholic. It's a common belief that chocolate does make you happy, so why not indulge? Chocolate is made from the seeds of the cacao tree, which is native to Central and South America. In the sixteenth century, Hernán Cortés, the Spanish conquistador of Mexico, saw how fond the Aztec emperor, Montezuma, was of a drink called *xocoatl*. This drink, prepared from cocoa beans, was so dear that it was served in golden cups. The Aztecs even used cacao beans as money. The bitter taste of the natural beans was tempered by the Spaniards, who added sugar and water to make hot chocolate. These explorers then brought the drink back to Spain, where it quickly became a favorite of the noble class. The popularity of the drink spread throughout the world, and chocolate, as we know it today, evolved in the nineteenth century.

Table 16.9   At the Supermarket

Drinks	Las Bebidas	Pronunciation
cider	la sidra	lah see-drah
coffee (iced)	el café (helado)	ehl kah-feh (eh-lah-doh)
hot chocolate	el chocolate	ehl choh-koh-lah-teh
juice	el jugo	ehl hoo-goh
lemonade	la limonada	lah lee-moh-nah-dah
milk	la leche	lah leh-cheh
milk shake	el batido de leche	ehl bah-tee-doh deh leh-cheh
milk, malted	la leche malteada	lah leh-cheh mahl-teh-ah-dah
orangeade	la naranjada	lah nah-rahn-hah-dah
punch	el ponche	ehl pohn-cheh
soda	la gaseosa	lah gah-seh-oh-sah
tea (iced)	el té (helado)	ehl teh (eh-lah-doh)
tonic water	el tónico	ehl toh-nee-koh
water (mineral) (carbonated) (non-carbonated)	el agua (mineral) (con gas) (sin gas)	ehl ah-gwah (mee-neh-rahl) (kohn gahs) (seen gahs)
wine	el vino	ehl bee-noh

Cultural Tidbit

   Coffee is a very popular drink in Spanish-speaking countries throughout the world. Consider how many different ways there are of serving *café*.

   For breakfast, try a *café con leche* (kah-feh kohn leh-cheh), a large cup of coffee topped with a large amount of heated milk. The coffee that we are accustomed to drinking, coffee with just a little milk, is called *un cortado* (oon kohr-tah-doh). One way to beat the heat is to try *un blanco y negro* (oon blahn-koh ee neh-groh), a glass of iced coffee, sweetened with sugar and topped with a scoop of vanilla ice cream. Another way to avoid the hot weather is to try *un granizado de café* (ooh grah-nee-sah-doh deh kah-feh), iced coffee served over crushed ice. And if you prefer something on the strong side, try *un café solo* (oon kah-feh soh-loh) or *un exprés* (oon ehks-prehs), very strong black coffee (without milk), served in a demi-tasse cup (what we refer to as *espresso*).

Another very popular drink in Latin-American countries is ice cold shakes made with tropical fruits called *batidos* (bah-tee-dohs), *batidas* (bah-tee-dahs), or *licuados* (lee-kwah-dohs). Morning, noon, and night on the streets of every city and town there are stands dispensing these refreshing shakes. The main ingredients are fruit, milk, sugar, and crushed ice. If you want a really thick drink, a raw egg is added. You can try making one yourself in a blender by mixing all the ingredients for a couple of minutes.

As a Rule

If you want to be specific about a type of juice, use *jugo de* + name of the fruit:

   jugo de naranja   *orange juice*

   jugo de manzana   *apple juice*

Your Likes and Dislikes

Do you cringe at the sight of spinach but start to drool when you pick up the scent of a hamburger or frank cooking on a grill? Are you picky when you have to choose what you like to eat or will you eat just about anything to stop your stomach from growling? For each group listed here, tell what you love (*me encanta[n]*), like (*me gusta[n]*), and dislike (*me disgusta[n]*): fish, meat, dairy, fruits, breads, vegetables, drinks, dessert.

It's the Quantity That Counts

Because most of us are used to dealing with ounces, pounds, pints, quarts, and gallons, we've included a conversion chart to help you out until the metric system becomes second nature.

Table 16.10 Measuring Quantities of Food*

Solid Measures		Liquid Measures	
U.S. Customary System	Metric Equivalent	System	U.S. Customary Metric Equivalent
1 oz.	28 grams	1 oz.	30 milliliters
1/4 lb.	125 grams	16 oz. (1 pint)	475 milliliters
1/2 lb.	250 grams	32 oz. (1 quart)	950 milliliters (approximately 1 liter)
3/4 lb.	375 grams	1 gallon	3.75 liters
1.1 lb.	500 grams		
2.2 lb.	1,000 grams (1 kilogram)		

All weight and measurement comparisons are approximate

When I was a kid, no one ever told us about the metric system. So if you're a bit confused, trust me, I perfectly understand. We can make things a bit easier for ourselves by simply asking for a box, bag, can, etc. and by just memorizing the amounts we think we'll need: a pound, a quart, or whatever. Consult table 16.11 to easily get the right amount.

Table 16.11 Getting the Amount You Want

Amount	Spanish Translation	Pronunciation
a bag of	un saco de	oon sah-koh deh
a bar of	una barra de	oo-nah bah-rrah deh
a bottle of	una botella de	oo-nah boh-teh-yah deh
a box of	una caja de	oo-nah kah-hah deh
a bunch of	un atado de	oon ah-tah-doh deh
a can of	una lata de	oo-nah lah-tah deh
a dozen	una docena de	oo-nah doh-seh-nah deh

Amount	Spanish Translation	Pronunciation
a half pound of	una media libra de	oo-nah meh-dee-ah lee-brah deh
a jar of	un pomo de	oon poh-moh deh
a package of	un paquete de	oon pah-keh-teh deh
a piece of	un pedazo de	oon peh-dah-soh deh
a pound of	una libra de	oo-nah lee-brah deh
a quart of	un litro de	oon lee-troh deh
a slice of	un trozo de	oon troh-soh deh

If you want to get a feel for Spanish culture you're just going to have to go off your diet for a change. You know you want to taste that *dulce de zapote* (dool-seh deh sah-poh-teh) that your Mexican friend has prepared for you. Never mind the caloric content of the zapote pulp, orange juice, and sugar. You taste it and savor its creamy texture and tangy flavor. Your friend decides to give you more than "just a taste," which is all you really wanted. Don't allow yourself to completely blow your diet. Here are some expressions that will help you limit the quantity you receive:

As a Rule
Each of these expressions of quantity include the word *de* (of), which is always used.

una docena de huevos
a dozen eggs

una botella de agua
a bottle of water

Quantity	Spanish Translation	Pronunciation
a little	un poco de	oon poh-koh deh
a lot of	mucho(a)	moo-choh(ah)
enough	bastante, suficiente	bahs-tahn-teh soo-fee-see-ehn-teh
too much	demasiado	deh-mah-see-ah-doh

What's in the Fridge?

Happiness is checking into your hotel room and finding out that it is equipped with a small refrigerator. After unpacking, why not take a quick walk down to the nearest grocery store and stock up on some items you'd like to have on hand. What snacks would you purchase for that occasional craving?

Cultural Tidbit

Be advised: it is not customary to receive a shopping bag in individual neighborhood stores. Spanish shoppers usually bring along *un saco* (oon sah-koh), a bag in which they pack and carry their purchases. This bag is reusable and, therefore, environment-friendly. You may purchase one at a supermarket, drugstore, or variety store.

Demonstrating What You Want

When you go into a store do you sometimes drive the clerk crazy by pointing to this item and that one? Do you make demands because you must have that brand and not this one? And when you finally think you've made the best choice, do you notice that one over there and then spend several minutes debating your judgment? If that's the case, then you'll certainly need demonstrative pronouns.

These nifty little words are very useful and so easy to learn, because they are exactly the same as the demonstrative adjectives we studied in Chapter 15, except for an accent mark that must be added. Table 16.12 will help you select *this one*, *that one*, or you know, *that one, over there*.

Table 16.12   Demonstrative Pronouns

Demonstrative Pronoun	Masculine	Feminine
this one	éste	ésta
these	éstos	éstas
that one (near speaker)	ése	ésa
those (near speaker)	ésos	ésas
that one (away from speaker, over there)	aquél	aquélla
those (away from speaker, over there)	aquéllos	aquéllas

➤ Demonstrative pronouns are used to indicate a person, place, or thing when the noun itself is not mentioned.

Prefiero ésta.   *I prefer this one.*

➤ Demonstrative pronouns agree in number and gender with the nouns they replace.

esta botella y aquélla   *this bottle and that (one)*

Este vino es rojo, ése blanco, y aquél rosado.
This wine is red, that one white, and that one (over there) rosé.

Getting What You Want

In a small, neighborhood store there will always be someone eager to help you. Be prepared for the questions that you might be asked and the proper way to give an answer that will get you what you want:

¿Qué desea?	¿En qué puedo servirle?
keh deh-seh-ah	ehn keh pweh-doh sehr-beer-leh
What would you like?	*May I help you?*

Your answer might begin one of these ways:

Deseo…	¿Podria darme…?	Por favor.
deh-seh-oh	poh-dree-ah dahr-meh	pohr fah-bohr
I would like…	*Could you give me…?*	*Please.*

You might then be asked:

¿Y con ése?	¿Es todo?
ee kohn eh-seh	ehs toh-doh
And with that?	*Is that all?*

An appropriate response would be to either give additional items that you want, or to answer:

Sí, es todo, gracias.
see ehs toh-doh grah-see-ahs
Yes, that's all, thank you.

You're on your own. Tell a shopkeeper that you would like a pound of ham, a liter of soda, a chocolate bar, a box of cookies, a bag of candy, a half pound of turkey.

The Treat's on Alexandra

Alexandra Bernal, a lovely student of mine from Colombia, prepared this delicious flan for our Foreign Language Day celebration. Although I usually prefer something chocolatey, I found her recipe for this caramel custard to be extremely tasty. You, too, can impress your friends with this wonderful treat. It's great and easy to prepare. You will need:

2 12 oz. cans of evaporated milk	2 eggs
1 14 oz. can of sweetened condensed milk	3 tablespoons of sugar

Mix the evaporated milk, the condensed milk, and the 2 eggs in a blender. In the meantime, melt the sugar in a pan set over a low flame. The sugar will caramelize and turn to a honey brown color. Put the sugar on the bottom of a 8″ or 9″ diameter mold. Then add the mixed ingredients on top of the sugar. Put the mold in a waterbath (a shallow pan containing water). Bake in a 350° oven for one hour. Allow to cool. Refrigerate for at least 24 hours. Invert the mold to serve the flan. Then, enjoy!

The Least You Need to Know

➤ Use the verb *ir* + *a* + the definite article to express which store you are going to.

➤ Purchasing the correct amount of food in Spanish-speaking countries requires a knowlege of the metric system.

➤ Demonstrative pronouns (*éste*, *ése*, *aquél*) agree in number and gender with the nouns they replace. Use *éste* to replace nouns that are closest, *ése* to replace nouns that are farther away, and *aquél* for nouns that are the farthest from the speaker and person being addressed.

Eating Out

Let's say you're in Madrid. You shopped all morning and then stopped at a local store to pick up some snacks. You used what you learned about the metric system in Chapter 16 to purchase appropriate quantities of all your favorite goodies. Before you took your siesta, you lounged around your room munching on *tacos*, *tortillas*, and sipping *piña coladas*.

But now you've awakened and your stomach is growling again. It's time to venture out and find an enjoyable eating spot. Perhaps you will stop at a *tapas* bar for some appetizers and a drink before your main meal, or maybe it's late and you're ready for dinner. This chapter will teach you how to order food from a Spanish menu, even if your diet is limited and requires certain restrictions. And, if you are not perfectly satisfied with every aspect of your meal, you will be able to send food back and get exactly what you want.

Pick a Meal You Like

Whether you are just a little hungry and crave a small bite, or you're ravenous and in search of a quality meal, there are a variety of establishments that will cater to your needs and your pocketbook. If you are going out for breakfast, lunch, or dinner or just an in-between snack and want an informal setting, why not try one of the options in the following list. If you prefer a more formal meal, then go to the nearest *restaurante* (rehs-tow-rahn-teh).

➤ *Un café (oon kah-feh).* A small neighborhood restaurant where residents socialize.

➤ *Una cafetería (oo-nah kah-feh-teh-ree-ah).* Not at all the self-service type of establishment you would expect, but a small, informal café serving snacks and drinks.

➤ *Un bar, una tasca, una taberna (oon bahr, oo-nah tahs-kah, oo-nah tah-behr-nah).* Pubs or bars in which drinks and small snacks known as *tapas (tah-pahs)* or *pinchos (peen-chohs)* are served.

➤ *Una fonda, una hostería, una venta, una posada (oo-nah fohn-dah, ohs-teh-ree-ah, behn-tah, poh-sah-dah).* Inns specializing in regional dishes.

➤ *Un merendero, un chiringuito (oon meh-rehn-deh-roh, chee-reen-gee-toh).* Outdoor stands, usually at the beach, selling seafood, drinks, and ice cream.

➤ *Una cervecería (oo-nah sehr-beh-seh-ree-ah).* A pub that specializes in German beer in the barrel, as well as wine.

➤ *Una hacienda (oo-nah ah-see-ehn-dah).* A ranch-style restaurant found in Spanish America.

➤ *Una cantina (oo-nah kahn-tee-nah).* A men's bar (sorry ladies, there's nothing sneaky or illicit going on, the men simply want their privacy) found in Spanish America.

Which Restaurant?

Every country provides a tourist guide that advertises a wide variety of restaurants from which to choose. Imagine that you have to pick the place where you and your travelling companion are going to eat. What will it be? Explore the ads and determine what each restaurant has to offer.

LA CASITA
Parrillada Argentina

*Ahora en Miami se puede disfrutar
la mejor parrillada Argentina.*

Churrasco•Bife Chorizo
Tira de Asado•Morcilla
Chinchulines con el sabor y el
estilo de La Casita

La Princesa

PRIMERA CASA DE PESCADOS
Y MARISCOS
EN EL CORAZON DE MADRID

Lagasca, 60   Reservas: 276 80 35
276 05 75

---

*Restaurante
de Madrid*

EDIFICIO
SERRANO, 240
• ALTA COCINA DE MERCADO
• SALONES PRIVADOS
• GARAJE PROPIO CON APARCACOCHES
• CENAS AMENIZADAS CON MUSICA
DE PIANO EN VIVO

Especial Navidad y Noche Fin De Año
Reservas: 250 41 03-259 27 75

Cena Romantica
Para Dos

excluye
Por Pareja $49.50   El Impuesto
y Propina

La Cena Incluye
Vino y Bebida,
Piano En Vivo
y Una Rosa Complementaria
Para Las Damas

Abierto Los 9 Dias

RESTAURANTE
El Rincón

Deguste nuestro menú, con una cuidada
selección de platos, a un precio ajustado
MUSICA EN VIVO, CON SOLISTA
VIERNES Y SABADOS

Nuevos teléfonos

555 23 86-501 60 00
Plaza Colón, 2

(Parking en el edificio)

La Cava

Especialidad asados al
horno de leña. carnes rojas
a la brasa y pescados
SALONES PRIVADOS

De Alburquerque

C/ Alburquerque, 81. Reservas: 555 21 77

Cultural Tidbit

El desayuno (ehl deh-sah-yoo-noh), Spanish breakfast, is usually served between 7 a.m. and 9 a.m. It is usually quite light and consists of coffee with milk, and bread with butter and/or jam and sometimes cheese. A special favorite is *churros y chocolate* (choo-rrohs ee choh-koh-lah-teh). *Churros* (fritters) are made by frying long skinny strips of dough in very hot oil and then cutting the strips into small pieces and sprinkling them with sugar. Special machines called *churreros* squeeze the dough to get the proper shape. Although they are usually consumed at breakfast, churros can be eaten at any time. The *chocolate* is the delicious hot chocolate that is generally served with this treat.

Between 10:30 a.m. and noon, a mid-morning snack—referred to as *el almuerzo* (ehl ahl-mwehr-soh) in Mexico—is customary. People generally have a *batido* or *licuado* (fruit shake) or a regional snack at this time.

Lunch is eaten much later in the Spanish-speaking world than it is here and it is considered the main meal of the day. Generally eaten between 1:30 and 3:00, lunch is referred to as *la comida* (lah koh-mee-dah) in Spain and Mexico and as *el almuerzo*

continues

in South America and the Caribbean. Expect a full meal that includes soup, meat or fish, vegetables, salad, and dessert.

There is usually a late afternoon snack, *la merienda* (lah meh-ree-ehn-dah), (referred to as *once* in Chile) served between 5:00 and 6:00 in the evening. This usually consists of coffee or tea and pastry.

Supper is called *la cena* (lah seh-nah) in Spain and Mexico and *la comida* in Spanish America. Eaten rather late, sometimes not until 9:00 p.m., this meal tends to be very light.

Spanish cuisine is quite different from that of Mexico and Spanish America. Spanish cooking is Mediterranean style and uses many of the ingredients found in Greek and Italian cooking: spices and olive oil. In Spanish America, expect to experience different flavors produced by the different condiments and spices used there.

Should you decide to eat in a popular restaurant, you might find it necessary to reserve a table. When you call, you will be asked for a lot of information. Make sure you know what to say:

Quisiera hacer una reservación.
kee-see-eh-rah ah-sehr oo-nah
reh-sehr-bah-see-ohn
I would like to reserve a table.

para esta noche
pah-rah ehs-tah noh-cheh
for this evening

para mañana (el sábado) por la noche
pah-rah mah-nyah-nah (ehl sah-bah-doh)
pohr lah noh-cheh
for tomorrow (Saturday) evening

para dos personas
pah-rah dohs pehr-soh-nahs
for two people

para las ocho y media
pah-rah lahs oh-choh ee meh-dee-ah
for 8:30 p.m.

en la terraza (el rincón), por favor
ehn lah teh-rrah-sah (ehl reen-kohn)
pohr fah-bohr
on the terrace, please (outdoors)

cerca de la ventana
sehr-kah deh lah behn-tah-nah
near the window

We're Eating Out

Practice what you've just learned by reserving a table for Friday evening, at 9:00 p.m., for six people. Also request a table outdoors.

But let's say that you did not reserve a table and show up at a restaurant unannounced. *El jefe del comedor* (ehl heh-feh dehl koh-meh-dohr), the headwaiter, will most certainly ask:

¿Una mesa para cuántas personas?
oo-nah meh-sah pah-rah kwahn-tahs pehr-soh-nahs
A table for how many?

Your response should contain all the necessary information:

Una mesa para tres, por favor.
oo-nah meh-sah pah-rah trehs pohr fah-bohr
A table for three, please.

It's just been one of those days. You dropped your fork and as you bent down to retrieve it you spilled water on your suit and had to mop it up with your napkin. Your elbow hit your empty plate and that's on the floor now, too. After all of this, a new place setting is needed. Table 17.1 gives you the vocabulary needed when asking the waiter for cutlery, as well as other items that will come in handy.

Table 17.1 A Table Setting

Tableware	Spanish Translation	Pronunciation
bowl	el tazón	ehl tah-sohn
carafe	la garrafa	lah gah-rrah-fah
cup	la taza	lah tah-sah
dinner plate	el plato	ehl plah-toh
fork	el tenedor	ehl teh-neh-dohr
glass	el vaso	ehl bah-soh
knife	el cuchillo	ehl koo-chee-yoh
menu	el menú	ehl meh-noo
napkin	la servilleta	lah sehr-bee-yeh-tah
pepper shaker	el pimentero	ehl pee-mehn-teh-roh
place setting	el cubierto	ehl koo-bee-ehr-toh
salt shaker	el salero	ehl sah-leh-roh
saucer	el platillo	ehl plah-tee-yoh
soup dish	el sopero	ehl soh-peh-roh
soup spoon	la cuchara	lah koo-chah-rah

continues

Table 17.1   Continued

Tableware	Spanish Translation	Pronunciation
tablecloth	el mantel	ehl mahn-tehl
teaspoon	la cucharita	lah koo-chah-ree-tah
waiter	el camarero	ehl kah-mah-reh-roh
waitress	la camarera	lah kah-mah-reh-rah
wine glass	la copa	lah koh-pah

Cultural Tidbit

Many Spanish restaurants offer a price-fixed menu that may be referred to as any one of the following: *Menú Turistico*, *Menú del Día*, or *Plato Combinado*. The dinner consists of an appetizer, soup, main course, salad, dessert, and drink for a pre-determined price. While your choice of dishes may be restricted, this still offers an excellent value for the money. Ordering from the menu is, without exception, a more expensive option. On many occasions you will also find that the tip is included in the bill. Look for the words: *servicio incluído*.

Is there something missing from your table? Do you want to make a request of the head waiter, waiter, or wine steward? If you do, the following phrases will help you get want you want.

➤ Use an indirect object pronoun. Remember that the verb *faltar* agrees with the number of things lacking. If it's just one, use *falta*. For more than one, *faltan*:

Showing Need	Pronunciation	Translation
Me falta(n)	meh fahl-tah(n)	I need
Te falta(n)	teh fahl-tah(n)	You need
Le falta(n)	leh fahl-tah(n)	He, she, you need(s)
Nos falta(n)	nohs fahl-tah(n)	We need
Os falta(n)	ohs fahl-tah(n)	You need
Les falta(n)	lehs fahl-tah(n)	They, you need

➤ Use the verb *necesitar*, to need:

Showing Need	Pronunciation	Translation
Necesito	neh-seh-see-toh	I need
Él necesita	ehl neh-seh-see-tah	He needs
Ella necesita	eh-yah neh-seh-see-tah	She needs
Necesitamos	neh-seh-see-tah-mohs	We need
Necesitáis	neh-seh-see-tah-ees	You need
Ellos necesitan	eh-yohs neh-seh-see-tahn	They need
Ellas necesitan	eh-yahs neh-seh-see-tahn	They need

Now, use what you've learned to tell your server that you need: a salt shaker, a napkin, a fork, a knife, a plate, or a spoon.

Camerero—What Do You Suggest?

Let's assume, then, that you've had your drink at a pub or bar before arriving at the restaurant. You'll probably want to order right away. Here are some phrases that will help you ask the waiter for the specials of the day or for his own personal recommendations:

¿Cuál es el plato del día?
kwahl ehs ehl plah-toh dehl dee-ah
What is today's specialty?

¿Cuál es la especialidad de la casa?
kwahl ehs lah ehs-peh-see-ah-lee-dahd deh lah kah-sah
What is the house specialty?

¿Qué recomienda Ud.?
keh reh-koh-mee-ehn-dah oo-stehd
What do you recommend?

This Menu Is Greek to Me

A Spanish menu could prove a bit difficult to understand unless you are acquainted with certain culinary terms. If your waiter is too busy or speaks too fast, you might wind up with something you didn't really want or don't particularly like. Table 17.2 gives you the terms you need to interpret what's being offered to you.

Table 17.2 What's on the Menu?

Salsas (Sauces)	Pronunciation	Description
ají de queso	ah-hee deh keh-soh	cheese sauce
adobo	ah-doh-boh	chili sauce made with sesame seeds, nuts, and spices
mole	moh-leh	chili sauce made with sesame seeds, cocoa, and spices
pipián	pee-pee-ahn	chili and pumpkin seed sauce spiced with coriander and served with bread crumbs
salsa cruda	sahl-sah kroo-dah	an uncooked tomato sauce dip
salsa de perejil	sahl-sah deh peh-reh-heel	parsley sauce
salsa de tomatillo verde	sahl-sah deh toh-mah-tee-yoh behr-deh	Mexican green tomato sauce

Chilies (Chiles)	Pronunciation	Description
ancho	ahn-choh	medium hot
chipotle	chee-poht-leh	hot, smokey-flavored
jalapeño	hah-lah-peh-nyoh	hot, meaty-flavored
pasilla	pah-see-yah	hot, rich, sweet-flavored
pequín	peh-keen	hot
pimiento	pee-mee-ehn-toh	peppery
poblano	poh-blah-noh	medium hot, rich-flavored
serrano	seh-rrah-noh	hot

Tortillas (Tortillas)		
burrito	boo-rree-toh	flour tortilla with a cheese and meat filling served with salsa
chalupas	chah-loo-pahs	cheese or ground pork filling, served with a green chili sauce

Tortillas (Tortillas)

chilaquiles	chee-lah-kee-lehs	baked layers of tortillas, filled alternately with beans, meat, chicken, and cheese
enchiladas	ehn-chee-lah-dahs	soft corn tortillas, filled with meat, rice, and cheese, and topped with spicy sauce
flautas	flow-tahs	rolled, flute-shaped, deep-fried tortilla sandwich
quesadillas	keh-sah-dee-yahs	deep-fried tortillas covered with cheese, tomato, and pepper
tacos	tah-kohs	crisp toasted tortillas filled with meat, poultry, or beans, topped with shredded lettuce, cheese, and sauce
tamal	tah-mahl	cooked corn husks stuffed with meat, chicken, and chile peppers, known as *tamales* in English
tostada	tohs-tah-dah	tortilla chip with different pepper and cheese toppings

Cultural Tidbit

The *tortilla mexicana*, a flat pancake made of corn meal, is the tortilla with which most of us are familiar. In Mexico, the tortilla is served in place of bread and is an important part of every meal. The tortilla may also be rolled and stuffed with various ingredients and then fried and covered with sauce and cheese. *Huevos rancheros*, a well-known Mexican breakfast, consists of a tortilla filled with a fried egg and covered with a spicy tomato sauce. The tortilla is also used like a cracker to scoop up dips such as *guacamole*.

In Spain, the *tortilla española* is a type of thick omelette made with potatoes, eggs, and onions. It may be cut into pieces and served as an appetizer.

You may or may not have stopped at a tapas bar for drinks and some hors d'oeuvres. In any event, you might choose to sample an appetizer from the restaurant before beginning your main course. Then it's on to the soup and main course. Tables 17.3 to 17.5 list the interesting prospects available to you.

Table 17.3 Appetizers (Los Aperetivos—lohs ah-peh-reh-tee-bohs)

Appetizer	Spanish Translation	Pronunciation
artichokes	alcachofas	ahl-kah-choh-fahs
avocado spread	guacamole	gwah-kah-moh-leh
clams	almejas	ahl-meh-hahs
crayfish	cigales	see-gah-lehs
eggs	huevos	oo-eh-bohs
melon	melón	meh-lohn
mushrooms	champiñones	chahm-pee-nyoh-nehs
mussels	moluscos	moh-loos-kohs
oysters	ostras	ohs-trahs
sardines	sardinas	sahr-dee-nahs
shrimp	camarones	kah-mah-roh-nehs
smoked eels	anguilas ahumadas	ahn-gee-lahs ah-oo-mah-dahs
snails	caracoles	kah-rah-koh-lehs
spicy sausage	chorizo	choh-ree-soh
squid	calamares	kah-lah-mah-rehs
tortilla chips	tostadas	tohs-tah-dahs

Cultural Tidbit

In Spain, salads are often served as appetizers and may contain a mixture of vegetables and seafood. In Spanish America, the salad is often served with the main course. Your *ensalada* (ehn-sah-lah-dah) may come with lettuce, *lechuga* (leh-choo-gah); tomato, *tomate* (toh-mah-teh); olives, *aceitunas* (ah-seh-ee-too-nahs); and cucumber, *pepino* (peh-pee-noh).

Table 17.4 Soups (Las Sopas—lahs soh-pahs)

Soup	Pronunciation	Description
gazpacho	gahs-pah-choh	puréed, uncooked tomatoes, served cold
potaje madrileño	poh-tah-heh mah-dree-leh-nyoh	thick, puréed cod, spinach, and chickpeas

Soup	Pronunciation	Description
sopa de ajo	soh-pah deh ah-hoh	garlic soup
sopa de albóndigas	soh-pah deh ahl-bohn-dee-gahs	meatball soup
sopa de cebolla	soh-pah deh seh-boh-yah	onion soup
sopa de fideos	soh-pah deh fee-deh-ohs	noodle soup
sopa de gambas	soh-pah deh gahm-bahs	shrimp soup
sopa de mariscos	soh-pah deh mah-rees-kohs	seafood soup
sopa de pescado	soh-pah deh pehs-kah-doh	fish soup
sopa de verduras	soh-pah deh behr-doo-rahs	soup made from puréed green vegetables

Cultural Tidbit

Parrillada refers to grilled meat and the expression *a la parrillada* means that the meat is grilled or barbecued. This term is very popular in Latin American countries, such as Argentina, where the beef is locally raised and is, therefore, plentiful.

Table 17.5   Meats (Las Carnes—lahs kahr-nehs)

Meat	Spanish Translation	Pronunciation
bacon	el tocino	ehl toh-see-noh
beef	la carne de vaca	lah kahr-neh deh bah-kah
blood pudding	la morcilla	lah mohr-see-yah
chop, cutlet	la chuleta	lah choo-leh-tah
filet mignon	el lomo fino	ehl loh-moh fee-noh
goat	el cabrito	ehl kah-bree-toh
ham	el jamón	ehl hah-mohn
hamburger	la hamburguesa	lah ahm-boor-geh-sah

continues

219

Table 17.5 Continued

Meat	Spanish Translation	Pronunciation
lamb	el cordero	ehl kohr-deh-roh
pork	el cerdo	ehl sehr-doh
roast	el asado	ehl ah-sah-doh
roast beef	el rosbif	ehl rohs-beef
sausage	la salchicha	lah sahl-chee-chah
sirloin	el lomillo	ehl loh-mee-yoh
steak	el bistec	ehl bees-tehk
steak, charcoal grilled	el churrasco	ehl chuh-rrahs-koh
stew	el estofado, el guisado	ehl ehs-toh-fah-doh, ehl gee-sah-doh
veal	la ternera	lah tehr-neh-rah

As a Rule
Remember to use the appropriate direct object pronoun to refer to the noun you are using.
¿Ud. recomienda la paella?—
¿Ud. *la* recomienda?—
¿Ud. toma el lomillo? Sí, *lo* tomo.

Cultural Tidbit
When your meal arrives, good manners dictate that you wish your fellow diners *buen provecho* (bwehn proh-beh-choh), a hearty appetite.

That's the Way I Like It

Even if you know how to order your hamburger or veal chops, you want to be certain that your entree is cooked to your specifications. The waiter might ask:

¿Comó lo (la, los, las) quiere?
koh-moh loh (lah, lohs, lahs) kee-eh-reh
How do you want it (them)?

Do you prefer your fish baked or broiled? Do you want your meat medium-rare or well-done? If you want to ensure that your food is prepared to your liking, use table 17.6 to express your wants and needs.

Table 17.6 Proper Preparation

Meats and Vegetables

Preparation	Spanish Translation	Pronunciation
baked	asado	ah-sah-doh
boiled	cocido	koh-see-doh
breaded	empanado	ehm-pah-nah-doh
broiled	a la parrilla	ah lah pah-rree-yah
fried	frito	free-toh
grilled	asado a la parrilla	ah-sah-doh ah lah pah-rree-yah
marinated	escabechado	ehs-kah-beh-chah-doh
medium	término medio	tehr-mee-noh meh-dee-oh
medium rare	un poco rojo pero no crudo	oon poh-koh roh-hoh peh-roh noh kroo-doh
poached	escalfado	ehs-kahl-fah-doh
rare	poco asado	poh-koh ah-sah-doh
roasted	asado	ah-sah-doh
steamed	al vapor	ahl bah-pohr
very rare	casi crudo	kah-see kroo-doh
well-done	bien asado (hecho, cocido)	bee-ehn ah-sah-doh (eh-choh, koh-see-doh)

Eggs

Preparation	Spanish Translation	Pronunciation
fried	fritos	free-tohs
hard-boiled	duros	doo-rohs
poached	escalfados	ehs-kahl-fah-dohs
scrambled	revueltos	reh-bwehl-tohs
soft-boiled	pasados por agua	pah-sah-dohs pohr ah-gwah
omelette	una tortilla	oo-nah tohr-tee-yah
plain omelette	una tortilla a la francesa	oo-nah tohr-tee-yah ah lah frahn-seh-sah
herb omelette	una tortilla con hierbas	oo-nah tohr-tee-yah kohn ee-ehr-bahs

Spice It Up

You should expect that there will be a variety of spices used in Spain and in the Spanish American countries. Menu descriptions or your waiter will usually be able to help you determine if the dish will be to your liking—bland or spicy. Table 17.7 will help you become acquainted with many of the spices you might encounter.

Table 17.7   Herbs, Spices, and Condiments

Spice	Spanish Translation	Pronunciation
basil	la albahaca	lah ahl-bah-ah-kah
bay leaf	la hoja de laurel	lah oh-hah deh lah-oo-rehl
butter	la mantequilla	lah mahn-teh-kee-yah
caper	el alcaparrón	ehl ahl-kah-pah-rrohn
chives	el cebollino	ehl seh-boh-yee-noh
dill	el eneldo	ehl eh-nehl-doh
garlic	el ajo	ehl ah-hoh
ginger	el jenjibre	ehl hehn-hee-breh
honey	la miel	lah mee-ehl
ketchup	la salsa de tomate	lah sahl-sah deh toh-mah-teh
mint	la menta	lah mehn-tah
mustard	la mostaza	lah mohs-tah-sah
nutmeg	la nuez moscada	lah noo-ehs mohs-kah-dah
oil	el aceite	ehl ah-seh-ee-teh
oregano	el orégano	ehl oh-reh-gah-noh
paprika	el pimentón dulce	ehl pee-mehn-tohn dool-seh
parsley	el perejil	ehl peh-reh-heel
pepper	la pimienta	lah pee-mee-ehn-tah
rosemary	el romero	ehl roh-meh-roh
saffron	el azafrán	ehl ah-sah-frahn
salt	la sal	lah sahl
sesame	el ajonjolí	ehl ah-hohn-hoh-lee
sugar	el azúcar	ehl ah-soo-kahr

Special Diets

Does your diet require certain restrictions? Are you a person with specific likes and dislikes that you want your server to be aware of? If so, then you'll want to remember the following phrases:

Phrase	Spanish Translation	Pronunciation
I am on a diet.	Estoy a régimen.	ehs-toh-ee ah reh-hee-mehn
I'm a vegetarian.	Soy vegetariano(a).	soh-ee beh-heh-tah-ree-ah-noh(ah)
Do you serve kosher food?	¿Sirven Uds. comida permitida por la religión judia?	seer-behn oo-steh-dehs koh-mee-dah pehr-mee-tee-dah pohr lah reh-lee-hee-ohn hoo-dee-ah
I can't eat anything made with...	No puedo comer nada con...	noh pweh-doh koh-mehr nah-dah kohn
I can't have any...	No puedo tomar...	noh pweh-doh toh-mahr
dairy products	productos lácteos	proh-dook-tohs lahk-teh-ohs
alcohol	alcohol	ahl-koh-ohl
saturated fats	grasas saturadas	grah-sahs sah-too-rah-dahs
shellfish	mariscos	mah-rees-kohs
I'm looking for a dish...	Estoy buscando un plato...	ehs-toh-ee boos-kahn-doh oon plah-toh
high in fiber	con mucha fibra	kohn moo-chah fee-brah
low in cholesterol	con poco colesterol	kohn poh-koh koh-lehs-teh-rohl
low in fat	con poca grasa	kohn poh-kah grah-sah
low in sodium	con poca sal	kohn poh-kah sahl
non-dairy	non lácteo	nohn lahk-teh-oh
salt-free	sin sal	seen sahl
sugar-free	sin azúcar	seen ah-soo-kahr
without artificial coloring	sin colorantes artificiales	seen koh-loh-rahn-tehs ahr-tee-fee-see-ah-lehs
without preservatives	sin preservativos	seen preh-sehr-bah-tee-bohs

Back to the Kitchen

The dish you ordered just doesn't seem right. Perhaps something is missing. Maybe you ordered it rare and it looks and tastes like shoe leather. The waiter said it wouldn't be too hot and you can't seem to get enough water to cool your palate. If there's a problem, you'll want to be able to communicate exactly what it is. Table 17.8 will help you send back that disappointing dish and get something more to your liking.

Table 17.8 Possible Problems with Your Food

Problem	Spanish Translation	Pronunciation
… is cold	está frío	ehs-tah free-oh
… is too rare	está demasiado crudo	ehs-tah deh-mah-see-ah-doh kroo-doh
… is over-cooked	está sobrecocido	ehs-tah soh-breh-koh-see-doh
… is tough	está duro	ehs-tah doo-roh
… is burned	está quemado	ehs-tah keh-mah-doh
… is too salty	está muy salado	ehs-tah moo-ee sah-lah-doh
… is too sweet	está muy dulce	ehs-tah moo-ee dool-seh
… is too spicy	está demasiado picante	ehs-tah deh-mah-see-ah-doh pee-kahn-teh
… is spoiled	está pasado	ehs-tah pah-sah-doh
… is bitter (sour)	está agrio (cortado)	ehs-tah ah-gree-oh (kohr-tah-doh)
… is dirty	está sucio	ehs-tah soo-see-oh

Fancy Endings

Finally, it's time for dessert and there are some interesting Spanish specialties from which to choose. Table 17.9 will help you make your decision.

Table 17.9 Divine Desserts

Dessert	Spanish Translation	Pronunciation
caramel custard	el flan	ehl flahn
cookies	las galletas	lahs gah-yeh-tahs
gelatin	la gelatina	lah heh-lah-tee-nah
ice cream	el helado	ehl eh-lah-doh
pie	el pastel	ehl pahs-tehl
rice pudding	el arroz con leche	ehl ah-rrohs kohn leh-cheh
sponge cake	el bizcocho	ehl bees-koh-choh
tart	la tarta	lah tahr-tah
yogurt	el yogur	ehl yoh-goor

Cultural Tidbit

When it is necessary to make a distinction: if you are eating salad (*ensalada*), then be sure to order *galletas saladas*, crackers. For dessert, you will want to order *galletas dulces*, cookies, because they are sweet.

If you are ordering ice cream, the following terms will help you get the type and flavor, *el sabor* (ehl sah-bohr), you prefer:

Ice Cream	Spanish Translation	Pronunciation
cone	un barquillo	oon bahr-kee-yoh
cup	una taza	oo-nah tah-sah
chocolate	de chocolate	deh choh-koh-lah-teh
vanilla	de vainilla	deh bah-ee-nee-yah
strawberry	de fresa	deh freh-sah
pistachio	de pistacho	deh pees-tah-choh
walnut	de nueces	deh noo-eh-sehs

A Toast with White, Red, or Rosé

Spaniards usually drink wine with dinner. The wines you might order include:

Wine	Spanish Translation	Pronunciation
red wine	el vino tinto	ehl bee-noh teen-toh
rosé wine	el vino rosado	ehl bee-noh roh-sah-doh
white wine	el vino blanco	ehl bee-noh blahn-koh
dry wine	el vino seco	ehl bee-noh seh-koh
sweet wine	el vino dulce	ehl bee-noh dool-seh
sparkling wine	el vino espumoso	ehl bee-noh ehs-poo-moh-soh
champagne	el champán	ehl chahm-pahn

Cultural Tidbit

Spain is one of the top wine producers in the world. *Rioja,* a premier Burgundy and Bordeaux-type red table wine, is one of the world's finest, because of its unmistakable bouquet and flavor. Its quality is protected by strict official regulations governing the seal of origin.

Sherry is the most international Spanish wine due to its high volume of exportation. The four different kinds of this Andalusian wine are Manzanilla, Amontillado, Fino, and Los Dulces. *Fino* and *Manzanilla* are dry aperitifs. The others are served with dessert or as after-dinner drinks.

Sangria, the popular fruit punch made from red wine, brandy, sugar, and soda is not served at dinner. It is a popular picnic or afternoon wine.

Catalán cava is an excellent sparkling wine grown in Catalonia.

Beer (*cerveza*), although not traditionally Spanish, is currenly popular in Spain. It is not generally served with meals but is quite popular in tapas bars.

Each region in Spain produces its own liqueur.

If you do not choose to have wine as an accompaniment to your meal, you will, of course, want to order something else. You might even find that you would like to order different drinks with different courses. Table 17.10 lists other beverages you might enjoy with or after dinner.

Table 17.10   Beverages

Beverage	Spanish Translation	Pronunciation
coffee	un café	oon kah-feh
with milk	con leche	kohn leh-cheh
espresso	exprés	ehks-prehs
with cream	con crema	kohn kreh-mah
black	solo	soh-loh
iced	helado	eh-lah-doh
decaffeinated	descafeinado	dehs-kah-feh-ee-nah-doh
tea	un té	oon teh
with lemon	con limón	kohn lee-mohn
with sugar	con azúcar	kohn ah-soo-kahr
herbal	herbario	ehr-bah-ree-oh

Beverage	Spanish Translation	Pronunciation
soda	una soda	oo-nah soh-dah
mineral water	un agua mineral	oon ah-gwah mee-neh-rahl
carbonated	con gas	kohn gahs
non-carbonated	sin gas	seen gahs
juice	un jugo	oon hoo-goh
milk	una leche	oo-nah leh-cheh
skim milk	desnatada	dehs-nah-tah-dah

You Only Want Some, Not All?

De is used after nouns of quantity:

> un vaso de leche   *a glass of milk*   una botella de agua   *a bottle of water*

There is no Spanish equivalent for *some*. To express what you would like simply use the word *quisiera* (kee-see-eh-rah), "I would like," and a noun. In general, some is understood when a noun is used.

> Quisiera carne, por favor.   *I'd like some meat, please.*

It Was Delicious

So how was that meal? Would you tell your friends about it and recommend it highly or would you rate it just so-so? If you were really happy with your meal and found the food to be quite exceptional, you might want to exclaim your pleasure by using the word *¡Qué...!* to express "What a...!"

> ¡Qué comida!   *What a meal!*   ¡Que servicio!   *What service!*

To make the exclamation more intense, add an adjective that agrees with the noun and place the word *tan* (tahn) or *más* (mahs) (both mean *so* in this context, although we do not use *so* in our English translation of the phrase) before the adjective.

> ¡Qué comida tan rica!   *What a rich meal!*

> ¡Qué servicio más excelente!   *What excellent service!*

> ¡Qué platos tan sabrosos!   *What tasty dishes!*

How Was It?

Of course the meal was great. Tell the person who recommended the restaurant to you how much you enjoyed it. Use the *que* + noun + *tan (más)* + adjective structure to express how you felt about what you ate and drank: soups, steak, wine, salad, and dessert.

Don't forget to ask for the check at the end of your meal:

La cuenta, por favor.
lah kwehn-tah pohr fah-bohr
The check, please.

The Least You Need to Know

➤ You can read a Spanish menu if you know the right terms for the foods you like to eat: appetizers, soups, meats, fish, poultry, vegetables, and desserts, and the way you like them prepared.

➤ Use *un* or *una* to specify a single portion.

➤ *De* is used after nouns of quantity.

➤ There is no Spanish equivalent to express our English word, *some*. Just use the noun without any article to get your meaning across or use *quisiera* + a noun.

➤ To make an exclamation, use *¡Qué + noun + tan (más) + an adjective* that agrees with the noun.

Chapter 18

I Want to Have Fun!

In This Chapter

➤ Things to do to have fun

➤ Extending, accepting, and refusing invitations

➤ Using adverbs to describe abilities

You've visited countless tourist attractions, collected souvenirs, and purchased gifts for those you love. The meals you've eaten have been superb and your appetite is truly sated. Now you want to either have some fun, engage in your favorite sport, or simply lay back and relax.

You can go off to the sea to swim, snorkel, parasail, or windsurf. Or would you prefer to ski or hike on snow-covered mountains? Are you drawn to the links for a round of golf or to the courts for a friendly tennis match? Are you a film *aficionado* or a theater buff? An opera lover or a fan of the ballet? Do you like to gamble and want to spend some time with a one-armed bandit in a Dominican casino? After studying Chapter 18, you'll be able to do all of this, invite someone to join you, and even describe your skills and talents.

Do You Live for Sports?

I love a challenging tennis match and my racquet has seen nearly as many countries as I have. My husband prefers the pool and likes nothing better than trying to surpass his daily record of completed laps. Whether you're into sports or would rather spend some relaxing time at the poolside or the beach, you'll need certain words and expressions to discuss your preferences. Outdoor activities and sports are listed in table 18.1. Note that the verbs *hacer** and *jugar + a + definite article*** are commonly used to express participation in a sport. Any verb in parentheses is used in place of jugar or hacer to express that you are playing that particular sport. If you want to express that you like or dislike a sport, use the phrase *(No) Me gusta + definite article (el, la, los, las) + sport.*

Table 18.1   Sports

Sport	Spanish Translation	Pronunciation
aerobics	los aeróbicos*	lohs ah-eh-roh-bee-kohs
baseball	el beísbol **	ehl beh-ees-bohl
basketball	el baloncesto,** el básquetbol **	ehl bah-lohn-sehs-toh, ehl bahs-keht-bohl
bicycling	el ciclismo * (montar en bicicleta)	ehl see-klees-moh (mohn-tahr ehn bee-see-kleh-tah)
boating	(dar) un paseo en barco	(dahr) oon pah-seh-oh ehn bahr-koh
bodybuilding	el fisi culturismo*	ehl fee-see kool-too-rees-moh
canoeing	el piragüismo*	ehl pee-rah-gwees-moh
cycling	el ciclismo*	ehl see-klees-moh
diving	el clavado	ehl klah-bah-doh
fishing	la pesca (ir de pesca)	lah pehs-kah (eer deh pehs-kah)
football	el fútbol americano**	ehl foot-bohl ah-meh-ree-kah-noh
golf	el golf**	ehl gohlf
horseback riding	la equitación*	lah eh-kee-tah-see-ohn
ice skating	el patinaje sobre hielo* (patinar)	ehl pah-tee-nah-heh soh-breh ee-eh-loh (pah-tee-nahr)
jai alai	el jai alai**	ehl hah-ee ah-lah-ee
jogging	el footing* (trotar)	ehl foo-teeng (troh-tahr)
mountain climbing	el alpinismo*	ehl ahl-pee-nees-moh

Sport	Spanish Translation	Pronunciation
ping-pong	el ping-pong**	ehl peeng-pohng
sailing	la navegación* (navegar)	lah nah-beh-gah-see-ohn (nah-beh-gahr)
scuba (skin) diving	el buceo	ehl boo-seh-oh
skating	el patinaje*	ehl pah-tee-nah-heh
ski	el esquí* (esquiar)	ehl ehs-kee (ehs-kee-ahr)
soccer	el fútbol**	ehl foot-bohl
surfing	el surf* (surfear)	ehl soorf (soor-feh-ahr)
swimming	la natación* (nadar)	lah nah-tah-see-ohn (nah-dahr)
tennis	el tenis**	ehl teh-nees
volleyball	el volíbol**	ehl boh-lee-bohl
waterskiing	el esquí acuático*	ehl ehs-kee ah-kwah-tee-koh

*When using the verb jugar + a + definite article, remember that **a** contracts with **el** to form **al**.*

Juego al tenis.   I play tennis.

As a Rule

To speak about more than one sport that you like, use *me gustan* (meh goos-tahn).

Me gustan el volíbol y el tenis.

Cultural Tidbit

Every four years the Campeonato Mundial de Fútbol (World Soccer Championship) attracts several billion T.V. viewers around the world. No other sporting event is as popular. Half of the championships have been won by European teams, but the rest have been won by teams from Latin America. It's no wonder then that soccer, *el fútbol* (ehl foot-bohl), is the most popular sport in the world, including Spain and Spanish America. Mexico City boasts one of the largest stadiums in the world. The Estadio Azteca holds more than 100,000 spectators.

Shall We Play?

Are you the type of person who likes sports that involve team competition or do you prefer to engage in a one-person activity that affords lots of exercise? Using me encanta, me gusta, and detesto, express how you feel about these sports, given the choice: horseback riding, sailing, swimming, skiing, soccer, golf, and tennis.

Cultural Tidbit

Want to get the exercise you need to work off that huge dinner you ate last night? Why not run with the bulls in Pamplona, Spain? Once a year, from July 6th through the 14th, in this Spanish city, the Feria de San Fermín is celebrated. Every morning at 8:00 the crowds wait in suspense as a flare is fired into the air. Two minutes later, six bulls are released onto the Calle de Santo Domingo and make their way to the bullfighting arena. The bulls chase the fleeing participants, as the spectators scream enthusiastically. All notion of time is lost as the people try to avoid being gored by the bulls. Some would-be toreadores even try their hand at bullfighting. Many unsuccessful matadors have paid with their lives. Casualties are not uncommon, as those involved get carried away and lose sight of the fact that the object of the game is to survive the run. After the run, the street becomes swarmed with observers and participants who revel and party all day and night.

How About Coming Along?

If you prefer to play with a partner, you might find it necessary to extend an invitation to someone you don't know very well. To ask someone to join you, you may use the stem-changing verbs *querer* (ie) (to want) or *poder* (ue) (to be able to) and the infinitive of the verb jugar (ue) (to play). Remember that these verbs change within the shape of the shoe: within the stem of the verb, *e* changes to *ie*, and *o* changes to *ue* in all present-tense forms except nosotros and vosotros. Here's a quick memory refresher from Chapter 12.

querer—to want, wish

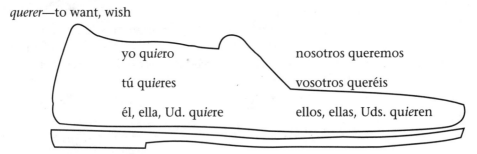

yo quiero   nosotros queremos

tú quieres   vosotros queréis

él, ella, Ud. quiere   ellos, ellas, Uds. quieren

poder—to be able

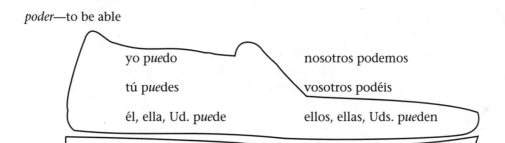

yo p*ue*do   nosotros podemos

tú p*ue*des   vosotros podéis

él, ella, Ud. p*ue*de   ellos, ellas, Uds. p*ue*den

Now you are ready to ask someone to join you. But first you have to find out if they play or enjoy the same activity as you. If the answer is "yes," then go ahead and extend an invitation using this structure:

¿Le (Te) gusta + (jugar +) definite article + sport?

Such as:

¿Le (Te) gusta jugar al tenis? *Do you like to play tennis?*

¿Le (Te) gusta el alpinismo? *Do you like to go mountain climbing?*

Or you may ask something like:

¿Quiere (Quieres) acompañarme (acompañarnos)? *Do you want to join me (us)?*

¿Puede (Puedes) acompañarme (acompañarnos)? *Can you accompany me (us)?*

As a Rule

If you are going to play any sport in which there is a match you would say:

Voy a jugar un partido de…
boh-ee ah hoo-gahr oon pahr-tee-doh deh
I'm going to play a game of…

If you want to say that you are going to engage in an activity, refer to table 18.1 and use ir + a + the infinitive of the verb in parentheses, or ir + a + hacer + a sport. For example:

Voy a nadar.   Voy a hacer la equitación.
boh-ee ah nah-dahr   boh-ee ah ah-sehr lah eh-kee-tah-see-ohn
I'm going to go swimming.   *I'm going to go horseback riding.*

continues

233

Note the irregularities:

Voy de pesca.	Voy a jugar al ping-pong.
boh-ee deh pehs-kah.	boh-ee ah hoo-gahr ahl peeng-pohng
I'm going fishing.	*I'm going to play ping-pong.*

It's time to get some exercise. Remember that each sport is played in a very particular environment: a court, a field, a course, a rink, etc. Table 18.2 will help you choose the proper venue for the sport that interests you:

Table 18.2 Where to Go

Sports Venue	Spanish Translation	Pronunciation
beach	la playa	lah plah-yah
course (golf)	el campo	ehl kahm-poh
court	la cancha	lah kahn-chah
court (jai alai)	el frontón	ehl frohn-tohn
field	el campo	ehl kahm-poh
gymnasium	el gimnasio	ehl heem-nah-see-oh
mountain	la montaña	lah mohn-tah-nyah
ocean	el océano	ehl oh-seh-ah-noh
park	el parque	ehl pahr-keh
path	el camino	ehl kah-mee-noh
pool	la piscina	lah pee-see-nah
rink	la pista	lah pees-tah
sea	el mar	ehl mahr
slope	la pista	lah pees-tah
stadium	el estadio	ehl ehs-tah-dee-oh
track	la pista	lah pees-tah

As a Rule

When a sentence contains one subject noun or pronoun, be sure to conjugate the verb that immediately comes after it. Any verb or verbs that then follow remain in the infinitive. Express *at*, *in*, and *to the* by using *a* + definite article (*al, a la*).

Yo quiero jugar al golf.

If the sentence contains two subject nouns or pronouns, a verb must be conjugated after each.

Susana va a la playa pero ella no quiere nadar.

¿Quiere (Quieres) ir al parque a jugar un partido de fútbol?
kee-eh-reh (kee-eh-rehs) eer ahl pahr-keh ah hoo-gahr oon pahr-tee-doh deh foot-bohl
Do you want to go to the park to play soccer?

¿Puede (puedes) acompañarme a la playa?
pweh-deh (pweh-dehs) ah-kohm-pah-nyahr-meh ah lah plah-yah
Can you go with me to the beach?

Do the Inviting

Today is a beautiful day for all of those who love sports. Imagine that you're in the mood to get some exercise. Phone a friend and invite him/her to go with you to the proper place so that you can go: hiking, skiing, swimming, skating, mountain climbing, or golfing.

Saying Yes

It's always a very friendly gesture to graciously accept an invitation that is offered to you. Perhaps you've been asked to play doubles tennis, to accompany someone on a sightseeing trip, or to eat dinner at someone's house. Whatever the situation, the following phrases will help you in all your social encounters:

Phrase	Pronunciation	Meaning
Con mucho gusto.	kohn moo-choh goos-toh	With pleasure.
Por supuesto.	pohr soo-pwehs-toh	Of course.
Claro.	klah-roh	Of course.

continues

continued

Phrase	Pronunciation	Meaning
Es una buena idea.	ehs oo-nah bweh-nah ee-deh-ah	That's a good idea.
Magnífico.	mahg-nee-fee-koh	Great!
De acuerdo.	deh ah-kwehr-doh	O.K. (I agree.)
Sin duda.	seen doo-dah	There's no doubt about it.
¿Por qué no?	pohr keh noh	Why not?
Si tú quieres (Ud. quiere).	see too kee-eh-rehs (oo-stehd kee-eh-reh)	If you want to.
Con placer.	kohn plah-sehr	Gladly.

Saying No and Giving a Reason

There are times when you really would like to accept an invitation but truly cannot. Maybe you have a previous appointment. Perhaps you're tired and would just like to be alone for a while. Of course, you wouldn't want to offend anyone so you would politely turn down the invitation. Here's how to do just that:

Phrase	Pronunciation	Meaning
Es imposible.	ehs eem-poh-see-bleh	It's impossible.
No tengo ganas.	noh tehn-goh gah-nahs	I don't feel like it.
No puedo.	noh pweh-doh	I can't.
No estoy libre.	noh ehs-toh-ee lee-breh	I'm not free.
No quiero.	noh kee-eh-roh	I don't want to.
Lo siento.	loh see-ehn-toh	I'm sorry.
Estoy cansado.	ehs-toh-ee kahn-sah-doh	I'm tired.
Estoy ocupado.	ehs-toh-ee oh-koo-pah-doh	I'm busy.

Showing That You Don't Care

We've all received invitations that we can't decide whether to accept. If you can't make up your mind or are just feeling indifferent towards an idea, use one of these phrases:

Phrase	Pronunciation	Meaning
Depende.	deh-pehn-deh	It depends.
No me importa.	noh meh eem-pohr-tah	It's all the same to me.
Lo que Ud. prefiera (tú prefieras).	loh keh oo-stehd preh-fee-eh-rah (too preh-fee-eh-rahs)	Whatever you want.
Lo que Ud. quiera (tú quieras).	loh keh oo-stehd kee-eh-rah (too kee-eh-rahs)	Whatever you want.
No tengo preferencia.	noh tehn-goh preh-feh-rehn-see-ah	I don't have any preference.
Yo no sé.	yoh noh seh	I don't know.
Tal vez.	tahl behs	Perhaps. (Maybe.)

Other Diversions

You like sports and you're also a very cultured, refined person. Now it's time for a change of pace. Why not try some other activities that would be equally rewarding and fulfilling. If you want to suggest a different pursuit use table 18.3. If you choose to see an opera, a ballet, or a concert don't forget to bring along *los gemelos*, binoculars.

Table 18.3 Places to Go and Things to Do

El Lugar	The Place	La Actividad	The Activity
ir a la opera	go to the opera	escuchar a los cantadores	listen to the singers
ir a la playa	go to the beach	nadar, tomar sol	swim, sunbathe
ir a una discoteca	go to the disco	bailar	dance
ir a un ballet	go to the ballet	ver a los bailadores	see the dancers
ir a un casino	go to the casino	jugar	play, gamble
ir al centro comercial	go to the mall	mirar los escaparates	windowshop
ir al cine	go to the movies	ver una película	see a film
ir a un concierto	go to a concert	escuchar a la orquesta	listen to the
ir al teatro	go to the theater	ver un drama	to see a play
ir de excursión	go on an excursion	ver los sitios	see the sights

continues

Table 18.3 Continued

El Lugar	The Place	La Actividad	The Activity
quedarse en su habitación (casa)	stay in one's room (home)	jugar a los naipes jugar a las damas jugar al ajedrez leer una novela	play cards play checkers play chess read a novel

Will You or Won't You?

Imagine that you're on a cruise and your winning personality has attracted many new friends. You've received many invitations from your newfound acquaintances for when you reach the first port. One person wants you to go shopping in town, while another has suggested visiting famous ruins outside the city. Your traveling companion would like to go to a movie, but someone special has asked you to a famous (and expensive) restaurant and a trendy disco. Use the phrases you've learned in this chapter to give a suitable reply to all these invitations.

By the Sea

Were you ever so excited to finally see the sea that you jumped into the ocean without a second thought? You swim for a while and enjoy that relaxing feeling. When you finally come out, you realize you forgot to get a towel. Now you're standing there dripping wet, shivering, with embarrassing goosebumps all over your body. If you want to have a pleasant day at the beach or pool, remember to take along these items:

Beach Items	Spanish Translation	Pronunciation
beach ball	una pelota de playa	oo-nah peh-loh-tah deh plah-yah
beach chair	un sillón de playa	oon see-yohn deh plah-yah
beach towel	una toalla de playa	oo-nah toh-ah-yah deh plah-yah
cooler	una nevera portatil	oo-nah neh-beh-rah pohr-tah-teel
radio	una radio	oo-nah rah-dee-oh
sunglasses	las gafas de sol	lahs gah-fahs deh sohl

At the Movies and on T.V.

You're all played out, you're all walked out, and your belly is full. If you're a film buff you may want to catch the latest film or even your favorite show on T.V. If you want some quiet entertainment, ask the following questions and consult table 18.4.

¿Qué tipo de película están pasando?
keh tee-poh deh peh-lee-koo-lah ehs-tahn pah-sahn-doh
What kind of film are they showing?

¿Qué hay en la televisión?
keh ah-ee ehn lah teh-leh-bee-see-ohn
What's on T.V.?

Table 18.4 Movies and Television Programs

Type of Program	Spanish Translation	Pronunciation
adventure film	una película de aventura	oo-nah peh-lee-koo-lah deh ah-behn-too-rah
cartoon	los dibujos animados	lohs dee-boo-hohs ah-nee-mah-dohs
comedy	una comedia	oo-nah koh-meh-dee-ah
documentary	un documental	oon doh-koo-mehn-tahl
drama	un drama	oon drah-mah
game show	un juego	oon hoo-eh-goh
horror movie	una película de horror	oo-nah peh-lee-koo-lah deh oh-rrohr
love story	una película de amor	oo-nah peh-lee-koo-lah deh ah-mohr
mystery	un misterio	oon mees-teh-ree-oh
news	las noticias	lahs noh-tee-see-ahs
police story	una película policíaca	oo-nah peh-lee-koo-lah poh-lee-see-ah-kah
science fiction film	una película de ciencia ficción	oo-nah peh-lee-koo-lah deh see-ehn-see-ah feek-see-ohn
soap opera	una telenovela	oo-nah teh-leh-noh-beh-lah
spy movie	una película de espía	oo-nah peh-lee-koo-lah deh ehs-pee-ah
talk show	un programa de entrevistas	oon proh-grah-mah deh ehn-treh-bees-tahs
weather	el parte meteorológico, el pronóstico	ehl pahr-teh meh-teh-oh-roh-loh-hee-koh, ehl proh-nohs-tee-koh
western	una película del Oeste, un western	oo-nah peh-lee-koo-lah dehl oh-ehs-teh, oon wehs-tehrn

Cultural Tidbit

In Spanish movie theaters, an usher, *un(a) guía* (oon [oo-nah] gee-ah) will help you select a seat to your liking. Don't worry, no tip is necessary, it's their job. Don't be surprised to see commercials (which could last for as long as fifteen minutes) before the main feature. Just like back home, there's an ample selection of candy, drinks, ice cream, and popcorn. The following explanations will help you when choosing a movie or theater:

Prohibida para menores de 18 años (a menos de que este acompañado por un adulto).   *Forbidden for those under 18 unless accompanied by an adult.*

Mayores de 13 años.   *You must be older than 13.*

Versión original.   *Original version, subtitled.*

Versión doblada (doh-blah-dah) al español.   *Dubbed in Spanish.*

Tarifa reducida.   *Reduced rate.*

Many American movies are shown in Spanish-speaking countries and they are usually dubbed in Spanish. In some countries, like Mexico, the government controls box office prices to ensure that almost everyone can afford a movie ticket.

What's Your Opinion?

Use the following phrases to express your enjoyment of a film or program:

Positive Review	Spanish Translation	Pronunciation
I love it!	¡Me encanta!	meh ehn-kahn-tah
It's a good movie.	¡Es una buena película!	ehs oo-nah bweh-nah peh-lee-koo-lah
It's amusing!	¡Es divertida!	ehs dee-behr-tee-dah
It's great!	¡Es fantástica!	ehs fahn-tahs-tee-kah
It's moving!	¡Me conmueve!	meh kohn-moo-eh-beh
It's original!	¡Es original!	ehs oh-ree-hee-nahl

If you are less than thrilled with the show, try these phrases:

Negative Review	Spanish Translation	Pronunciation
I hate it!	¡La odio!	lah oh-dee-oh
It's a bad movie!	¡Es una película mala!	ehs oo-nah peh-lee-koo-lah mah-lah
It's a loser!	¡Es un desastre!	ehs oon dehs-ahs-treh
It's garbage!	¡Es una porquería!	ehs oo-nah pohr-keh-ree-ah
It's the same old thing!	¡Es lo mismo de siempre!	ehs loh mees-moh deh see-ehm-preh
It's too violent!	¡Es demasiado violenta!	ehs deh-mah-see-ah-doh bee-oh-lehn-tah

At a Concert

You've gone to Spain simply because your favorite rock group will be performing there. Or maybe you're more into classical guitar or chamber music. One young student of mine received an all-expense paid trip to Europe to sing opera with a choir. Whatever your taste in music, table 18.5 will help you with the names of the musical instruments you will hear.

Table 18.5 Musical Instruments

Instrument	Spanish Translation	Pronunciation
accordion	el acordeón	ehl ah-kohr-deh-ohn
cello	el violoncelo	ehl bee-oh-lohn-seh-loh
clarinet	el clarinete	ehl klah-ree-neh-teh
drum	el tambor	ehl tahm-bohr
drum set	la batería	lah bah-teh-ree-ah
flute	la flauta	lah flow-tah
guitar	la guitarra	lah gee-tah-rrah
harp	el arpa	ehl ahr-pah
horn	el cuerno	ehl kwehr-noh
oboe	el oboe	ehl oh-boh-eh
piano	el piano	ehl pee-ah-noh
piccolo	el piccolo	ehl pee-koh-loh

continues

Table 18.5   Continued

Instrument	Spanish Translation	Pronunciation
saxophone	el saxofón	ehl sahk-soh-fohn
trombone	el trombón	ehl trohm-bohn
trumpet	la trompeta	lah trohm-peh-tah
violin	el violín	ehl bee-oh-leen

Jugar vs. Tocar

Whether we're talking about a sport or an instrument, in English, we use the verb "to play" when we are engaging in one of these activities. In Spanish, however, a distinction is made. The verb *jugar* + a + definite article (al, a la, a los, a las) is used before the name of a sport or game. Jugar is a stem-changing shoe verb that changes *u* to *ue* in all forms except nosotros and vosotros. Take a quick refresher course or refer to Chapter 12.

jugar—to play

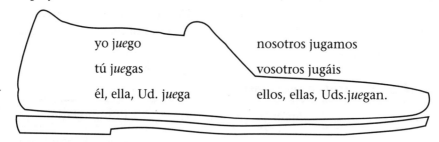

yo j*ue*go   nosotros jugamos

tú j*ue*gas   vosotros jugáis

él, ella, Ud. j*ue*ga   ellos, ellas, Uds. j*ue*gan.

Jugamos a los naipes.
hoo-gah-mohs ah lohs nah-ee-pehs
We play cards.

Juego al tenis.
hoo-eh-goh ahl teh-nees
I play tennis.

Use the verb *tocar* when you are talking about playing a musical instrument.

Me gusta tocar el piano.
meh goos-tah toh-kahr ehl pee-ah-noh
I like to play the piano.

Do You Do Things Well?

Adverbs are often used to describe how well you do something, such as "He plays the classical guitar beautifully" (in English most adverbs end in *ly*). In Spanish, adverbs are used for the same purpose, and they generally end in *mente*.

To form many adverbs, add *mente* to the feminine, singular form of the adjective. This works quite well as long as you look for the proper letter at the end of the adjective and remember the feminine forms. As you remember from Chapter 9: to form the feminine of adjectives that end in *o*, change *o* to *a*; for adjectives that end in *a*, *e*, or a consonant, add nothing. Table 18.6 shows you just how easy this is.

Table 18.6   Adverbs Formed from Feminine Adjectives

Feminine Adjective	Adverb	Meaning
atenta	atentamente	attentively
cariñosa	cariñosamente	affectionately
completa	completamente	completely
especial	especialmente	especially
fácil	fácilmente	easily
final	finalmente	finally
frecuente	frecuentemente	frequently
inteligente	inteligentemente	intelligently
lenta	lentamente	slowly
rápida	rápidamente	quickly
triste	tristemente	sadly

When you find it necessary to describe an action with two or more adverbs, add *mente* only to the last one. The other adverbs are shown in the feminine singular adjective form, to which it is assumed that *mente* would be added, had they stood alone. For example:

Enrique habla clara, lenta, fácil y elocuentemente.

Henry speaks clearly, slowly, easily, and eloquently.

As a Rule

If you can't think of the adverb, or if one does not exist, use the preposition con + noun:

Con + Noun	Adverb	Meaning
con alegría	alegremente	happily
con cortesía	cortésmente	courteously
con cuidado	cuidadosamente	carefully
con habilidad	hábilmente	skillfully
con paciencia	pacientemente	patiently

Is your Spanish good? Do you speak the language well? How about your accent, is it good or bad? I know that you can't pronounce Spanish poorly if you use the pronunciation guide. Be careful with the adverbs *well* and *badly*, that have distinct forms from the adjectives *good* and *bad*.

Adjective	Meaning	Adverb	Meaning
bueno	good	bien	well
malo	bad	mal	badly

Ella es buena y habla bien el español.
eh-yah ehs bweh-nah ee ah-blah bee-ehn ehl ehs-pah-nyohl
She is good and she speaks Spanish well.

Son malos músicos y tocan mal la guitarra.
sohn mah-lohs moo-see-kohs ee toh-kahn mahl lah gee-tah-rrah
They are bad musicians and they play the guitar poorly.

Some adverbs and adverbial expressions are not formed from adjectives at all, and, therefore, do not end in *mente*. Table 18.7 provides some of the most common adverbs that follow this rule.

Table 18.7 Adverbs and Adverbial Expressions Not Formed from Adjectives

Adverb/Adverbial Expression	Pronunciation	Meaning
ahora	ah-oh-rah	now
allá	ah-yah	there
aquí	ah-kee	here
peor	peh-ohr	worse
mejor	meh-hohr	better
más	mahs	more
menos	meh-nohs	less
a menudo	ah meh-noo-doh	often
muy	moo-ee	very
siempre	see-ehm-preh	always
también	tahm-bee-ehn	also, too
tan	tahn	as, so
tarde	tahr-deh	late
temprano	tehm-prah-noh	soon, early
todavía	toh-dah-bee-ah	still, yet
ya	yah	already

Position of Adverbs

Adverbs are generally placed after the verb they modify. Sometimes, however, the position of the adverb is variable and is usually placed where we would logically put an English adverb. Notice the position of the adverbs in the following examples:

Juega bien al fútbol.
hoo-eh-gah bee-ehn ahl foot-bohl
He plays soccer well.

Juega muy bien al fútbol.
hoo-eh-gah moo-ee bee-ehn ahl foot-bohl
He plays soccer very well.

Generalmente juega bien al fútbol.
geh-neh-rahl-mehn-teh hoo-eh-gah bee-ehn ahl foot-bohl
Usually he plays soccer well.

How Do You Do It?

How's your flamenco dancing? Do you make a perfect flan? Can you sing like a nightingale or do you wail like a sick cat? Naturally, our abilities differ. We're all good at some things and awful at others. How do you think you measure up? Express how you feel you perform these activities by using adverbs:

Example: **hablar español**—Hablo español lentamente.

hablar español (speak Spanish)	trabajar (work)
cocinar (cook)	bailar (dance)
pensar (think)—pensar is a shoe verb	nadar (swim)

The Least You Need to Know

➤ The verbs *hacer* + noun, *ir* + *a* + infinitive, or *jugar un partido de* + team sport are used to express participation in a sport.

➤ *Querer* and *poder* + a verb infinitive can be used to propose, accept, and refuse invitations. Don't forget, both of these are shoe verbs.

➤ *Jugar* + *a* + definite article (*al, a la, a los, a las*) is used to talk about playing a game. *Tocar* is used to talk about playing a musical instrument.

➤ Many adverbs are formed by adding *mente* to adjectives ending in a vowel.

Part 4
Problems

Chapter 19

Getting a Great Hairstyle and Other Personal Services

In This Chapter

➤ Personal services

➤ Problems and solutions

➤ Using pronouns after prepositions

➤ Making comparisons

You're having the time of your life traveling throughout the Spanish-speaking world. However, you've been gone so long that little by little, problems are starting to surface. First of all, have you looked at yourself in the mirror lately? It's time for a change. Also, your new tweed jacket has a hole in it and you just dropped your glasses and broke the frame. And if all of this isn't enough, your shoes need resoling and the flash in your camera no longer works. Don't fret! Ask around or consult *las páginas amarillas* (lahs pah-hee-nahs ah-mah-ree-yahs), the yellow pages. Just explain the problem and expert technicians will see to all of them. This chapter will help you get the job done.

I'm Having a Bad Hair Day

Imagine that you've spent the day relaxing in the sun and now it's time to prepare for an important conference, meeting, or date that you've planned for this evening. Upon returning to your room you cast a quick glance at yourself in the mirror. Good grief! You have terminal "hat head," or your beautiful curls are as flat as a board. For a quick fix-me-up, run to the nearest *peinador* (peh-ee-nah-dohr), hairstylist.

Gone are the days when men were treated solely *a la barbería* (ah lah bahr-beh-ree-ah), at the barbershop, while women went *al salón de belleza* (ahl sah-lohn deh beh-yeh-sah), to the beauty parlor. Thanks to the modern unisex trend, many establishments cater to the needs of everyone, because men and women frequently demand the same services. Use the following sentences when your hair needs help:

Puede darme	Quisiera…	por favor
pweh-deh dahr-meh	kee-see-eh-rah	pohr fah-bohr
Can you give me…	*I would like…*	*please*

Do you want a quick fix-up or a whole new look? Whatever you desire, try a salon that will provide the services listed in table 19.1.

Table 19.1 Hair Care

Type of Service	Spanish Translation	Pronunciation
a blunt cut	un corto en cuadrado	oon kohr-toh ehn kwah-drah-doh
a coloring (vegetable)	un tinte (vegetal)	oon teen-teh beh-heh-tahl
a facial	un masaje facial	oon mah-sah-heh fah-see-ahl
a haircut	un corte de pelo	oon kohr-teh deh peh-loh
a manicure	una manicura	oo-nah mah-nee-koo-rah
a pedicure	una pedicura	oo-nah peh-dee-koo-rah
a permanent	una permanente	oo-nah pehr-mah-nehn-teh
a set	un marcado	oon mahr-kah-doh
a shampoo	un champú	oon chahm-poo
a trim	un recorte	oon reh-kohr-teh
a waxing	una depilación	oo-nah deh-pee-lah-see-ohn
highlights	reflejos	reh-fleh-hohs
layers	un corte en degradación	oon kohr-teh ehn deh-grah-dah-see-ohn

Do you need other services? Table 19.2 gives you the phrases you need so that you can explain exactly what you want. Use this phrase to preface your request:

Podría... por favor
poh-dree-ah... pohr fah-bohr
Could you... please.

Table 19.2 Other Services

Type of Service	Spanish Translation	Pronunciation
blow-dry my hair	secarme el pelo	seh-kahr-meh ehl peh-loh
curl my hair	rizarme el pelo	ree-sahr-meh ehl peh-loh
shave	afeitarme	ah-feh-ee-tahr-meh
my beard	la barba	lah bahr-bah
my mustache	el bigote	ehl bee-goh-teh
my head	la cabeza	lah kah-beh-sah
straighten my hair	estirarme el pelo	ehs-tee-rahr-meh ehl peh-loh
trim my bangs	recortarme el flequillo	reh-kohr-tahr-meh ehl fleh-kee-yoh
trim	recortarme	reh-kohr-tahr-meh
my beard	la barba	lah bahr-bah
my mustache	el bigote	ehl bee-goh-teh
my sideburns	las patillas	lahs pah-tee-yahs

Saying What You Like

We all know what it's like to go to a hair salon and explain in very clear English exactly what we want. However, a half hour later, when the hairstylist is done, we end up shrieking at the mirror. That was *not* what we had asked for. Imagine how difficult it could prove to be to get what you want when there is a language barrier. Learn the following phrases and the information in tables 19.3 and 19.4 so that you can easily make known your styling and coloring preferences.

Quisiera un peinado....
kee-see-eh-rah oon peh-ee-nah-doh
I'd like a ... style.

Prefiero mi pelo....
preh-fee-eh-roh mee peh-loh
I prefer my hair....

Table 19.3 Hairstyles

Hairstyle	Spanish Translation	Pronunciation
long	largo	lahr-goh
medium	mediano	meh-dee-ah-noh
short	corto	kohr-toh
wavy	ondulado	ohn-doo-lah-doh
curly	rizado	ree-sah-doh
straight	lacio (liso)	lah-see-oh (lee-soh)

Table 19.4 Asking for the Perfect Hair Color

Hair Color	Spanish Translation	Pronunciation
auburn	rojizo	roh-hee-soh
black	negro	neh-groh
blond	rubio	roo-bee-oh
brunette	castaño	kahs-tah-nyoh
chestnut brown	pardo	pahr-doh
red	pelirrojo	peh-lee-rroh-hoh
a darker color	un color más oscuro	oon koh-lohr mahs oh-skoo-roh
a lighter color	un color más claro	oon koh-lohr mahs klah-roh
the same color	el mismo color	ehl mees-moh koh-lohr

I'm Having Problems

When you need to have certain services performed or when something you own needs repair, you'll want to have some key phrases on hand. Make use of the following sentences when you go to the dry cleaner, the shoemaker, the optometrist, the jeweler, or the camera store.

¿A qué hora abre Ud.?
ah keh oh-rah ah-breh oo-stehd
At what time do you open?

¿A qué hora cierra Ud.?
ah keh oh-rah see-eh-rrah oo-stehd
At what time do you close?

¿Qué días abre (cierra) Ud.?
keh dee-ahs ah-breh (see-eh-rrah) oo-stehd
What days are you open? closed?

¿Puede arreglarme …?
pweh-deh ah-rreh-glahr-meh …
Can you fix…for me?

¿Puede arreglarmelo (la, los, las) hoy?
pweh-deh ah-rreh-glahr-meh-loh (lah, lohs, lahs)
oh-ee
Can you fix it (them) today?

¿Puede arreglarmelo (la, los, las) temporalmente (mientras yo espero)?
pweh-deh ah-rreh-glahr-meh-loh (lah, lohs, lahs) tehm-poh-rahl-mehn-teh (mee-ehn-trahs yoh ehs-peh-roh)
Can you fix it (them) temporarily (while I wait)?

¿Me puede dar un recibo?
meh pweh-deh dahr oon reh-see-boh
May I have a receipt?

As a Rule
Use the verb *remendar*, to repair, when you are referring to clothing or shoes.

¿Puede remendarme este vestido?

¿Puede remendarme estos zapatos?

At the Dry Cleaner's—A la Tintorería

My friends think I'm crazy, but I like to travel with one of those compact travel irons. I can't stand that rumpled look. My husband believes that hanging anything in a damp bathroom will do the trick just fine. When you unpack, do you hate the way your clothes come out? Or, have you ever found a stain that you missed? No problem. Every country has dry cleaning and laundry establishments that can deal with all your spots, stains, wrinkles, and tears. Here's how to explain your problem:

Tengo un problema.
tehn-goh oon proh-bleh-mah
I have a problem.

¿Cuál es el problema?
kwahl ehs ehl proh-bleh-mah
What's the problem?

Hay...
ah-ee
There is (are)...

Problem	Spanish Translation	Pronunciation
a hole	un roto	oon rroh-toh
a missing button	(le falta) un botón	(leh-fahl-tah) oon boh-tohn
a spot, stain	una mancha	oo-nah mahn-chah
a tear	un desgarrón	oon dehs-gah-rrohn

Cultural Tidbit

Don't expect to find as many dry cleaners and laundromats in the Spanish-speaking world as in the United States. And don't expect the quick same-day service that has spoiled so many of us. Although laundries in foreign countries are usually quite good, they work much slower than what we are accustomed to. Plan on waiting a few days, or perhaps even a week, to get your stains removed and your clothes cleaned. If you're lucky, in big cities you might find a dry cleaner who can have your laundry ready in a day. Your best bet is to travel with as many permanent press clothes as possible.

Congratulations, you've successfully explained your problem. Now you're ready to state what you'd like done about it:

¿Puede lavarme este (esta, estos, estas)...en seco?
pweh-deh lah-bahr-meh ehs-teh (ehs-tah, ehs-tohs, ehs-tahs) ehn seh-koh
Can you (dry) clean this (these)...for me?

As a Rule
If you'd like a service performed *for* someone else, use the appropriate indirect object: *te* (for you), *le* (for him, her, you), *nos* (for us), *os* (for you), *les* (for them).

¿Puede tejerle este abrigo? *Can you please weave this coat for him?*

¿Puede remendarme este (esta, estos, estas)...?
pweh-deh reh-mehn-dahr-meh ehs-teh (ehs-tah, ehs-tohs, ehs-tahs)
Can you please mend this (these)...for me?

¿Puede plancharme este (esta, estos, estas)...?
pweh-deh plahn-chahr-meh ehs-teh (ehs-tah, ehs-tohs, ehs-tahs)
Can you please press this (these)...for me?

¿Puede almidonarme este (esta, estos, estas)…?
pweh-deh ahl-mee-doh-nahr-meh ehs-teh (ehs-tah, ehs-tohs, ehs-tahs)
Can you please starch this (these)…for me?

¿Puede tejerme este (esta, estos, estas)…?
pweh-deh teh-hehr-meh ehs-teh (ehs-tah, ehs-tohs, ehs-tahs)
Can you please weave this (these)…for me?

At the Laundry—En la Lavandería

Whether you're on the road or enjoying a leisurely vacation in a hotel, your laundry will pile up. If it can't wait until you get home, you could save a lot of money by doing it yourself at a laundromat. The following phrases will help you get the information you need.

Quiero lavarme la ropa.
kee-eh-roh lah-bahr-meh lah roh-pah
I'd like to wash my clothes.

Quisiera que me laven la ropa.
kee-see-eh-rah keh meh lah-behn lah roh-pah
I'd like to have my clothes washed.

You don't want anyone to see that ring around your collar. Or perhaps you're embarrassed by that tomato-sauce stain on your white shirt. Maybe you think that no one does a better job than you, or you're afraid that your new wool sweater will shrink. If you're intent on doing the job yourself, here are some phrases that might prove useful:

¿Hay una lavadora (secadora) libre?
ah-ee oo-nah lah-bah-doh-rah (seh-kah-doh-rah) lee-breh
Is there a free washing machine (dryer)?

¿Dónde puedo comprar jabón en polvo?
dohn-deh pweh-doh kohm-prahr hah-bohn ehn pohl-boh
Where can I can buy soap powder?

Please Do My Laundry

If you're not up to washing your own clothes, fill out a laundry slip, which is usually left in every hotel room. Once you complete the form, leave your clothes in the sack that's provided. Imagine that you've let things pile up and you have to fill out a laundry slip. Read this notice that accompanies your laundry slip. What does it tell you?

HABITACIÓN

NOTA: Su ropa será aceptada bajo las siguientes condiciones:

No somos responsables por botones o adornos que no resistan el lavado o aplanchado.

En caso de pérdida o daño, el hotel responderá hasta diez veces el valor del servicio encomendado a la lavandería.

No nos hacemos responsables por materiales sintéticos, ni por articulos dejados por más de 3 meses.

Cerrado los sábados, domingos y días de fiesta.

Servicios urgentes serán cargados con 50% sobre costo.

At the Shoemaker's—En la Zapatería

Have you walked so much that your shoes need new soles? Perhaps you're going out on the town and it's time for a shine. Or if you're a jeans and sneakers type of person, maybe it's time for some new laces. Use the following phrases to help you:

¿Puede remendarme...?
pweh-deh reh-mehn-dahr-meh
Can you repair...for me?

estos zapatos	este tacón
ehs-tohs sah-pah-tohs	ehs-teh tah-kohn
these shoes	*this heel*
estas botas	esta suela
ehs-tahs boh-tahs	ehs-tah sweh-lah
these boots	*this sole*

¿Vende cordones de zapatos?
behn-deh kohr-doh-nehs deh sah-pah-tohs
Do you sell shoelaces?

Quisiera una limpieza de zapatos.
kee-see-eh-rah oo-nah leem-pee-eh-sah deh sah-pah-tohs
I'd like a shoe shine.

I Need These Shoes

You just looked at the dress shoes you're planning to wear for a very important engagement. They are in serious need of repair and you need them for tomorrow night. You look in the yellow pages and come across this ad. What service does this *zapatería* provide?

ZAPATERÍA

BERNAL

Buscamos y Llevamos

Calle de la Cruz 154

Viejo San Juan

At the Optician's—En la Optica

Those of us who wear contact lenses know that they tend to disappear or rip at the most inopportune moments. And for those who rely on glasses, well a broken lens or frame when you are on vacation could be a real disaster. Familiarize yourself with the following useful phrases:

¿Puede arreglarme estos lentes (estas gafas)?
pweh-deh ah-rreh-glahr-meh ehs-tohs lehn-tehs (ehs-tahs gah-fahs)
Can you repair these glasses for me?

El lente (la montura) está roto(a).
ehl lehn-teh (lah mohn-too-rah) ehs-tah rroh-toh(tah)
The lens (the frame) is broken.

¿Puede darme otra lentilla (otro lente) de contacto?
pweh-deh dahr-meh oh-trah lehn-tee-yah (oh-troh lehn-teh) deh kohn-tahk-toh
Can you replace this contact lens?

¿Tiene lentes progresivos?
tee-eh-neh lehn-tehs proh-greh-see-bohs
Do you have progressive lenses?

¿Vende lentes (gafas) de sol?
behn-deh lehn-tehs (gah-fahs) deh sohl
Do you sell sunglasses?

At the Jeweler's— En la Joyería

What luck! The battery of your watch just went dead right in the middle of your trip. That's my kind of luck too. If it's inconvenient to go without your watch, you might have to stop into a jewelry store or a watchmaker's *la relojería* (la reh-loh-heh-ree-ah), for a quick repair.

Cultural Tidbit

One of the most interesting and avant-garde jewelry designers today is Paloma Picasso, daughter of the famous Spanish-born painter, Pablo Picasso and his companion of ten years, Françoise Gilot, a Frenchwoman. Best known for her chic, exotic, and oftentimes colorful jewelry designs that are prominently displayed in Tiffany's, New York, Paloma (Spanish for *dove*) Picasso has also created a famous perfume bearing her name. Although she spent most of her life living in France, Paloma married Argentine playwright-director Rafael López-Sanchez who acts as her business manager and for whom she designs stage sets.

¿Puede arreglarme este reloj?
pweh-deh ah-rreh-glahr-meh ehs-teh reh-loh
Can you repair this watch?

Mi reloj no funciona.
mee reh-loh noh foon-see-oh-nah
My watch doesn't work.

Mi reloj está parado.
mee reh-loh ehs-tah pah-rah-doh
My watch has stopped.

¿Vende pulsos (baterías)?
behn-deh pool-sohs (bah-teh-ree-ahs)
Do you sell bands (batteries)?

It's My Watch

You're going to be late for a very important date, all because your battery died. Fortunately, there's a jewelry shop right outside your hotel. You decide to stop by for a quick repair, you hope. Explain the problem you're having and what you'd like done.

At the Camera Shop—En la Tienda del Fotógrafo

If you're like me, then you take your camera and a huge supply of film on every trip you take. You wouldn't want to miss one of those precious moments. And besides, when you get back, you like to look at the shots you snapped. In a way, this allows you to relive the vacation many times over. If you need more supplies, repair, or simply want to develop your film, the following words will help you.

Photo Supply	Spanish Translation	Pronunciation
a camera	una cámara	oo-nah kah-mah-rah
film	una película	oo-nah peh-lee-koo-lah
slides	las diapositivas	lahs dee-ah-poh-see-tee-bahs
a video camera	una videocámara	oo-nah bee-deh-oh-kah-mah-rah

If you have special needs, you might ask:

¿Vende películas a color (en blanco y negro) de 20 (36) exposiciones?
behn-deh peh-lee-koo-lahs ah koh-lohr (ehn blahn-koh ee neh-groh) deh beh-een-teh (treh-een-tah ee seh-ees) ehks-poh-see-see-oh-nehs
Do you sell rolls of 20 (36) exposure film in color (black-and-white)?

¿Vende películas para diapositivas?
behn-deh peh-lee-koo-lahs pah-rah dee-ah-poh-see-tee-bahs
Do you sell film for slides?

Quisiera que me revele este carrete (rollo).
kee-see-eh-rah keh meh reh-beh-leh ehs-teh kah-rreh-teh (roh-yoh)
I would like to have this film developed.

I Can't Wait to See My Pictures!

You took some great shots and you want to see them right away. You read an ad in the paper and decided to bring your film in for developing. What did the ad promise you?

Other Services

Besides needing repairs, you may find that there are other services you need. Should you lose important papers or documents, or need special assistance, you might find yourself in need of the police or the American embassy. Don't be shy to ask for a translator, if necessary. Although you've become quite good at this, if you're nervous or upset, you might not be able to get your thoughts across in any language. The phrases that follow should help you get started.

¿Dónde está...?
dohn-deh ehs-tah
Where is…

la comisaria de policía
lah koh-mee-sah-ree-ah
  deh poh-lee-see-ah
the police station?

el consulado americano
ehl kohn-soo-lah-doh
  ah-meh-ree-kah-noh
the American consulate?

la embajada americana
lah ehm-bah-hah-dah
  ah-meh-ree-kah-nah
the American embassy?

Yo perdí...
yoh pehr-dee
I lost...

mi pasaporte
mee pah-sah-pohr-teh
my passport

mi cartera
mee kahr-teh-rah
my wallet

Ayúdeme, por favor.
ah-yoo-deh-meh pohr fah-bohr
Help me, please.

Necesito un interprete.
neh-seh-see-toh oon
  een-tehr-preh-teh
I need an interpreter.

Hay alguien aquí que hable inglés?
ah-ee ahl-gee-ehn ah-kee keh
  ah-bleh een-glehs
Does anyone here speak English?

Prepositional Pronouns

A prepositional pronoun is used to replace a noun as the object of a preposition. This pronoun always follows the preposition. Table 19.5 shows subject pronouns with their corresponding prepositional pronouns.

Table 19.5   Prepositional Pronouns

Subject	Prepositional Pronoun	Meaning
yo	mí	me
tú	ti	you (familiar)
él	él	him, it
ella	ella	her, it
Ud.	Ud.	you (formal)
nosotros (as)	nosotros (as)	us
vosotros (as)	vosotros (as)	you (familiar)
ellos	ellos	them
ellas	ellas	them
Uds.	Uds.	you (formal)

Make sure to use the correct pronoun in a prepositional phrase. This should prove to be rather easy because the only prepositional pronouns that differ from subject pronouns are *mi* and *ti*.

Este regalo no es para ti, es para mí.   *This present isn't for you, it's for me.*

No podemos partir sin ellos.   *We can't leave without them.*

Because indirect object pronouns often need clarification in Spanish, it is common to add the preposition *a + prepositional pronoun* to avoid confusion.

As a Rule
Mí and *ti* combine with the preposition *con* (kohn), with, as follows:

Él va al centro conmigo.
He's going downtown with me.

No puedo ir contigo.
I can't go with you.

Le doy a él la respuesta.   *I give him the answer.*

Le doy a ella la respuesta.   *I give her the answer.*

Le doy a Ud. la respuesta.   *I give you the answer.*

A + prepositional pronoun may be added to stress to whom an action has importance:

A mí me gusta el chocolate.   *I like chocolate.*

A él no le encantan los deportes.   *He doesn't adore sports.*

Making Comparisons

Which airline company has the best airfare to a Spanish-speaking country? Which hotel has the best facilities? Which car rental will give you the best deal. Who is the most reliable tour guide in the city? Everyday we make comparisons. Sometimes we're looking for the most, and sometimes the least. Use table 19.6 to help you compare things.

Table 19.6 Comparison of Adjectives: Inequality

	Adjective	Pronunciation	Meaning
POSITIVE	triste	trees-teh	sad
COMPARATIVE	más triste	mahs trees-teh	sadder
	menos triste	meh-nohs trees-teh	less sad
SUPERLATIVE	el (la, los, las) *xxx* más triste(s)	ehl (lah, lohs, lahs) *xxx* mahs trees-teh(s)	the saddest *xxx*
	el (la, los, las) *xxx* menos triste(s)	ehl (lah, lohs, lahs) *xxx* meh-nohs trees-teh(s)	the least sad *xxx*

Que may or may not be used after the comparative. When used, *que* expresses *than*.

¿Quién es más sincero?   *Who is more sincere?*

Roberto es más sincero (que Rafael).
Roberto is more sincere (than Rafael).

Amalia es menos sincera (que Ana).
Amalia is less sincere (than Ana).

The preposition *de + definite article* (del, de la, de los, de las) may be used to express *in (of)* the.

Este hombre es simpático.
This man is nice.

Este hombre es más simpático que él.
This man is nicer than he.

Este hombre es el más simpático (del pueblo).
This man is the nicest (in the city).

Esas mujeres son ricas.

Esas mujeres son las más ricas.

Aquellas mujeres son las menos ricas (de la cuidad).

As a Rule

The comparative and superlative forms of the adjectives used must agree in gender and number with the nouns they describe.

Julio es menos *fuerte* que su amigo.

Juanita es más *linda* que su hermana.

Estas camisetas son *las* menos *caras.*

Esos coches son *los* más *deportivos.*

Pitfall

Beware of irregular comparisons. Never use *más* or *menos* with the adjectives *bueno, malo.* There are special comparative forms that express *better* and *best*:

POSITIVE		COMPARATIVE		SUPERLATIVE	
Spanish	English	Spanish	English	Spanish	English
bueno (a, os, as)	good	mejor (es)	better	el (la) mejor, los (las) mejores	best
malo (a, os, as)	bad	peor (es)	worse	el (la) peor, los (las) peores	worst

When *grande* and *pequeño* refer to age (older or younger), do not use más or menos. Use the following comparitive forms instead:

continues

POSITIVE		COMPARATIVE		SUPERLATIVE	
Spanish	English	Spanish	English	Spanish	English
grande	big	mayor (es)	older	el (la) mayor, los (las) mayores	oldest
pequeño	small	menor (es)	younger	el (la) menor, los (las) menores	youngest

As a Rule
Mejor and peor generally come before the noun they modify:

mi mejor amiga   *my best friend*

mi peor enemigo   *my worst enemy*

Mayor and menor generally go after the noun they modify:

mi hermano mayor   *my older brother*

mi hermana menor   *my younger sister*

Each person in my family has quite different artistic talents. When my husband picks up a pencil and piece of paper, his drawings are quite good. My son, Michael has the second-best genes and, probably because he's a lefty, seems rather talented. I have the worst ability, which I passed on to my other son, Eric. He draws horribly. And me, I'm the worst in the family. No one can ever tell exactly what it is I've put on the paper. At least I make everyone laugh. Not only can people be compared, but the way in which they do things may also be compared. Table 19.7 shows how to make comparisons using adverbs (to describe actions).

Table 19.7 Comparison of Adverbs: Inequality

	Adverb	Pronunciation	Meaning
POSITIVE	rápidamente	rah-pee-dah-mehn-teh	rapidly
COMPARATIVE	más rápidamente	mahs rah-pee-dah-mehn-teh	more rapidly
	menos rápidamente	meh-nohs rah-pee-dah-mehn-teh	less rapidly
SUPERLATIVE	más rápidamente (que)	mahs rah-pee-dah-mehn-teh (keh)	more rapidly (than)
	menos rápidamente (que)	meh-nohs rah-pee-dah-mehn-teh (keh)	less rapidly (than)

You've done a lot of sight-seeing on your trip. Did you find the modern museums as entertaining as those that hold the treasures of antiquity? Did you spend as much time visiting the Picasso exhibits as you did the ones by Velázquez? If all things are equal, then it becomes necessary to form a comparison of equality using either adjectives or adverbs. To do this, follow this formula:

tan + adjective or adverb + *como*—as … as

> Él es tan elegante como su amigo.
> *He is as elegant as his friend.*

> Ella trabaja tan diligentemente como él.
> *She works as hard as he does.*

Absolutely Superlative

When no comparison is involved and you want to express that something is absolutely superlative, you may attach *ísimo, ísima, ísimos,* or *ísimas* (according to the number and gender of the noun being described) to the adjective. If the adjective ends in a vowel, drop the vowel before adding the superlative ending. The *ísimo* ending gives the same meaning as if you had used *muy* + adjective. In the following sentences, the sentences on the right, in italics, mean the same thing as the sentences on the left:

> El hotel es muy grande.   *Es un hotel grandísimo.*

> Esta película es muy popular.   *Es una película popularísima.*

Adjectives with certain endings make the following changes: *c* changes *c* to *qu*, *g* changes *g* to *gu*, and *z* becomes *c* before adding *ísimo*. Notice the changes in the following, equivalent sentences:

Es un postre muy ri*c*o.   Es un postre ri*qu*ísimo.

Es una avenida muy lar*g*a.   Es una avenida lar*gu*ísima.

El tigre es muy fero*z*.   El tigre es fero*c*ísimo.

Adverbs can also be made absolutely superlative, but you probably won't be hearing or saying this often because the words seem to be tongue twisters. If you'd like to give it a shot, add *mente* to the feminine form of the adjective adding in *ísima*:

> Él trabaja lentísimamente.   *He works very slowly.*

As a Rule
There's no distinction made between the comparative and superlative forms of adverbs. For the comparative and superlative use *que* to express *than*:

Yo camino rápidamente.
I walk fast.

Carlos camina más rápidamente.
Carlos walks faster.

Carlos camina más rápidamente que yo.
Carlos walks faster than I.

Pitfall
Never use the expression *muy mucho*. If you want to express very much, use *muchísimo*.

Me gusta muchísimo este libro.   *I like this book very much.*

Compare Yourself

How do you compare to those you know? Are you shorter? Thinner? More charming? Do you dance better? Work more seriously? Listen more patiently? Use what you've learned to compare yourself to friends or family members.

The Least You Need to Know

➤ Prepositional pronouns are used after prepositions and for emphasis. They also help to clarify the identity of the indirect object pronoun.

➤ Use *más* (more) or *menos* (less) before adjectives or adverbs to make comparisons or state the superlative.

➤ Use *tan* (as) before adjectives and adverbs + *como* to express that things are equal.

➤ Use *ísimo* (*ísima, ísimos, ísimas*) to form the absolute superlative of adjectives and adverbs.

Chapter 20

Quick, Call a Doctor!

In This Chapter

➤ Your body

➤ Symptoms, complaints, and illnesses

➤ Expressing *how long*

➤ All about *decir* (to say, tell)

➤ Using reflexive verbs

Minor, everyday hassles were treated in the last chapter. You should now feel assured that you can make yourself look presentable and obtain necessary repair services with a fair amount of expediency. All you really need is a few short, simple phrases and terms. In this chapter you'll learn the words and expressions that will help you deal with a more serious problem—an illness.

Of course you think that it can't happen to you. People travel far and wide all the time without ever having to visit a doctor. But let's face it, at the most inopportune moment, people get sick or have freak incapacitating accidents: my best friend passed a kidney stone in France; my son shattered a tooth in the Dominican Republic; my mother fell and fractured her wrist in Puerto Rico; and I got violently seasick on a two-day cruise to nowhere. Life's medical annoyances can really bring us down when all we want to do is relax and have a good time. The situation becomes even more exasperating and frustrating when we can't communicate what is wrong. In this chapter you will learn how to express what ails you and explain how long you've had your symptoms.

What a Body!

Have you ever been to Mexico? I drool over the sexy ads for Cancún, and I covet a genuine turquoise jewelry collection. Why haven't I flown the coop and jumped on an Aeronaves de México flight during the winter snows? The answer is simple: Montezuma's Revenge (a.k.a. severe diarrhea). I know my stomach. If I just look at a glass of water, I'll wind up in *un consultorio* (oon kohn-sool-toh-ree-oh), a doctor's office. Or worse yet, I'll spend the entire week in *el baño* (ehl bah-nyoh). Logically, I know that I can travel with a bottle of Lomotil and always keep mineral water on hand. But I've heard too many horror stories from friends who ate salad (washed in tap water) or had drinks on the rocks (with ice cubes made from local water). Everyone says that today, with modern technology and advanced hygienic conditions, the curse of Montezuma is a thing of the past. Perhaps one day you'll see me on that flight. But if we go, we'll want to learn the words in table 20.1 so that we can tell somebody we're sick and where it hurts…just in case.

Table 20.1 Parts of the Body

Body Part	Spanish Translation	Pronunciation
ankle	el tobillo	ehl toh-bee-yoh
arm	el brazo	ehl brah-soh
back	la espalda	lah ehs-pahl-dah
body	el cuerpo	ehl kwehr-poh
brain	el cerebro	ehl seh-reh-broh
chest	el pecho	ehl peh-choh
chin	la barbilla	lah bahr-bee-yah
ear	la oreja	lah oh-reh-hah
eye	el ojo	ehl oh-hoh
face	la cara	lah kah-rah
finger	el dedo	ehl deh-doh
foot	el pie	ehl pee-eh
hand	la mano	lah mah-noh
head	la cabeza	lah kah-beh-sah
heart	el corazón	ehl koh-rah-sohn
knee	la rodilla	lah roh-dee-yah
leg	la pierna	lah pee-ehr-nah
mouth	la boca	lah boh-kah
nail	la uña	lah oo-nyah
neck	el cuello	ehl kweh-yoh

Body Part	Spanish Translation	Pronunciation
nose	la nariz	lah nah-rees
skin	la piel	lah pee-ehl
shoulder	el hombro	ehl ohm-broh
spine	la espina	lah ehs-pee-nah
stomach	el estómago	ehl ehs-toh-mah-goh
throat	la garganta	lah gahr-gahn-tah
toe	el dedo del pie	ehl deh-doh dehl pee-eh
tongue	la lengua	lah lehn-gwah
tooth	el diente	ehl dee-ehn-teh
wrist	la muñeca	lah moo-nyeh-kah

Jet lag is no joke. In the 1970s, when it was popular to backpack to Europe on five dollars a day, my husband and I decided to do just that before we started our family. We arrived in England during an extremely hot spell, and spent our first three nights in an unbearably hot trailer—that's what happens when you go without reservations. We hardly slept a wink. When the sun came up, we'd be exhausted, but we'd go out sightseeing.

Our next stop was Paris. We had another hot room, without a bath, in the red-light district. Sleep still wouldn't come. At the end of 1 1/2 weeks of traveling, when we were delirious from lack of sleep, we finally went to the doctor. The kind man prescribed a sleep aid. Finally, we were able to resume a normal life. If you run into a problem and have to seek medical help, the obvious first question will be: "What's the matter with you?," "*¿Qué le pasa?*" (keh leh pah-sah). To say what hurts or bothers you, use the expression *tener dolor de (en) + the part that hurts*:

Tengo dolor de cabeza.
tehn-goh doh-lohr deh kah-beh-sah.
I have a headache.

Tiene dolor en el brazo.
tee-eh-neh doh-lohr ehn ehl brah-soh.
He has pain in his arm.

As a Rule

Remember that when you say what ails you or anyone else, you must conjugate the verb *tener*, to have, so that it agrees with the subject. Although the Spanish use tener to express what's bothering them, our English may not include the word "have."

continues

¿Tienes dolor en los pies?
tee-eh-nehs doh-lohr ehn lohs pee-ehs
Do your feet hurt?

If you have to go to the dentist, use the expression:

Tengo dolor de muelas.
tehn-goh doh-lohr deh mweh-lahs
I have a toothache.

You may also choose to talk about your symptoms by using the shoe verb *doler* (doh-lehr), to hurt. You will notice that *doler* is a stem-changing verb. This should not present too much of a problem because doler is used in the same way as the verb *gustar*, which means that you'll really only have to use two verb forms: *duele* (dweh-leh) and *duelen* (dweh-lehn). Why is that? *Doler* means that something is hurting (to) you and is, therefore, a verb that requires an indirect object pronoun. You must use the appropriate indirect object pronoun to refer to those who might be in pain (*me* [to me], *te* [to you], *le* [to him/her/you], *nos* [to us], *os* [to you], *les* [to them/you]). The subject of the sentence, is the body part that is giving the pain.

Let's take a closer look at how this works. Let's say you've been playing volleyball for the first time in a very long while. At the end of the day your whole body aches. You might say to a friend (the italicized sentences are how we would get the same point across in English, but the bold sentences are direct translations):

Me duele la cabeza.   *My head hurts.*   **(My head is hurting to me.)**

Me duelen los pies.   *My feet hurt.*   **(My feet are hurting to me.)**

Feel free to speak or ask about others who were also involved in the game. Once again, don't let the reverse word order fool you. Remember to choose an indirect object pronoun that refers to the person in pain. The subject will follow the verb *doler* and must, therefore, agree with it. Let's see how this works:

¿Te duele el brazo?   *Does your arm hurt?*

¿Le duele el estómago?   *Does his (her, your) stomach hurt?*

Nos duelen las piernas.   *Our legs hurt.*

¿Os duelen los dedos?   *Do your fingers hurt?*

No les duelen las manos.   *Their (Your) hands don't hurt.*

As a Rule

If you want the indirect object pronoun to clearly and specifically express who is in pain, you may add the preposition a + name or prepositional pronoun.

A Julio le duelen las espaldas.   *Julio's shoulders hurts.*

A ellos le duele la garganta.   *Their throat hurts.*

Notice that it is unnecessary to use a possessive adjective (*mi(s)*, *tu(s)*, *su(s)*, *nuestro(a)(s)*, *vuestro(a)(s)*, *su(s)*) before the name of the body part. This is considered repetitive, since the indirect object pronoun states to whom the pain is occurring.

Perhaps you have symptoms that are indicative of something a bit more complicated than an ache or pain. Maybe there's a problem that requires further medical attention. A list of possible symptoms and conditions is given in table 20.2. These words will surely come in handy when you need to provide a more detailed description of your aches and pains. Use the word *tengo* (tehn-goh), I have, to preface your complaint.

Table 20.2 Other Symptoms and Conditions

Symptoms and Conditions	Spanish Translation	Pronunciation
abscess	un absceso	oon ahb-seh-soh
blister	una ampolla	oo-nah ahm-poh-yah
broken bone	un hueso roto	oon weh-soh roh-toh
bruise	una contusión	oo-nah kohn-too-see-ohn
bump	una hinchazón	oo-nah een-chah-sohn
burn	una quemadura	oo-nah keh-mah-doo-rah
chills	un escalofrío	oon ehs-kah-loh-free-oh
cough	una tos	oo-nah tohs
cramps	un calambre	oon kah-lahm-breh
diarrhea	una diarrea	oo-nah dee-ah-rreh-ah
fever	una fiebre	oo-nah fee-eh-breh
indigestion	una indigestión	oo-nah een-dee-hehs-tee-ohn
lump	un bulto	oon bool-toh
migraine	una jaqueca	oo-nah hah-keh-kah
pain	un dolor	oon doh-lohr

continues

Table 20.2 Continued

Symptoms and Conditions	Spanish Translation	Pronunciation
rash	una erupción	oo-nah eh-roop-see-ohn
sprain	una torcedura	oo-nah tohr-seh-doo-rah
swelling	una inflamación	oo-nah een-flah-mah-see-ohn
wound	una herido	oo-nah eh-ree-doh

Other useful phrases to help describe your illness include:

Yo toso.
yoh toh-soh
I'm couging.

Yo no puedo dormir.
yoh noh pweh-doh dohr-meer
I can't sleep.

Yo estornudo.
yoh ehs-tohr-noo-doh
I'm sneezing.

Yo estoy agotado(a).
yoh ehs-toh-ee ah-goh-tah-doh(dah)
I'm exhausted.

Yo tengo náuseas.
yoh tehn-goh now-seh-ahs
I'm nauseous.

Me duele todo el cuerpo.
meh dweh-leh toh-doh ehl kwehr-poh
I hurt everywhere.

Yo estoy sangrando.
yoh ehs-toh-ee sahn-grahn-doh
I'm bleeding.

Me siento mal.
meh see-ehn-toh mahl
I feel bad.

I Hurt

Now use all that you've learned so far to describe your symptoms and complaints to a doctor. Pretend you have flu-like symptoms, an allergy, a sprained ankle, and, finally, a migraine.

This Is What You Have

Obviously, you won't be the only one doing the talking when you visit the doctor. You will also be asked to fill out forms, tell about any medications you're taking, and answer other questions about your symptoms and general health. The doctor or nurse may ask you if you have some of the symptoms or illnesses listed in table 20.3:

As a Rule
Remember that de contracts with el to become del with masculine singular nouns.

¿Ha tenido...?
ah teh-nee-doh
Have you had...?

¿Sufre Ud. de...?
soo-freh oo-stehd deh...
Do you suffer from...?

Table 20.3 Symptoms and Illnesses

Symptom/Illness	Spanish Translation	Pronunciation
allergic reaction	una reacción alérgica	oo-nah reh-ahk-see-ohn ah-lehr-hee-kah
angina	la angina	lah ahn-hee-nah
appendicitis	la apendicitis	lah ah-pehn-dee-see-tees
asthma	el asma	ehl ahs-mah
bronchitis	la bronquitis	lah brohn-kee-tees
cancer	el cáncer	ehl kahn-sehr
cold	un resfriado, un catarro	oon rehs-free-ah-doh, oon kah-tah-rroh
diabetes	la diabetes	lah dee-ah-beh-tehs
dizziness	el vértigo	ehl behr-tee-goh
dysentery	la disentería	lah dee-sehn-teh-ree-ah
exhaustion	la fatiga	lah fah-tee-gah
flu	la gripe	lah gree-peh
German measles	la rubeola	lah roo-beh-oh-lah
gout	la gota	lah goh-tah
heart attack	un ataque al corazón	oon ah-tah-keh ahl koh-rah-sohn
hepatitis	la hepatitis	lah eh-pah-tee-tees
measles	el sarampión	ehl sah-rahm-pee-ohn
mumps	las paperas	lahs pah-peh-rahs
pneumonia	la pulmonía	lah pool-moh-nee-ah
polio	la poliomielitis	lah poh-lee-oh-mee-eh-lee-tees
smallpox	la viruela	lah bee-roo-eh-lah
stroke	un ataque de apoplejía	oon ah-tah-keh deh ah-poh-pleh-hee-ah
sunstroke	una insolación	oo-nah een-soh-lah-see-ohn
tetanus	el tétano	ehl teh-tah-noh
tuberculosis	la tuberculosis	lah too-behr-koo-loh-sees
whooping cough	la tosferina	lah tohs-feh-ree-nah

How Long Have You Felt This Way?

One of the most frequent questions a doctor asks is: "How long have you been feeling this way?" It's important for the person giving you medical help to know for how long you've been experiencing your symptoms. The following phrases offer you two ways in which that question might be asked, and the ways for you to give an appropriate answer. The first question and answer phrases are the most common and probably the easiest to use.

¿Cuánto tiempo hace que + *present tense verb*?
kwahn-toh tee-ehm-poh ah-seh keh …
(For) how long (has) have + present tense verb?

You would answer this question in the form of:

Hace + *time* + que + *present tense*
ah-seh … keh
I've been + present tense + *for* + time.

The second way you might be asked how long you've been sick is:

¿Desde cuándo + *present tense*?
dehs-deh kwahn-doh …
(For) How long has (have) + present tense.

You would answer this question like:

present tense of verb + desde hace + *time*
… dehs-deh ah-seh …
… *for* …

Here are some examples of what you might be asked, and how you would respond to the questions.

¿Cuánto tiempo hace que sufre?
kwahn-toh tee-em-poh ah-seh keh soo-freh
(For) How long have you been suffering?

Hace dos días (que sufro).
ah-seh dohs dee-ahs (keh soo-froh)
(I've been suffering) For two days.

¿Desde cuándo sufre?
dehs-deh kwahn-doh soo-freh
(For) How long have you been suffering?

(Sufro) desde hace ayer.
soo-froh dehs-deh ah-seh ah-yehr
(I've been suffering) Since yesterday.

I'm Not a Hypochondriac

Now use all the variations to explain how long you been suffering. Talk about a cough you've had for two weeks, a headache that's stuck around for three days, or the stomach ache that's been bugging you for nearly a month.

What Do You Tell the Doctor?

When something is really bothering you, and you're somewhat frightened, what do you *tell* the doctor? Do you say what is truly bothering you or are you afraid to enumerate all your symptoms? In order to express what you say or tell someone, use the irregular verb *decir* (to tell, say). You will notice that decir is a go-go shoe verb. The yo form ends in *go*, and the *e* from the stem changes to *i* in all forms except nosotros and vosotros.

decir—to tell, say

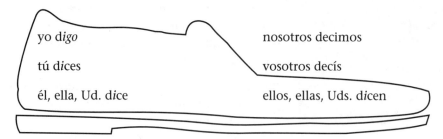

yo d*igo*	nosotros decimos
tú d*i*ces	vosotros decís
él, ella, Ud. d*i*ce	ellos, ellas, Uds. d*i*cen

Me, Myself, and I

Use the irregular, stem-changing shoe verb *sentirse* (sehn-teer-seh) to express how you feel. Do you notice something strange about this verb, something that just doesn't look right? Besides the *ie* stem-change, this verb does not end like most others—there's *se* attached to the infinitive ending. This *se* is a special pronoun, called a reflexive pronoun that may serve as either a direct or indirect object pronoun. Quite simply, a reflexive pronoun shows that the subject is performing an action upon itself. The subject and the reflexive pronoun refer to the same person(s) or thing(s), for example, *She* washes *herself*; *They* enjoy *themselves*. Don't panic about these verbs. They are quite easy to use and will be explained more fully in the next section. For the time being, lets see how you would conjugate a reflexive verb using the correct reflexive pronouns:

As a Rule
To express "that" after *decir*, use *que*:

Él dice que no estoy muy enfermo.
ehl dee-seh keh noh ehs-toh-ee moo-ee ehn-fehr-moh
He says that I'm not very sick.

sentirse—to feel

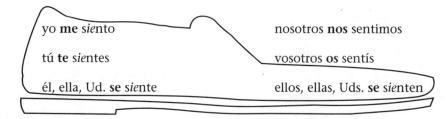

yo **me** s*i*ento	nosotros **nos** sentimos
tú **te** s*i*entes	vosotros **os** sentís
él, ella, Ud. **se** s*i*ente	ellos, ellas, Uds. **se** s*i*enten

Now you can express how you feel:

Me siento bien.	Me siento mejor.
meh see-ehn-toh bee-ehn	meh see-ehn-toh meh-hohr
I feel well.	*I feel better.*
Me siento mal.	Me siento peor.
meh see-ehn-toh mahl.	meh see-ehn-toh peh-ohr
I feel bad.	*I feel worse.*

As a Rule
Reflexive verbs can always be identified by the *se* that follows the infinitive and to which it is attached. Sentirse (used reflexively) tells about a person's state of health—how he or she feels. *Me siento bien.* I feel well. The verb *sentir* (used non-reflexively) refers to our sense of touch. *Siento algo en mi espalda.* I feel something on my shoulder.

You've seen the doctor, gotten a prescription, *una receta* (oo-nah reh-seh-tah), and you're ready to leave. Wait! Not so fast! Don't forget a very important question that might save you some money:

¿Puede darme un recibo para mi seguro médico?
pweh-deh dahr-meh oon reh-see-boh pah-rah mee seh-goo-roh meh-dee-koh
May I please have a receipt for my medical insurance?

Reflexive? Yes or No?

Are you the kind of person who is always doing favors for someone else and generally tend to put yourself last? Or do you tend to think of yourself first, because who else will do that if you don't? Are you *generoso* or *egoísta* when it comes to yourself and others? In Spanish, when you perform an action *upon* or *for* yourself, that action (verb) is reflexive and requires a reflexive pronoun. In many instances, you can use the same verb, without the reflexive pronoun and perform the action *upon* or *for* someone else. In these cases, an object pronoun—direct or indirect is used.

Yo me lavo.   *I wash myself.*

Lavo a mi niño.   *I wash my son.*

Yo lo lavo.   *I wash him.*

In the last example, the direct object pronoun *lo* expresses *him*.

Me compro un libro.   *I buy myself a book.*

Compro un libro a Ana.   *I buy Ann a book.*

Le compro un libro.   *I buy her a book.*

In the last example, the indirect object pronoun *le* expresses *for her*.

There are some verbs that are usually or always used reflexively. Table 20.4 provides a list of the most common reflexive verbs:

Table 20.4 Common Reflexive Verbs

Reflexive Verb	Pronunciation	Meaning
acordarse (ue)*[de]	ah-kohr-dahr-seh [deh]	to remember
acostarse (ue)*	ah-kohs-tahr-seh	to go to bed
alegrarse	ah-leh-grahr-seh	to be glad
apurarse	ah-poo-rahr-seh	to hurry
bañarse	bah-nyahr-seh	to bathe oneself
callarse	kah-yahr-seh	to be silent
cepillarse	seh-pee-yahr-seh	to brush (hair, teeth)
despertarse (ie)*	dehs-pehr-tahr-seh	to wake up
desvestirse (i)*	dehs-behs-teer-seh	to undress
divertirse (ie)*	dee-behr-teer-seh	to have fun
ducharse	doo-chahr-seh	to take a shower
engañarse	ehn-gah-nyahr-seh	to be mistaken
enojarse	eh-noh-hahr-seh	to become angry
equivocarse	eh-kee-boh-kahr-seh	to be mistaken
fiarse [de]	fee-ahr-seh [deh]	to trust
fijarse [en]	fee-hahr-seh [ehn]	to notice
irse	eer-seh	to go aweh
lavarse	lah-bahr-seh	to wash oneself
levantarse	leh-bahn-tahr-seh	to get up
llamarse	yah-mahr-seh	to be called, named
maquillarse	mah-kee-yahr-seh	to put on make-up
olvidarse [de]	ohl-bee-dahr-seh [deh]	to forget
pararse	pah-rah-seh	to stop oneself
peinarse	peh-ee-nahr-seh	to comb one's hair
ponerse	poh-nehr-seh	to put on, become, place oneself
quedarse	keh-dahr-seh	to remain
quejarse	keh-hahr-seh	to complain
quitarse	kee-tahr-seh	to remove
reírse [de]	reh-eer-seh [deh]	to laugh [at]
sentarse (ie)*	sehn-tahr-seh	to sit down
sentirse (ie)*	sehn-teer-seh	to feel
vestirse (i)*	behs-teer-seh	to get dressed

As a Rule

The verbs followed by an * are all shoe verbs and, therefore, require appropriate spelling changes. Refer to Chapter 12 to refresh your memory. Here are some examples of conjugated shoe verbs, in sample sentences:

Yo me acuesto   *I go to bed.*

Yo me divierto.   *I have fun.*

Yo me visto.   *I get dressed.*

Verbs followed by [a], [de], or [en] require the use of those prepositions to make their intentions understood. For example:

Yo me apresuro a partir.   *I hurry to leave.*

Yo no me olvido de nada.   *I don't forget anything.*

Yo me fío de él.   *I trust him.*

My husband is a very fortunate man. He has only about three things to do in the morning before leaving for work and can fly out the door in ten to fifteen minutes. Before I leave in the morning, it seems that I do at least one hundred things: I wash myself, I dry my hair, I get dressed, I eat breakfast, and I brush my teeth. That's why I need an hour and fifteen minutes between the time I wake up and when I walk out the door. When a reflexive verb is used in Spanish, it is understood that the subject is performing the action *for* or *upon* itself, because the reflexive pronoun indicates so. It then becomes unnecessary to use the possessives adjective *my* (*mi, mis*), *your* (*tu, tus*), etc. when referring to parts of the body, because it is obvious upon whom the action is being performed. The definite article is used instead. For example:

Yo me cepillo los dientes.
yoh meh seh-pee-yoh lohs dee-ehn-tehs
I brush my teeth.

Ella se pinta las uñas.
eh-yah seh peen-tah lahs oo-nyahs
She polishes her nails.

Where to Put the Reflexive Pronoun

By now you know that the word order in Spanish differs greatly from what we are accustomed to in English. It seems that a lot of things are backwards in Spanish. In English we tend to put reflexive pronouns after verbs. You might tell a friend: "I always look at *myself* in the mirror before I go out." In Spanish, this may or may not be the case. Fortunately, the rules for the placement of pronouns in Spanish are quite consistent. Reflexive pronouns are placed in the same position as the direct and indirect object pronouns you have already studied in Chapter 15. For example:

Yo me divierto.   Yo no me divierto.

Voy a divertirme.   *or*   Me voy a divertir.

Estoy divirtiéndome.   *or*   Me estoy divirtiendo

In an affirmative command, reflexive pronouns change position and are placed immediately after the verb and are joined to it.

¡Levántese!   *but*   ¡No se levante!

¡Apúrense!   *but*   ¡No se apuren!

As a Rule

When using the present progressive and attaching the pronoun to the present participle (*estar* + *present participle* + *pronoun*) or when forming an affirmative command, remember to count back three vowels from the end and then add an accent.

Estamos peinándonos.   *We're combing our hair.*

Están cepillándose el pelo.   *They're brushing their hair.*

¡Quédese aquí!   *Stay here!*

¡Siéntese, por favor!   *Please sit!*

Practicing Reflexive Verbs

Use what you've learned so far to describe all the things you do before leaving the house in the morning. (Yo me despierto.) Then, talk about the things you do before going to bed at night. (Yo me cepillo los dientes.)

Commanding with Reflexives

You're traveling in a group with some of your best friends. Siesta time is over and you've decided to go out and have some fun. In your haste to get ready, everyone is telling everyone else what to do. Practice forming reflexive commands by telling your friends to do and not to do the following: wake up, get up, take a bath, hurry up, get dressed, comb hair, brush teeth, have fun.

For example: **brush hair**

Cepíllense el pelo. No se cepillen el pelo.

The Least You Need to Know

➤ Knowing how to describe the different parts of the body in Spanish will help you describe your symptoms and feelings should you fall ill while on vacation.

➤ To ask *how long* something has been going on, use "¿Cuánto tiempo hace que + *present tense*?" or "¿Desde cuándo + *present tense*?" To answer, use "Hace + *time* + que + *present tense*" or "*present tense* + desde hace + *time*."

➤ Reflexive verbs, identified by the reflexive pronouns that accompany them, are used to show that the subject is acting upon itself.

Did I Bring Along the...?

In Chapter 20, you learned how to express your good health, as well as any problems you might encounter. Perhaps you're experiencing some minor aches and pains or signs and symptoms that are bothersome, but don't require a visit to the doctor. Whether you want to simply purchase a box of cough drops or need a prescription filled, you'll want to make a quick stop at *una farmacia* (oo-nah fahr-mah-see-ah), a drugstore.

On our last trip, I inadvertently left our toiletry case at home. My husband, who always remains undaunted by life's small unpleasantries, gently reminded me that toothbrushes, toothpaste, razors, shaving cream, hairbrushes, combs, and so on. are rather universal items. My blunder was only a minor inconvenience and certainly not a reason to spoil a delightful vacation. This chapter will help you purchase some of your toiletry and medical needs, and also show you how to talk about the past using the preterite (past) tense.

From Finding Drugs to Finding Toothpaste

If it's medicine you need, look for a green cross, the universal symbol for pharmacies *(farmacias)*.

If you are looking for a tube of lipstick or a bottle of your favorite perfume, you must go to *una perfumería* (oo-nah pehr-foo-meh-ree-ah), which specializes in toiletries.

When you need to have a prescription filled, you can ask for the nearest pharmacy:

¿Dónde está la farmacia (de guardia) más cercana?
dohn-deh ehs-tah lah fahr-mah-see-ah (deh gwahr-dee-ah) mahs sehr-kah-nah
Where's the nearest (all-night) pharmacy?

And then speak to the druggist:

Necesito medicina.
neh-seh-see-toh meh-dee-see-nah
I need medication.

¿Podría preparar esta receta (en seguida)?
poh-dree-ah preh-pah-rahr ehs-tah reh-seh-tah (ehn seh-gee-dah)
Could you please fill this prescription (immediately)?

¿Cuánto tiempo tardará?
kwahn-toh tee-ehm-poh tahr-dah-rah
How long will it take?

If you're simply looking for something over-the-counter, table 21.1 will help you find it in the farmacia, the perfumería, or even the supermercado. Begin by saying to a clerk: *Busco...* (boos-koh), I'm looking for..., or *Necesito...* (neh-seh-see-toh), I need:

Table 21.1 Drugstore Items

FOR MEN AND WOMEN

Drugstore Needs	Spanish Translation	Pronunciation
alcohol	el alcohol	ehl ahl-koh-hohl
antacid	el antiácido	ehl ahn-tee-ah-see-doh
antihistamine	el antistamínico	ehl ahn-tee-stah-mee-nee-koh
antiseptic	el antiséptico	ehl ahn-tee-sehp-tee-koh
aspirin	la aspirina	lah ahs-pee-ree-nah
band-aid	la curita	lah koo-ree-tah
brush	el cepillo	ehl seh-pee-yoh
condoms	los condones	lohs kohn-doh-nehs
cotton (absorbent)	el algodón hidrófilo	ehl ahl-goh-dohn ee-droh-fee-loh

FOR MEN AND WOMEN

Drugstore Needs	Spanish Translation	Pronunciation
cough drops	las pastillas para la tos	lahs pahs-tee-yahs pah-rah lah tohs
cough syrup	el jarabe para la tos	ehl hah-rah-beh pah-rah lah tohs
deodorant	el desodorante	ehl deh-soh-doh-rahn-teh
depilatory	el depilitorio	ehl deh-pee-lee-toh-ree-oh
eye drops	las gotas para los ojos	lahs goh-tahs pah-rah lohs oh-hohs
first-aid kit	el botiquín de primeros auxilios	ehl boh-tee-keen deh pree-meh-rohs owk-see-lee-ohs
gauze	la gasa	lah gah-sah
heating pad	la almohadilla de calefacción	lah ahl-moh-ah-dee-yah deh kah-leh-fahk-see-ohn
ice pack	la bolsa de hielo	lah bohl-sah deh ee-eh-loh
laxative (mild)	el laxante (ligero)	ehl lahk-sahn-teh (lee-heh-roh)
mirror	el espejo	ehl ehs-peh-hoh
moisturizer	la crema hidratante	lah kreh-mah ee-drah-tahn-teh
mouthwash	el enjuagador bucal	ehl ehn-hwah-gah-dohr boo-kahl
nail file	la lima	lah lee-mah
nose drops	las gotas para la nariz	lahs goh-tahs pah-rah lah nah-rees
razor (electric)	la rasuradora eléctrica	lah rah-soo-rah-doh-rah eh-lehk-tree-kah
razor blade	la hoja de afeitar	lah oh-hah deh ah-feh-ee-tahr
safety pin	el seguro, el imperdible	ehl seh-goo-roh, ehl eem-pehr-dee-bleh
scissors	las tijeras	lahs tee-heh-rahs
shampoo (anti-dandruff)	el champú anti-caspa	ehl chahm-poo ahn-tee kahs-pah
shaving cream	la crema de afeitar	lah kreh-mah deh ah-feh-ee-tahr
sleeping pills	las pastillas para dormir	lahs pah-stee-yahs pah-rah dohr-meer
talcum powder	el polvo de talco	ehl pohl-boh deh tahl-koh
thermometer	un termómetro	oon tehr-moh-meh-troh
tissues	los pañuelos de papel	lohs pah-nyoo-eh-lohs deh pah-pehl
toothbrush	el cepillo de dientes	ehl seh-pee-yoh deh dee-ehn-tehs
toothpaste	la pasta dentífrica	lah pahs-tah dehn-tee-free-kah
tweezers	las pinzas	lahs peen-sahs
vitamins	las vitaminas	lahs bee-tah-mee-nahs

continues

Table 21.1 Continued

FOR BABIES	Spanish Translation	Pronunciation
bottle	un biberón	oon bee-beh-rohn
diapers (disposable)	los pañales (desechables)	lohs pah-nyah-lehs (deh-seh-chah-blehs)
pacifier	un chupete	oon choo-peh-teh

What's On Sale

You're vacationing in Puerto Rico and, believe it or not, there's a huge Walgreen's across the street from your fancy hotel! Why pay exorbitant mini-bar prices when everything you'd ever want or need is just a few feet away, and on sale, too? Look below and ask for some of the things you might want to pick up.

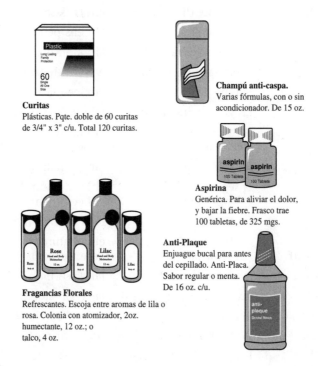

Curitas
Plásticas. Pqte. doble de 60 curitas de 3/4" x 3" c/u. Total 120 curitas.

Champú anti-caspa.
Varias fórmulas, con o sin acondicionador. De 15 oz.

Aspirina
Genérica. Para aliviar el dolor, y bajar la fiebre. Frasco trae 100 tabletas, de 325 mgs.

Anti-Plaque
Enjuague bucal para antes del cepillado. Anti-Placa. Sabor regular o menta. De 16 oz. c/u.

Fragancias Florales
Refrescantes. Escoja entre aromas de lila o rosa. Colonia con atomizador, 2oz. humectante, 12 oz.; o talco, 4 oz.

Special Needs

Special organizations that cater to the needs of the physically challenged or pharmacies that specialize in *el alquiler de aparatos médicos* (ehl ahl-kee-lehr deh ah-pah-rah-tohs meh-dee-kohs), the rental of medical appliances, would either sell or have information concerning the special items featured in table 21.2.

¿Dónde puedo obtener...?
dohn-deh pweh-doh ohb-teh-nehr
Where can I get...

Table 21.2   Special Needs

Medical Appliance	Spanish Translation	Pronunciation
cane	el bastón	ehl bahs-tohn
crutches	las muletas	lahs moo-leh-tahs
hearing aid	el aparato para sordos	ehl ah-pah-rah-toh pah-rah sohr-dohs
seeing-eye dog	el perro guía	ehl peh-rroh gee-ah
walker	el andador	ehl ahn-dah-dohr
wheelchair	la silla de ruedas	la see-yah deh roo-eh-dahs

Would You Like to Come Along?

You just called the pharmacy ahead of time to order or locate a certain product. If you want to tell the pharmacist when you will be coming by to pick up what you need, you would use the verb *venir*, to come. The following diagram provides the forms of this irregular verb. Note that *venir* is a go-go verb, because its yo form ends in *go*. Venir is also similar to a shoe verb in that the nosotros and vosotros forms look like the infinitive, while the forms for the other subject pronouns do not.

venir—to come

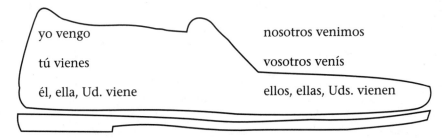

yo vengo   nosotros venimos

tú vienes   vosotros venís

él, ella, Ud. viene   ellos, ellas, Uds. vienen

Are You Living in the Past?

No matter how much time I put aside to pack or how many times I run to add something to my packing list, I invariably forget something important. This year it was my special

285

shampoo and conditioner needed to achieve that unique look. The hotel brand was a generic disaster. I also purposely left my hairdryer at home because the hotel brochure promised one in every room. They didn't lie but that was the slowest hairdryer I've ever used. If what you've forgotten is really important to you, you might go to a *farmacia* or *perfumería* to try to purchase something similar. In order to express what you *did* or *did not* do, you must use the past tense. In Spanish this tense is called the *pretérito*, the preterite.

Forming the Preterite

Forming the preterite of regular verbs is quite easy since all verbs within the families follow the same rules. A little more attention will have to be paid to those verbs that have spelling and stem changes and those that are totally irregular.

To form the preterite of regular verbs, drop the infinitive ending (*ar*, *er*, or *ir*) and add the following endings:

AR Verbs	Preterite Stem	Pronoun	Preterite Endings
hablar	habl	yo	é,
		tú	aste
		él, ella, Ud.	ó
		nosotros	amos
		vosotros	asteis
		ellos, ellas, Uds.	aron

ER and IR Verbs	Preterite Stem	Pronoun	Preterite Endings
vender	vend	yo	í
abrir	abr	tú	iste
		él, ella, Ud.	ió
		nosotros	imos
		vosotros	isteis
		ellos, ellas, Uds.	ieron

Verbs ending in *car*, *gar*, and *zar* drop the *ar* infinitive ending to form the preterite and have a spelling change only in the yo form. All other forms are regular.

CAR Verbs	Change	Yo Form	Other Forms
bus<u>car</u>	*c* changes to *qu*	yo bus**qu**é	buscaste, buscó, buscamos, buscasteis, buscaron

Some common *car* verbs that you might find useful are

Verb	Pronunciation	Meaning
aplicar	ah-plee-kahr	to apply
buscar	boos-kahr	to look for
colocar	koh-loh-kahr	to place, put
comunicar	koh-moo-nee-kahr	to communicate
equivocarse	eh-kee-boh-kahr-seh	to be mistaken
explicar	ehks-plee-kahr	to explain
fabricar	fah-bree-kahr	to manufacture, make
indicar	een-dee-kahr	to indicate
marcar	mahr-kahr	to mark, designate
pescar	pehs-kahr	to fish
sacar	sah-kahr	to take out
significar	seeg-nee-fee-kahr	to mean
tocar	toh-kahr	to touch, play (musical instrument)

GAR Verbs	Change	Yo Form	Other Forms
pa<u>gar</u>	*g* changes to *gu*	yo pa**gu**é	pagaste, pagó, pagamos, pagasteis, pagaron

Some common *gar* verbs that you might find useful are

Verb	Pronunciation	Meaning
apagar	ah-pah-gahr	to put out, turn off, extinguish
colgar	kohl-gahr	to hang
encargar	ehn-kahr-gahr	to put in charge, entrust
entregar	ehn-treh-gahr	to deliver

continues

continued

Verb	Pronunciation	Meaning
jugar	hoo-gahr	to play (sports, games)
llegar	yeh-gahr	to arrive
negar	neh-gahr	to deny
pagar	pah-gahr	to pay

ZAR Verbs	Change	Yo Form	Other Forms
go<u>zar</u>	*z* changes to *c*	yo go*c*é	gozaste, gozó, gozamos, gozasteis, gozaron

Some common *zar* verbs that you might find useful are

Verb	Pronunciation	Meaning
abrazar	ah-brah-sahr	to hug, embrace
almorzar	ahl-mohr-sahr	to eat lunch
avanzar	ah-bahn-sahr	to advance, to hurry
comenzar	koh-mehn-sahr	to begin, commence
cruzar	kroo-sahr	to cross
empezar	ehm-peh-sahr	to begin
gozar	goh-sahr	to enjoy
lanzar	lahn-sahr	to throw

As a Rule
The verbs *reír* (to laugh) and *sonreír* (to smile) form the preterite as follows:

(son)reír: (son)reí, (son)reíste, (son)rió, (son)reísteis, (son)rieron

Ir verbs that have a stem change in the present tense, also have a stem change in the preterite. In the present, an *e* in the stem could change to *ie* or *i*. In the preterite *e* only changes to *i*, and *o* changes to *u* only in the third person singular (él, ella, Ud.) and third person plural forms (ellos, ellas, Uds.). For a list of common verbs with these changes refer to Chapter 12. For all *ir* verbs where the endings are regular in the present, endings are regular in the past.

Here are some irregular *ir* verbs in the past tense:

Infinitive	Yo, Tú, Nosotros, Vosotros	Third Person Singular	Third Person Plural
preferir (to prefer)	preferí, preferiste, preferimos, preferisteis	prefirió	prefirieron
pedir (to ask)	pedí, pediste, pedimos, pedisteis	pidió	pidieron
dormir (to sleep)	dormí, dormiste, dormimos, dormisteis	durmió	durmieron

Verbs ending in *er* or *ir* and having a vowel immediately preceding the infinitive ending (except *traer*, to bring, and *atraer*, to attract—which are irregular and are explained later in the chapter) change *i* to *y* in the third person singular (él, ella, Ud.) and third person plural (ellos, ellas, Uds.) forms in the preterite. In all other forms, the *i* has an accent mark. For example:

Infinitive	Yo, Tú, Nosotros, Vosotros	Third Person Singular	Third Person Plural
caer (to fall)	caí, caíste, caímos, caísteis	cayó	cayeron
creer (to believe)	creí, creíste, creímos, creísteis	creyó	creyeron
leer (to read)	leí, leíste, leímos, leísteis	leyó	leyeron
oír (to hear)	oí, oíste, oímos, oísteis	oyó	oyeron
poseer (to possess)	poseí, poseíste, poseímos, poseísteis	poseyó	poseyeron

Verbs ending in *uir* also follow this rule, except that an accent appears on the *i* only in the *yo* form. See Chapter 12 for other verbs that fit in this category.

Infinitive	Yo, Tú, Nosotros, Vosotros	Third Person Singular	Third Person Plural
incluir (to include)	incluí, incluiste, incluimos, incluisteis	incluyó	incluyeron

The Preterite of Irregular Verbs

Some verbs are irregular in the preterite and their stems must be memorized. All irregular verbs in the preterite have the same endings, regardless of their infinitive endings. This means that there are no distinctions for verbs ending in *ar*, *er*, or *ir*. All endings are as follows:

Pronoun	Verb Ending	Pronoun	Verb Ending
yo	e	nosotros	imos
tú	iste	vosotros	isteis
él, ella, Ud.	o	ellos, ellas, Uds.	ieron

Table 21.3 lists the most common irregular verbs that you will be using with considerable frequency.

Table 21.3   Irregular Verbs in the Preterite

Infinitive	Preterite Stem	Preterite Forms
andar (to walk)	anduv	anduve, anduviste, anduvo, anduvimos, anduvisteis, anduvieron
caber (to fit)	cup	cupe, cupiste, cupo, cupimos, cupisteis, cupieron
estar (to be)	estuv	estuve, estuviste, estuvo, estuvimos, estuvisteis, estuvieron
hacer (to make, do)	hic, *hiz*	hice, hiciste, *hizo*, hicimos, hicisteis, hicieron
poder (to be able to)	pud	pude, pudiste, pudo, pudimos, pudisteis, pudieron
poner (to put)	pus	puse, pusiste, puso, pusimos, pusisteis, pusieron
querer (to want)	quis	quise, quisiste, quiso, quisimos, quisisteis, quisieron
saber (to know)	sup	supe, supiste, supo, supimos, supisteis, supieron
tener (to have)	tuv	tuve, tuviste, tuvo, tuvimos, tuvisteis, tuvieron
venir (to come)	vin	vine, viniste, vino, vinimos, vinisteis, vinieron

For the following verbs that are irregular in the preterite, the *ieron* ending for the third person plural forms (ellos, ellas, Uds.) becomes *eron* before the letter *j*:

Infinitive	Preterite Stem	Preterite Forms
decir (to say)	dij	dije, dijiste, dijo, dijimos, dijisteis, dijeron
producir (to produce)	produj	produje, produjiste, produjo, produjimos, produjisteis, produjeron
traer (to bring)	traj	traje, trajiste, trajo, trajimos, trajisteis, trajeron

Three very high-frequency verbs that are very irregular are *dar*, to give; *ir*, to go; and *ser*, to be. You will note in the following conjugations that accent marks are not used with these verbs, just as with the verb *ver*, to see.

Dar, although an *ar* verb, uses the preterite endings for *er* and *ir* verbs:

yo di	nosotros dimos
tú diste	vosotros disteis
él, ella, Ud. dio	ellos, ellas, Uds. dieron

Ir and ser have the same preterite forms, so you'll have to follow the conversation to know which one is being used. For both verbs use:

yo fui	nosotros fuimos
tú fuiste	vosotros fuisteis
él, ella, Ud. fue	ellos, ellas, Uds. fueron

The verb ver is conjugated in a regular fashion without the accents:

yo vi	nosotros vimos
tú viste	vosotros visteis
él, ella, Ud. vio	ellos, ellas, Uds. vieron

Talk About Yesterday

You're sitting in a cafe with some of your friends and the conversation turns to what you each did yesterday. Express what each person did in the past by giving the correct preterite form for the infinitive in parentheses.

1. Ud. (trabajar) mucho.

2. Carlota (comer) en el café.

3. Tú (escribir) un poema.

4. Yo (leer) un libro.

5. Nosotros (andar) por el parque.

6. Yo (jugar) al tenis.

7. Ellos (tener) una cita.

8. Yo (equivocarse).

9. Uds. (oír) las noticias.

10. Vosotros (decir) la verdad.

11. Ellas (dormir) hasta la una.

12. Yo (pagar) todas mis cuentas.

Asking and Answering Questions in the Past

A yes-no question concerning the past may very easily be formed by using *intonation*, the tags ¿verdad?, or ¿no?, or *inversion* in exactly the same way as would be done when asking a question concerning the present.

As a Rule
When using reflexive verbs in the preterite, remember to include the reflexive pronoun.

Nos levantamos temprano.
We got up early.

Me equivoqué.
I made a mistake.

¿Tú fuiste al cine?
Did you go to the movies?

Tú fuiste al cine, ¿verdad? (¿no?)
You went to the movies, didn't you?

¿Fuiste tú al cine?   *Did you go to the movies?*

To ask for information, simply put the question word at the beginning of the sentence:

¿Cuándo fuiste (tú) al cine?
When did you go to the movies?

¿Con quién fuiste al cine?
With whom did you go to the movies?

¿Cómo fuiste al cine?   *How did you go to the movies?*

To answer yes or no, or to give information, follow the normal pattern that was used for the present tense.

Sí, fui al cine.   *Yes, I went to the movies.*

No, no fui al cine.   *No, I didn't go to the movies.*

Fui al cine con Ana.   *I went to the movies with Ana.*

Fui al cine en coche.   *I went to the movies by car.*

Ask Questions

Yesterday was a holiday, the weather was beautiful and everyone was free to do as he or she wished. Some people like to relax on their day off, others do chores, while others go out and have a good time. Ask about your acquaintances and then record the answers given to you as indicated in parentheses.

Example: Ana/ir al parque (no).
Ud.: ¿Ana, fuiste al parque?
Ana: No, no fui al parque.

Paco y José/jugar al tenis (sí).
Ud.: ¿Jugaron Uds. al tenis?
Paco y Jose: Sí, jugamos al tenis.

1. Carlos/hacer una visita al museo (sí).

2. Pablo y Jorge/dar un paseo (no).

3. María/pescar en el mar (no).

4. Isabel y Pilar/almorzar en el centro (sí).

5. Adela/traer regalos a sus primos (sí).

6. Francisco y Rafael/servir refrescos a sus amigos (no).

What Didn't You Do Today?

Did you ever make a list of chores, only to find at the end of the day that your list was totally unrealistic? Let's say you made a list for today and now your day has come to an end. Tell what you did and did not accomplish.

The Least You Need to Know

➤ To get prescription drugs you must go to *una farmacia*. Toiletries may be purchased at *una perfumería*.

➤ Use the irregular verb *venir* to express "to come."

➤ The preterite (past tense) of regular verbs in Spanish is formed by dropping the infinitive endings and adding *é, aste, ó, amos, asteis*, and *aron* for *ar* verbs; and *í, iste, ió, imos, isteis*, and *ieron* for *er* and *ir* verbs.

➤ In the preterite yo form, *car* verbs change the *c* to *qu*; *gar* verbs change *g* to *gu*; and *zar* verbs change *z* to *c*.

➤ Stem changing verbs ending in *ir* change the stem vowel from *e* to *i* or the *o* to *u* in the third person singular and plural forms in the preterite.

➤ Verbs ending in *er* or *ir* that have a vowel immediately preceding the infinitive ending, change the *i* to *y* in the third person singular and plural forms.

➤ Irregular preterite stems must be memorized. Add the endings *e, iste, o, imos, isteis, ieron* (*eron* after *j*).

Chapter 22

When You Have to Make an Important Phone Call

In This Chapter

➤ Making a phone call

➤ Correct phone etiquette

➤ What to say when you're having trouble

➤ The imperfect

➤ The preterite vs. the imperfect

You're feeling rather chipper now that you've taken care of all your personal and medical needs. Chapter 21 really helped you put yourself back on course. Now you'd like to let everyone back home know how great everything is going. You truly miss the old gang and decide that it's time to phone home.

Most Americans don't sufficiently acknowledge a good thing when they have it: a superior phone system. To truly appreciate our excellent telecommunications network, one need only try to make a phone call in a foreign country. In many instances, a simple local call creates quite a challenge, and long distance, well that's another nightmare. Operator assistance is often necessary for even the most mundane tasks. Imagine how difficult it is to communicate with a foreign speaker when you cannot read his lips or observe his body language for the clues you need for better understanding. This chapter will teach you how to place a local or international call from within a foreign country, and how to deal with wrong numbers and other calling problems. You'll also learn about using reflexive verbs in the past.

How Does This Thing Work?

Making a long distance call from afar usually requires a somewhat complicated explanation of the phone system, some operator assistance, and a lot of patience—there's usually an awful lot of numbers to punch in. In some countries, special tokens may still have to be used and certain buttons pushed, just to complete a local call. When learning how to use the phone, consult table 22.1 so that you can correctly express the type of call you'd like to make.

Table 22.1   Types of Phone Calls

Type of Phone Call	Spanish Translation	Pronunciation
collect call	la llamada por cobrar,	lah yah-mah-dah pohr koh-brahr,
	la llamada con cargo	lah yah-mah-dah kohn kahr-goh
credit card call	la llamada con tarjeta de crédito	lah yah-mah-dah kohn tahr-heh-tah deh kreh-dee-toh
local call	la llamada local	lah yah-mah-dah loh-kahl
long-distance call	la llamada de larga distancia	lah yah-mah-dah deh lahr-gah dees-tahn-see-ah
out of the country call	la llamada internaciónal	lah yah-mah-dah een-tehr-nah-see-oh-nahl
person-to-person call	la llamada de persona a persona	lah yah-mah-dah deh pehr-soh-nah ah pehr-soh-nah

Become familiar with the different parts of the telephone featured in table 22.2 so that should you get directions in Spanish, you'll be able to easily understand them.

Table 22.2 The Telephone

Telephone Parts	Spanish Translation	Pronunciation
booth	la cabina (casilla) telefónica	lah kah-bee-nah (kah-see-yah) teh-leh-foh-nee-kah
button	el botón	ehl boh-tohn
coin return button	el botón de recobrar	ehl boh-tohn deh reh-koh-brahr
cordless phone (portable phone)	el teléfono inalámbrico	ehl teh-leh-foh-noh een-ah-lahm-bree-koh
dial	el disco	ehl dees-koh
keypad	las teclas	lahs teh-klahs
phone card	la tarjeta telefónica	lah tahr-heh-tah teh-leh-foh-nee-kah
public phone	el teléfono público	ehl teh-leh-foh-noh poo-blee-koh
receiver	el auricular	ehl ow-ree-koo-lahr
slot	la ranura	lah rah-noo-rah
speaker telephone	el teléfono altavoz	ehl teh-leh-foh-noh ahl-tah-bohs
telephone	el teléfono	ehl teh-leh-foh-noh
telephone book	la guía telefónica	lah gee-ah teh-leh-foh-nee-kah
telephone number	el número de teléfono	ehl noo-meh-roh deh teh-leh-foh-noh
token	la ficha	lah fee-chah
touch-tone phone	el teléfono de botónes	ehl teh-leh-foh-noh deh boh-toh-nehs

Now you are ready to phone home. Table 22.3 gives you the necessary words that will help you understand Spanish directions for placing a phone call.

Cultural Tidbit

The telephone system in Spain is almost entirely automatic and is connected to the international dialing system (you don't need operator assistance to place local, long distance, or overseas calls). Public pay phones, *cabinas telefónicas* (kah-bee-nahs teh-leh-foh-nee-kahs), are available in some post offices, cafés, stores, and on the streets of larger cities. Many of these phones offer instructions in several languages. A call can also be placed from the telephone exchange, *la central telefónica* (lah sehn-trahl teh-leh-foh-nee-kah) or from your hotel, which will probably impose a heavy surcharge. In the most important cities, there are special telephone offices open all day. They enable you to make a call to anywhere. Expect to be charged according to the area you are calling and the length of your call. Spanish telephones accept 5, 25, and 100 pesetas coins. Some telephone booths are primarily for local calls. If you want to call another city or country, you will have to locate a *cabina* that has a green stripe across the top and that is marked *interurbano* (een-tehr-oor-bah-noh), interurban or long distance.

Table 22.3 How to Make a Phone Call

Telephone Term	Spanish Translation	Pronunciation
to call back	volver* a llamar	bohl-behr ah yah-mahr
to dial	marcar	mahr-kahr
to hang up (the receiver)	colgar*	kohl-gahr
to insert the card	introducir la tarjeta	een-troh-doo-seer lah tahr-heh-tah
to know the area code	saber la clave de área	sah-behr lah klah-beh deh ah-reh-ah
to leave a message	dejar un mensaje	de-hahr oon mehn-sah-heh
to pick up (the receiver)	descolgar	dehs-kohl-gahr
to telephone	telefonear	teh-leh-foh-neh-ahr
to wait for the dial tone	esperar el tono, la señal	ehs-peh-rahr ehl toh-noh, lah seh-nyahl

* These verbs are stem-changing shoe verbs. The o will change to ue in the present tense for all forms except nosotros and vosotros.

Using a Public Phone

Read the directions explaining how to use money or a credit card to place a call. Then continue with the instructions on how to place calls that are local, long distance, and international.

Como llamar por teléfono en una cabina

1. Descuelga el auricular del teléfono.

2. Deposita las monedas necesarias o introduce la tarjeta de crédito para pagar la tarifa indicada.

3. Espera hasta escuchar la señal de marcar.

4. Marca el número.

5. Habla con la persona.

6. Después de terminar, cuelga el auricular y saca la tarjeta.

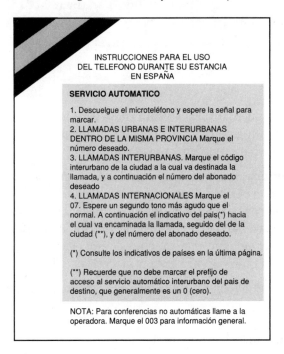

INSTRUCCIONES PARA EL USO
DEL TELEFONO DURANTE SU ESTANCIA
EN ESPAÑA

SERVICIO AUTOMATICO

1. Descuelgue el microteléfono y espere la señal para marcar.
2. LLAMADAS URBANAS E INTERURBANAS DENTRO DE LA MISMA PROVINCIA Marque el número deseado.
3. LLAMADAS INTERURBANAS. Marque el código interurbano de la ciudad a la cual va destinada la llamada, y a continuación el número del abonado deseado
4. LLAMADAS INTERNACIONALES Marque el 07. Espere un segundo tono más agudo que el normal. A continuación el indicativo del país(*) hacia el cual va encaminada la llamada, seguido del de la ciudad (**), y del número del abonado deseado.

(*) Consulte los indicativos de países en la última página.

(**) Recuerde que no debe marcar el prefijo de acceso al servicio automático interurbano del país de destino, que generalmente es un 0 (cero).

NOTA: Para conferencias no automáticas llame a la operadora. Marque el 003 para información general.

If you need the area code for the country you'd like to call, consult the telephone directory, *la guía telefónica* (lah gee-ah teh-leh-foh-nee-kah). If you want to call home to the U.S. or Canada:

1. Wait for the dial tone.

2. Dial **07**, wait for a second tone.

3. Dial the country code, el código territorial (ehl koh-dee-goh teh-rree-toh-ree-ahl), + **1** + the city code + the phone number you desire.

You should be connected with little trouble.

Cultural Tidbit

If you want to place a long distance call within Spain, you must first dial the city code, *el indicativo* (ehl een-dee-kah-tee-boh) before you dial the number you want. In Spain, the bigger cities like Madrid have seven-digit numbers (for example: 2 10 48 23, which is read "dos diez, cuarenta y ocho, veintitrés") while smaller cities have six-digit numbers (for example 24 67 31, read "veinticuatro, sesenta y siete, treinta y uno"). In the rest of the Spanish-speaking world, telephone numbers have five or six digits.

Special Needs

Many telephone products are available for those with limited visual, auditory, and motor skills. Read the following description of what is available to the physically challenged. Can you figure out what services are provided?

> Ahora las personas con impedimentos de audición o del habla pueden comunicarse por teléfono con personas oyentes a cualquier hora y día del año. La Autoridad de Teléfonos comenzó a ofrecer el Servicio de Relevo de Telecomunicaciones (SRT) para llamadas. El personal del Centro de Relevo, llamado Asistente de Comunicaciones (AC), recibirá el mensaje en texto enviado por el audioimpedido y lo leerá en voz alta al oyente a través de otra línea, y viceversa.
>
> Toda llamada es manejada con la más estricta confidencialidad y sin límite de tiempo.

Did you understand that there are special operators who will take messages from and receive messages for those who are hearing impaired or who cannot speak and relay them to or accept them from others? Did you notice that this service is strictly confidential and is available at any time? If you did, then you're really becoming a pro!

Who's Calling, Please?

Did you ever notice that it is more difficult to understand people over the telephone than if they were speaking to you face-to-face, especially if they are speaking a different language. Body language, facial expressions and gestures enable us to better comprehend the message the speaker is conveying. And how many times has each of us not immediately recognized the voice of a loved one when he or she called? Many, to be sure. Telephones, even with new, advanced technology, distort voices and sounds. It would prove quite helpful for you to familiarize yourself with the Spanish expressions used for making and answering a phone call. Table 22.4 will show you how to begin a typical telephone conversation.

Table 22.4 Making a Phone Call

Expressions Used When Making a Call	Meaning	Expressions Used When Answering a Call	Meaning
Diga. Oiga. Bueno.	Hello.	Diga. Oiga. Bueno.	Hello.
..., por favor	..., please	¿De parte de quién? ¿Quién habla?	Who's calling?
Soy ... Habla ...	It's ...	Soy ...	This is ...
¿Está ...?	Is ... in (there)?	No cuelgue, por favor.	Hold on.
Quisiera hablar con ...	I would like to speak to ...	Un momento.	Just a moment
¿Cuándo regresará?	When will he (she) be back?	Él/Ella no está.	He/She is not in.
Volveré a llamar más tarde.	I'll call back later.	¿Quiere dejar un mensaje?	Do you want to leave a message?

301

As a Rule

In English, when we want to express that someone is going to do something again, we generally use the prefix *re*. For example: retry, recall, recycle, redo. In Spanish, the idiomatic expression *volver(ue) a + infinitive* is used to get this meaning across. The verb volver must be conjugated.

Vuelva a llamar más tarde.   *Call back later.*

Yo siempre vuelvo a llamar cuando él no está.   *I always call back when he's not there.*

Whoops, I'm Having a Problem

There are many problems you can run into when making a phone call: a wrong number, a busy signal, a hang up. Here are some examples of phrases you may say or hear should you run into any difficulties:

¿Qué número está llamando?
keh noo-meh-roh ehs-tah yah-mahn-doh
What number are you calling?

Hay un error. (Yo tengo) Ud. tiene un número equivocado.
ah-ee oon eh-rrohr. (yoh tehn-goh) oo-stehd tee-eh-neh oon noo-meh-roh eh-kee-boh-kah-doh
It's a mistake. (I have) You have the wrong number.

Se nos cortó la línea.
seh nohs kohr-toh lah lee-neh-ah
We got cut off (disconnected).

La línea está ocupada.
la lee-neh-ah ehs-tah oh-koo-pah-dah
The line is busy.

Remarque Ud. el número, por favor.
reh-mahr-keh oo-stehd ehl noo-meh-roh, pohr fah-bohr
Please redial the number.

El teléfono está descompuesto (dañado, fuera de servicio).
ehl teh-leh-foh-noh ehs-tah dehs-kohm-pwehs-toh (dah-nyah-doh, fweh-rah deh sehr-bee-see-oh)
The telephone is out of order.

No puedo oír nada.
noh pweh-doh oh-eer nah-dah
I can't hear you.

Vuelva a llamarme más tarde.
bwehl-bah ah yah-mahr-meh mahs tahr-deh
Call me back later.

While You Were Out

While you were out sightseeing, the receptionist at the front desk took a message for you from a colleague. What information do you know?

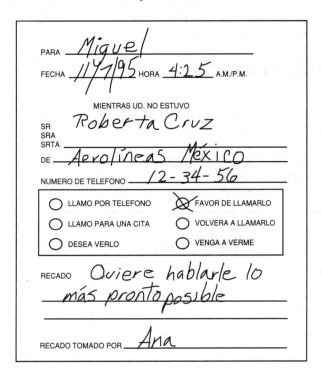

What Was Going On?

We *shopped* till we *dropped*. So when we *returned* to our cozy hotel room, my husband decided to take a nap. I **was sitting** in a chair reading a book when all of a sudden the lights *went out*. I *wondered* what *happened*. I *looked* out the window and I *saw* that everything **was** dark. I didn't **know** what to do. Night **was falling** and I **was getting** hungry. I *woke* my husband and we *decided* to find our way out in the darkness. It **was** so hard to walk. We really **couldn**'t see two feet in front of us. When we *got* to the stairs, we **were** relieved to see that someone from the hotel **was guiding** the guests with flashlights from the fifth floor to the lobby. So we *made* the best of it and *ate* at a charming restaurant nearby.

This really happened to us, in the not so distant past in a luxury hotel in Puerto Rico. In English, we speak or write easily in the past without giving much thought to what we are saying. In Spanish, however, it's not that simple because, there are two different simple past tenses: the *preterite (italicized in the preceding paragraph)* and the **imperfect** (**shown in bold**). This tends to make speaking in the past a bit confusing. Just remember, if you mistake one for the other, you'll still be understood. Sometimes either tense is correct. What's the difference? The preterite expresses specific actions or events that were completed in the past, whereas the imperfect expresses continuous or repeated actions, events, situations, or states in the past.

Formation of the Imperfect

Before going into a more detailed explanation, let's see how the imperfect is formed. There are only three irregular verbs in the imperfect and there are no changes necessary for verbs with spelling and stem changes.

➤ To form the imperfect of regular verbs, drop the infinitive ending (*ar*, *er*, or *ir*) and add the proper endings. The following verbs are conjugated as examples (the generic endings for all other verbs in the respective verb families are italicized):

AR Verbs (Sample)	Imperfect Stem	Conjugation
hablar	habl	yo habl*aba*
		tú habl*abas*
		él, ella, Ud. habl*aba*
		nosotros habl*ábamos*
		vosotros habl*abais*
		ellos, ellas, Uds. habl*aban*

ER & IR Verbs (Samples)	Imperfect Stem	Conjugation
vender	vend	yo vend*ía*
		tú vend*ías*
		él, ella, Ud. vend*ía*
		nosotros vend*íamos*
		vosotros vend*íais*
		ellos, ellas, Uds. vend*ían*
abrir	abr	yo abr*ía*
		tú abr*ías*
		él, ella, Ud. abr*ía*
		nosotros abr*íamos*
		vosotros abr*íais*
		ellos, ellas, Uds. abr*ían*

➤ The three irregular verbs are:

Infinitive	Meaning	Imperfect Endings
ir	to go	iba, ibas, iba, íbamos, ibais, iban
ser	to be	era, eras, era, éramos, erais, eran
ver	to see	veía, veías, veía, veíamos, veíais, veían

The Preterite vs. the Imperfect

Which tense should you use? And when? The preterite expresses an action that was completed at a specific time in the past. Thinking of a camera may help you understand this concept. The preterite represents an action that could be captured by an instammatic—the action happened and was completed.

Yo fui al cine ayer. *I went to the movies yesterday.*

The *imperfect* expresses an action that continued in the past over an indefinite period of time. Think again of a camera. The imperfect represents an action that could be captured by a *video* camera—the action continued to flow, it *was* happening, *used to* happen or *would* (meaning *used to*) happen. The imperfect is a descriptive tense. The two lists that follow provide a more in-depth look at the differences between the two tenses.

Yo iba al cine con mi abuelo.   *I used to go the movies with my grandfather.*

PRETERITE

1. Expresses specific, particular actions or events that were started and completed at a definite time in the past (even if the time isn't mentioned).

   Viajé con mi amigo.   *I traveled with my friend.*

2. Expresses a specific action or event that occurred at a specific point in time.

   Ayer yo salí a la una.   *Yesterday I went out at 1 o'clock.*

3. Expresses a specific action or event that was repeated a stated number of times.

   Fuimos al cine tres veces.   *We went to the movies three times.*

IMPERFECT

1. Describes ongoing or continuous actions in the past (which may or may not have been completed).

   Yo viajaba con mi amigo.   *I was traveling with my friend.*

2. Describes repeated or habitual actions that took place in the past.

   Generalmente yo salía a la una.   *I usually went out at 1 o'clock.*

3. Describes a person, place, thing, or state of mind.

   Estábamos contentos.   *We were happy.*

   El mar estaba peligroso.   *The sea was dangerous.*

   La puerta estaba abierta.   *The door was open.*

   Quería salir.   *I wanted to go out.*

Preterite or Imperfect?

It was a day just like any other, or so I thought. Little did I know that there was something unexpected in store for me. Complete my story with the correct form of the verb in the preterite or in the imperfect:

1 (ser) las cinco de la tarde. 2 (estar) lloviendo cuando yo 3 (salir) de mi oficina para regresar a casa. 4 (tomar) el autobús. 5 (llegar) delante de mi casa media hora más tarde. 6 (entrar) y 7 (subir) a mi apartamento. 8 (sacar) mis llaves pero no las

9 (necesitar). 10 (observar) que mi puerta 11 (estar) abierta. Yo no 12 (saber) por qué. 13 (tener) mucho miedo. 14 (estar) convencido de que alguien me 15 (robar). 16 (empujar) la puerta con cuidado y 17 (entrar) lentamente. No 18 (escuchar) nada. 19 (marchar) hacia el teléfono, cuando de repente todos mis amigos 20 (gritar) en voz alta: "Feliz cumpleaños." ¡Qué sorpresa!

The Least You Need to Know

➤ Use the information in the front of the Spanish yellow pages to guide you on how to make most of your telephone calls.

➤ A credit card will enable you to use most public phones in Spanish-speaking countries.

➤ The imperfect is formed by adding the endings *aba, abas, aba, ábamos, abais,* and *aban* to *ar* verbs, and *ía, ías, ía, íamos, íais,* and *ían* to *er* and *ir* verbs.

➤ The three irregular verbs in the imperfect: *ir, ser,* and *ver* must be memorized.

➤ The imperfect is used to describe what the subject *was* doing. The preterite states what the subject *did*.

Chapter 23

I Need the Nearest Post Office

In This Chapter

➤ Receiving and sending mail

➤ The difference between *saber* and *conocer*

➤ The present perfect tense

In the last chapter you learned how to successfully complete a phone call, carry on a polite conversation using proper phone etiquette, and deal with typical, everyday, telephone problems. You've just looked at your hotel telephone bill and have decided that it's too costly to phone home as often as you'd like. Writing letters is the simplest solution. So now we're off to the local post office.

Your friends will be deeply offended if you don't send them postcards. And you don't want to see the look in your mom's eyes if she doesn't receive a letter. You've bought yourself a great souvenir, but it's too heavy to lug on the plane. Shipping it sounds like a great idea. If you follow directions, fill out the proper forms, and apply the correct postage, you can rest assured that your mail will get to its destination in a timely fashion. In this chapter you'll learn how to send air, registered, and special delivery mail. You'll also learn how to write letters that state facts and describe your past and present activities and acquaintances.

Please, Mr. Postman

There's so much to write about that you hardly know where to begin. You've seen the Prado, run with the bulls in Pamplona, and basked in the sun on the Costa del Sol. You can't wait for your family and friends to read about your wonderful adventures. You don't want your postcards and letters to arrive home after you do. You want speedy delivery, so you're prepared to pay the extra price for airmail service. Naturally you'll want to keep a few essentials on hand, such as envelopes and stamps. Table 23.1 gives you the vocabulary you need to send your mail.

Table 23.1 Mail and Post Office Terms

Postal Terms	Spanish Translation	Pronunciation
address	la dirección	lah dee-rehk-see-ohn
addressee	el destinatario	ehl dehs-tee-nah-tah-ree-oh
air letter	el correo aéreo	ehl koh-rreh-oh ah-eh-reh-oh
commemorative stamp	el sello conmemorativo	ehl seh-yoh kohn-meh-moh-rah-tee-boh
envelope	el sobre	ehl soh-breh
letter	la carta	lah kahr-tah
mailbox	el buzón	ehl boo-sohn
money order	el giro postal	ehl hee-roh pohs-tahl
package	el paquete	ehl pah-keh-teh
parcel	el paquete	ehl pah-keh-teh
postcard	la tarjeta postal	lah tahr-heh-tah pohs-tahl
postage	el franqueo	ehl frahn-keh-oh
postal code	el código postal	ehl koh-dee-goh pohs-tahl
postal meter	la franqueadora postal	lah frahn-keh-ah-doh-rah pohs-tahl
postal worker	el cartero (la cartera)	ehl kahr-teh-roh (lah kahr-teh-rah)
postmark	el matasellos	ehl mah-tah-seh-yohs
rate	la tarifa de franqueo	lah tah-ree-fah deh frahn-keh-oh

Postal Terms	Spanish Translation	Pronunciation
sender	el remitiente	ehl reh-mee-tee-ehn-teh
sheet of stamps	la hoja de sellos	lah oh-hah deh seh-yohs
slot	la ranura	lah rah-noo-rah
stamp	el sello	ehl seh-yoh
window	la ventanilla	lah behn-tah-nee-yah

Cultural Tidbit

With over 600 offices all over the country, the Spanish Postal Service provides a wide range of modern and efficient services. The main offices located in Madrid, Barcelona, and Bilbao, as well as those in the international airports, are open 24 hours a day. You can also expect to find post offices, *Correos y Telégrafos* (koh-rreh-ohs ee teh-leh-grah-fohs) in railway stations, small villages, and ports.

The services provided by the Postal Service are two-fold in nature:

➤ Those pertaining strictly to different types of correspondence, such as letters, postcards, and packages.

➤ Those dealing with postal banking services such as postal and telegraphic money orders—unlike in other European cities, post offices in Spain do not normally handle telephone calls.

If you don't know in advance where you'll be staying and would like to pick up your mail personally (you'll need to show your passport as I.D. and pay a nominal fee for each item received), or if you want to have your mail forwarded to a certain address, you can register at the *Lista de Correos* (lees-tah deh koh-rreh-ohs), general delivery window.

If all you need is stamps, you can pick them up at *estancos* (ehs-tahn-kohs), establishments that are authorized to sell tobacco, stamps, and seals. When you're ready to send a letter or postcard home, look for the red and yellow mailboxes.

Getting Postal Service

You've written some postcards to your friends, dashed off a letter to your closest relatives, and even managed some business correspondence. If you need directions to the nearest post office or mailbox simply ask:

¿Dónde está el correo (buzón) más próximo?
Where is the nearest post office (mailbox)?

You'll find that just like back home, you'll have to fill out special forms and paperwork depending on the types of letters and packages you've decided to send. Postage rates will depend on how quickly you want your mail delivered. It's important to be able to correctly identify the type of service you need:

¿Cuál es la tarifa de franqueo de...?
kwahl ehs lah tah-ree-fah deh frahn-keh-oh deh
What is the postage rate for...?

Type of Delivery	Spanish Translation	Pronunciation
an insured letter	una carta asegurada	oo-nah kahr-tah ah-seh-goo-rah-dah
a letter to the United States	una carta a los Estados Unidos	oo-nah kahr-tah ah lohs ehs-tah-dohs oo-nee-dohs
an airmail letter	una carta por correo aéreo	oo-nah kahr-tah pohr koh-rreh-oh ah-eh-reh-oh
a registered letter	una carta certificada	oo-nah kahr-tah sehr-tee-fee-kah-dah
a special delivery letter	una carta urgente	oo-nah kahr-tah oor-hehn-teh

As a Rule
Remember to put the correct form of the demonstrative adjective (este, esta, estos, estas) before the noun you are using.

¿Cuánto cuestan estos sellos? *How much do these stamps cost?*

Other useful phrases include:

Quisiera mandar esta carta (este paquete) por correo regular (aéreo, urgente).
kee-see-eh-rah mahn-dahr ehs-tah kahr-tah (ehs-teh pah-keh-teh) pohr koh-rreh-oh reh-goo-lahr (ah-eh-reh-oh, oor-hehn-teh)
I would like to send this letter (this package) by regular mail (by airmail, special delivery).

Quisiera mandar este paquete contra reembolso.
kee-see-eh-rah mahn-dahr ehs-teh pah-keh-teh kohn-trah reh-ehm-bohl-soh
I would like to send this package C.O.D.

¿Cuánto pesa esta carta (este paquete)?
kwahn-toh peh-sah ehs-tah kahr-tah (ehs-teh pah-keh-teh)
How much does this letter (package) weigh?

¿Cuándo llegará (llegarán)?
kwahn-doh yeh-gah-rah (yeh-gah-rahn)
When will it arrive?

I Want to Send a Telegram

People generally send telegrams when there's important news to announce or acknowledge: your oldest son is finally getting married; the birth of a child or grandchild; a fabulous business deal; your best friend got an exciting promotion. When you want to send a telegram the following phrases might prove quite helpful:

Quisiera mandar un telegrama (a cobro revertido).
kee-see-eh-rah mahn-dahr oon teh-leh-grah-mah (ah koh-broh reh-behr-tee-doh)
I would like to send a telegram (collect).

¿Cuánto cuesta por palabra?
kwahn-toh kwehs-tah pohr pah-lah-brah
How much is it per word?

¿Puede darme un formulario (un impreso), por favor?
pweh-deh dahr-meh oon fohr-moo-lah-ree-oh (oon eem-preh-soh) pohr fah-bohr
May I please have a form?

¿Dónde están los formularios?
dohn-deh ehs-tahn lohs fohr-moo-lah-ree-ohs
Where are the forms?

Can You Read This?

Not only will you be doing some writing when you are in a foreign country, you will also find a lot to read. Perhaps you're interested in the local news and your hotel provides a complimentary newspaper each morning. Many people like to relax by thumbing through magazines and reading articles that are of interest. There may be an important sign that you need to read. If you see the word *aviso* (ah-bee-soh), then you know that there is some kind of warning that follows, like *agua no potable*, undrinkable water. Table 23.2 features items that you may read while visiting a Spanish-speaking country.

Table 23.2 Things to Read

Item to Be Read	Spanish Translation	Pronunciation
ad	un anuncio	oon ah-noon-see-oh
book	un libro	oon lee-broh
magazine	una revista	oo-nah reh-bees-tah
menu	una carta, un menú	oo-nah kahr-tah, oon meh-noo
newspaper	un periódico	oon peh-ree-oh-dee-koh
novel	una novela	oo-nah noh-beh-lah
pamphlet	un folleto	oon foh-yeh-toh
receipt	un recibo	oon reh-see-boh
sign	un letrero	oon leh-treh-roh
warning	un aviso	oon ah-bee-soh

What Do You Know About This?—Conocer & Saber

Do you know the name of a great Spanish restaurant? You do? What is its address? How about its phone number? You know the owner too? She's your second cousin and really knows how to prepare a mean paella? That's great. To express certain facts, information, relationships, and abilities you will need the two Spanish verbs that express *to know*, *saber* and *conocer*. First study the verbs and then read the paragraphs that follow for an explanation of how to use each verb properly.

saber—to know

yo sé (seh)	nosotros sabemos (sah-beh-mohs)
tú sabes (sah-behs)	vosotros sabéis (sah-beh-ees)
él, ella, Ud. sabe (sah-beh)	ellos, ellas, Uds. saben (sah-behn)

conocer—to know

yo conozco (koh-nohs-koh)	nosotros conocemos (koh-noh-seh-mohs)
tú conoces (koh-noh-sehs)	vosotros conocéis (koh-noh-seh-ees)
él, ella, Ud. conoce (koh-noh-seh)	ellos, ellas, Uds. conocen (koh-noh-sehn)

Conocer vs. Saber

If there are two ways to express *to know*, how are you supposed to know when to use each one? The important thing to remember is that the Spanish differentiate between knowing facts and how to do things (saber), and knowing (being acquainted with) people, places, things, and ideas (conocer).

The verb *saber* shows knowledge gained through learning or experience. It expresses that someone knows a fact or has actually memorized something. *Saber* means *to know how* when it is followed by an infinitive.

¿Sabe la dirección?
sah-beh lah dee-rehk-see-ohn
Do you know the address?

Yo sé donde está.
yoh seh dohn-deh ehs-tah
I know where it is.

¿Él sabe nadar?
ehl sah-beh nah-dahr
Does he know how to swim?

The verb *conocer* shows familiarity with a person, a place, or a thing.

If you can replace *to know* with *to be acquainted with* then you know to use the verb *conocer*.

¿Conoce a Marta?
koh-noh-seh ah mahr-tah
Do you know Martha? (Are you acquainted with her?)

¿Conoces este poema?
koh-noh-sehs ehs-teh poh-eh-mah
Do you know that poem? (Have you heard it—but you don't know the words?)

Notice the difference between:

> Yo sé la canción. *I know the song (by heart).*

> Yo conozco la canción. *I know the song (I'm familiar with it.).*

Would You Use Saber or Conocer?

Keep the differences between the two verbs in mind and you will quickly learn to use them properly. Show that you've gotten the hang of it by filling in the blanks with the correct form of *saber* or *conocer*.

1. Ellos _____ donde está el correo.

2. Yo no _____ su número de teléfono.

3. ¿_____ Ud. al señor Castro?

4. Nosotros _____ esquiar.

5. ¿_____ tú a esa mujer?

6. Ella _____ Madrid.

7. ¿_____ Uds. que yo soy cubana?

8. Vosotros _____ este monumento.

What Have You Done?—The Present Perfect Tense

"Good grief!," you exclaim when you realize that you have forgotten to call your loved ones to tell them that you have arrived safely. You have promised in the past to do the very same thing and you've always seemed to have let it slip your mind. That's because you've gotten so caught up in the excitement of your trip. In order to express what you *have* or *have not* done, you must use the present perfect tense in Spanish. This tense refers to an action that has already happened, either in the general past, or quite recently in relation to now: "I've started to study Spanish." It may also be used to speak about past events that carry over into the present: "I've always wanted to study that language (and I still want to know)."

The present perfect is a compound tense, which means that it is made up of more than one part. Two elements are needed to form the present perfect—a helping verb *haber* (ah-behr), to have, which expresses that something *has* taken place, and a past participle, which expresses exactly what the action was.

The present perfect tense is formed as follows:

(subject noun or pronoun) + helping verb + past participle

Pitfall

Do not get confused with the verb *tener* (to have) which is used to express have in a general sense, and *haber* (to have) which is only used as a helping verb in compound tenses.

Yo tengo muchos amigos. *I have many friends.*

Yo he telefoneado a mis amigos. *I have called my friends.*

The Helping Verb Haber

Since haber is the first verb to follow the subject or to be used without the subject, it must be conjugated. Table 23.3 gives the present tense of this helping verb:

Table 23.3 The Helping Verb Haber (to Have)

Conjugation of Haber	Pronunciation	Meaning
yo he	yoh eh	I have
tú has	too ahs	you have
él, ella, Ud. ha	ehl, eh-yah, oo-stehd ah	he, she, has; you have
nosotros hemos	nohs-oh-trohs eh-mohs	we have
vosotros habéis	bohs-oh-trohs ah-beh-ees	you have
ellos, ellas, Uds. han	eh-yohs, eh-yahs, oo-steh-dehs ahn	they, you have

Forming Past Participles

To this helping verb, you must now add a past participle. The helping verb is always conjugated, because it is the first verb. The past participle, therefore, remains the same, no matter what the subject may be.

➤ To form the past participles of regular verbs, drop the infinitive ending (*ar*, *er*, or *ir*) and add the following endings:

Sample AR verb	Past Participle Stem	Past Participle Ending
hablar	habl	ado

Sample ER & IR Verbs	Past Participle Stem	Past Participle Ending
vender	vend	ido
abrir	abr	ido

➤ Verbs ending in *er* or *ir* and having a vowel immediately preceding the infinitive ending add an accent mark on the *i* as follows:

Infinitive	Past Participle Stem	Past Participle
caer (to fall)	ca	caído
creer (to believe)	cre	creído

continues

317

continued

Infinitive	Past Participle Stem	Past Participle
leer (to read)	le	leído
oír (to hear)	o	oído
reír (to laugh)	re	reído
traer (to bring)	tra	traído

Here are some examples of *er* and *ir* verbs in past participle form:

Infinitive	Past Participle
abrir (to open)	abierto
cubrir (to cover)	cubierto
decir (to say, tell)	dicho
escribir (to write)	escrito
hacer (to do, make)	hecho
morir (to die)	muerto
poner (to put)	puesto
resolver (to resolve)	resuelto
romper (to break)	roto
ver (to see)	visto
volver (to return)	vuelto

Now let's take the formula we've learned and put the present perfect to use.

Yo he hablado con mi familia.   *I have spoken with my family.*

Nosotros hemos comido demasiado.   *We've eaten too much.*

Ud. ha recibido una carta.   *You have received a letter.*

Él ha hecho el trabajo.   *He has done the work.*

Ellos han visto El Prado.   *They have seen El Prado.*

As a Rule

In Spanish, the past participle cannot be separated from the helping verb by the word "no," an adverb, or a subject noun or pronoun when it is used in a question:

Jaime <u>no</u> **ha dicho** la verdad.   *James didn't tell the truth.*

Nosotros <u>siempre</u> **hemos llegado** <u>puntualmente</u>.   *We've always arrived on time.*

¿**Han llamado** <u>los muchachos</u>?   *Have the boys called?*

¿No **has comprendido** <u>tú</u>?   *Didn't you understand?*

Putting the Present Perfect to Work

It was a holiday weekend and most people had some spare time to themselves. Express what each person has or has not done to make the most of this opportunity by using the correct form of the helping verb haber and the past participle of the infinitive indicated:

Example: yo / mirar la televisión
Yo he mirado la televisión.

Ud. / no poner la mesa
Ud. no ha puesto la mesa.

1. nosotros / ir al cine

2. ellos / jugar al fútbol

3. tú / no trabajar

4. yo / leer una novela

5. Ud. / no escribir cartas

6. vosotros / no correr al centro

7. Uds. / no traer su ropa a la lavandería

8. ella / volver a casa temprano

The Least You Need to Know

➤ Go to a Spanish post office to mail letters and packages or to send money.

➤ *Saber* means to know a fact or how to do something. *Conocer* means to be acquainted with a person, place, or thing.

➤ The present perfect tense expresses what has happened in the general past or quite recently. It is made up of the conjugated form of the helping verb *haber* and a past participle.

Part 5
Let's Get Down
to Business

Chapter 24

Renting a Villa

In This Chapter

➤ Apartments and houses

➤ Rooms, furnishings, amenities, and appliances

➤ Using the conditional

Although you love the luxury of a well-appointed hotel, this might not prove to be cost efficient for you in the long run. It might be wise to consider purchasing or renting a place for yourself to stay in. Why not consider an apartment, a house, a condominium, or even a piece of time-sharing property? Should you make this decision, Chapter 24 will teach you how to get the furnishings, appliances, and amenities you want and need. You'll also learn how to express your plans in the future.

Could I Stay in a Villa?

Renting or buying a piece of real estate in a Spanish-speaking country is becoming more and more popular as time goes on. So if you've decided that you're ready to escape the rat race, and are looking for a change of scenery, you'll want to be able to pick up the real estate section of a Spanish newspaper and be able to read and understand what the ad offers and promises. You'll also want to be able to discuss the ad with the owner or real estate agent. Do you want cathedral ceilings? A two-car garage? A fireplace? Table 24.1, which lists the various features people look for in a home, will prepare you for your big move. Use *Necesito* (neh-seh-see-toh), I need, to express what you want.

Table 24.1 The House, the Apartment, the Rooms

Stuff for Your Home	Spanish Translation	Pronunciation
air conditioning (central)	el aire acondicionado (central)	ehl ah-ee-reh ah-kohn-dee-see-oh-nah-doh (sehn-trahl)
apartment	el apartamento	ehl ah-pahr-tah-mehn-toh
attic	el ático, el entretecho	ehl ah-tee-koh, ehl ehn-treh-teh-choh
backyard	el jardín	ehl hahr-deen
balcony	el balcón	ehl bahl-kohn
basement	el sótano	ehl soh-tah-noh
bathroom	el cuarto de baño	ehl kwahr-toh deh bah-nyoh
bedroom	el dormitorio	ehl dohr-mee-toh-ree-oh
cathedral ceiling	el vacio catedral	ehl bah-see-oh kah-teh-drahl
ceiling	el techo	ehl teh-choh
closet	el armario	ehl ahr-mah-ree-oh
courtyard	el patio	ehl pah-tee-oh
den	el estudio	ehl ehs-too-dee-oh
dining room	el comedor	ehl koh-meh-dohr
elevator	el ascensor	ehl ah-sehn-sohr

Stuff for Your Home	Spanish Translation	Pronunciation
family room	la sala de estar	lah sah-lah deh ehs-tahr
fireplace	la chimenea	lah chee-meh-neh-ah
floor	el suelo	ehl sweh-loh
floor (story)	el piso	ehl pee-soh
garage	el garaje	ehl gah-rah-heh
ground floor	la planta baja	lah plahn-tah bah-hah
hallway	el pasillo	ehl pah-see-oh
heating	la calefacción	lah kah-leh-fahk-see-ohn
electric	eléctrica	eh-lehk-tree-kah
gas	a gas	ah gahs
kitchen	la cocina	lah koh-see-nah
laundry room	la lavandería	lah lah-bahn-deh-ree-ah
lease	el contrato de arrendamiento	ehl kohn-trah-toh deh ah-rrehn-dah-mee-ehn-toh
living room	la sala	lah sah-lah
maintenance	el mantenimiento	ehl mahn-teh-nee-mee-yehn-toh
owner	el dueño	ehl dweh-nyoh
rent	el alquiler	ehl ahl-kee-lehr
roof	el techo	ehl teh-choh
room	el cuarto	ehl kwahr-toh
	la habitación	lah ah-bee-tah-see-ohn
security deposit	la fianza, la garantía	lah fee-ahn-sah, lah gah-rahn-tee-ah
shower	la ducha	lah doo-chah
staircase	la escalera	lah ehs-kah-leh-rah
storage room	la despensa	lah dehs-pehn-sah
tenant	el arrendatario	ehl ah-rrehn-dah-tah-ree-oh
terrace	la terraza	lah teh-rrah-sah
window	la ventana	lah behn-tah-nah

325

Home Sweet Home

You don't cook, so a microwave is a must. How else will you be able to heat up all those delectable leftovers? You're not in the habit of hanging laundry out on a line—a washer/dryer combination has to be available to you. Can you live without a television? What furniture do you need? Before you rent or buy a piece of property, it's always wise to find out what is included. Consult table 24.2 for a few pieces of furniture you may want. Use: *Hay...?* (ah-ee) Is (Are) there...? to ask your questions.

Table 24.2 Furniture and Accessories

Furniture and Accessories	Spanish Translation	Pronunciation
armchair	el sillón	ehl see-yohn
bed	la cama	lah kah-mah
bookcase	la estantería	lah ehs-tahn-teh-ree-ah
carpet	la moqueta	lah moh-keh-tah
chair	la silla	lah see-yah
clock	el reloj	ehl reh-loh
curtains	las cortinas	lahs kohr-tee-nahs
dishwasher	el lavaplatos	ehl lah-bah-plah-tohs
dresser	la cómoda	lah koh-moh-dah
dryer	la secadora	lah seh-kah-doh-rah
food processor	el procesador de cocina	ehl proh-seh-sah-dohr deh koh-see-nah
freezer	el congelador	ehl kohn-heh-lah-dohr
furniture	los muebles	lohs mweh-blehs
home appliances	los aparatos eléctricos	lohs ah-pah-rah-tohs eh-lehk-tree-kohs
lamp	la lámpara	lah lahm-pah-rah
microwave oven	el microondas	ehl mee-kroh-ohn-dahs
mirror	el espejo	ehl ehs-peh-hoh
oven	el horno	ehl ohr-noh
refrigerator	el refrigerador	ehl reh-free-heh-rah-dohr
rug	la alfombra	lah ahl-fohm-brah
sofa	el sofá	ehl soh-fah

Furniture and Accessories	Spanish Translation	Pronunciation
stereo	el estéreo	ehl ehs-teh-reh-oh
stove	la estufa	lah ehs-too-fah
table	la mesa	lah meh-sah
television	el televisor	ehl teh-leh-bee-sohr
large screen	con pantalla grande	kohn pahn-tah-yah grahn-deh
VCR	el VCR, la video cassette de grabadora	ehl bee-cee-ahr, lah bee-deh-oh kah-seht-teh deh grah-bah-doh-rah
washing machine	la lavadora	lah lah-bah-doh-rah

Buying Furniture

Is your place unfurnished? Then you'll surely have to pick up some furniture. We all have in mind the services, help, and guarantees that we expect from a store. Read the following ad to find out what attractive offers you could expect from the company.

MUEBLERÍA DE MADRID

Un valor seguro

Nosotros le garantizamos gratuitamente (free) sus muebles por 5 años y los cojines de las sillas por 2 años contra todo defecto de fabricación.

Nosotros venimos gratuitamente a su casa para tomar medidas, hacer estimados y para aconsejarle.

Nosotros le ofrecemos una garantía sin riesgos, gratuitamente, por un año.

Nosotros nos llevaremos sus muebles viejos despues de que compre muebles nuevos.

Nosotros garantizamos estos servicios y estas garantías sin incremento de precio, en todas nuestras tiendas, en todas partes de España.

Buying or Renting

Do you have any questions? Of course you do. That's certainly normal when you rent or buy a piece of property. To express your preferences or questions use the following phrases and expressions to help you get exactly what you want:

Busco...
boos-koh
I'm looking for...

los anuncios clasificado
lohs ah-noon-see-ohs
  klah-see-fee-kah-doh
the classified ads

los bienes raíces
lohs bee-eh-nehs rah-ee-sehs
*the real estate advertising
section*

una agencia inmobiliaria
oo-nah ah-hehn-see-ah
een-moh-bee-lee-ah-ree-ah
a real estate agency

Quisiera alquilar (comprar)...
kee-see-eh-rah ahl-kee-lahr
  (kohm-prahr)...
I would like to rent (buy)...

un apartmento
oon ah-pahr-tah-mehn-toh
an apartment

una casa
oo-nah kah-sah
a house

un condominio
oon kohn-doh-mee-nee-oh
a condominium

¿Es lujoso (lujosa)?
ehs loo-hoh-soh(sah)
Is it luxurious?

¿Cuánto es el alquiler?
kwahn-toh ehs ehl ahl-kee-lehr
What is the rent?

¿Hay robos?
ah-ee roh-bohs
Are there break-ins?

¿Hay copropiedad?
ah-ee koh-proh-pee-eh-dahd
Is there time-sharing?

¿Cuántos son los gastos de mantenimiento del apartamento (de la casa)?
kwahn-tohs sohn lohs gahs-tohs deh mahn-teh-nee-mee-ehn-toh dehl ah-pahr-tah-
mehn-toh (deh lah kah-sah)
How much is the maintenance of the apartment (house)?

¿Está incluído(a) ...?
ehs-tah een-kloo-ee-doh(dah) ...
Is ... included?

la calefacción
lah kah-leh-fahk-see-ohn
the heat

la climatización
lah klee-mah-tee-sah-see-ohn
the air-conditioning

¿De cuántas son las mensualidades?
deh kwahn-tahs sohn lahs mehn-soo-
ah-lee-dah-dehs
How much are the monthly payments?

¿Tengo que dejar un depósito?
tehn-goh keh deh-hahr oon deh-poh-see-toh
Do I have to leave a deposit?

la electricidad
lah eh-lehk-tree-see-dahd
the electricity

el gas
ehl gahs
the gas

Quisiera pedir una hipoteca.
kee-see-eh-rah peh-deer oo-nah ee-poh-
teh-kah
I'd like to apply for a mortgage.

Voy al banco.
boy al bahn-koh
I'm going to the bank.

Cultural Tidbit

Expect to find that houses in Spain and Spanish America differ somewhat from what we are accustomed to in the United States. Homes in Spanish-speaking countries are designed to protect the privacy of the family.

The front wall of many houses borders the sidewalk, so do not be surprised that there is no front yard. If someone wants to sit in the front, he puts a chair outside on the sidewalk.

Unlike our backyards, many Spanish-speaking people have an inner courtyard called *un patio* (oon pah-tee-oh), which is often surrounded by a high adobe wall. Most rooms face the patio, which is adorned with potted plants, flowers, and perhaps even a fountain. To get from the street to the inner patio, take a special path known as the *zaguán* (sah-gwahn).

Almost every home has wrought-iron window and balcony grills called *rejas* (reh-hahs). These bars allow the owner to safely leave his windows open and get a nice cool breeze. An old Spanish dating custom called *comiendo hierro* (koh-mee-ehn-doh ee-eh-rroh), eating iron, revolved around these iron grills. A young woman would stand at a street level window behind the reja. A young man, trying to court her, would get to know her better first by having extended conversations through the bars. Upon achieving a certain level of familiarity, the parents would then allow her suitor to enter the house and see their daughter.

Decisions, Decisions

Armed with a marker and a cup of coffee, you've decided to begin scanning the real estate ads in search of your dream get-away. There's so much to choose from in many different price ranges. Your friend cut this ad out from the paper that she thinks fits your criteria—what does this property offer you?

LA CASA GRANDE
3ra SECCION
Un Hogar Seguro y a su Alcance...
DESDE $80,000*

A sólo pasos del centro del pueblo áreas recreativas, restaurantes, centros comerciales, carreteras principales, playa y las más bellas vistas del áreas este de Puerto Rico.

• Modernas residencias con dos elegantes fachadas
• 3 dormitorios, baño y marquesina
• Solar básico de 300.30 m.c.
• SEPARELA CON $600

A Choice Is Made

You've made a wonderful choice and you've even gone to look at the property. Look at the floor plan that was distributed to you. How many bedrooms are there? Bathrooms? What extras are there? Where is the terrace located? What do you like about the layout? Is there anything you dislike?

What's in Store for the Future

A person planning to buy or rent property in the future usually has to financially prepare for it. In Spanish, the future may be expressed in one of three ways:

➤ Use a present tense form of the verb, usually in conjunction with other words that show that the future is implied:

¿Qué vuelo llega esta noche?   *What flight is arriving tonight?*

➤ Use the irregular verb *ir + a + infinitive*. Because the verb *ir* means *to go*, it is understandable that it is used to express what the speaker is going to do. Because *to go* will be the first verb used, it will have to be conjugated. The action that the speaker is going to perform will be expressed by the infinitive of the verb. Refresh your memory:

yo voy	nosotros vamos
tú vas	vosotros vaís
él, ella, Ud. va	ellos, ellas, Uds. van

As a Rule
The future endings are the same for all verbs, whether they belong to the *ar*, *er*, or *ir* family or are irregular. You will also notice that all of the future endings have accents except for the *nosotros* form.

Voy a ir al centro.
boh-ee ah eer ahl sehn-troh
I'm going to go to the city.

Ellos van a echar (mandar) la carta al correo.
eh-yohs bahn ah eh-chahr (mahn-dahr) lah kahr-tah ahl koh-rreh-oh
They are going to send the letter.

The Future Tense

The future may also be expressed by changing the verb to the future tense. The future tense tells what the subject *will* do or what action *will* take place in future time. The future of regular verbs is formed by adding the future endings to the infinitive of the verb.

Sample Verbs	Future Stem	Conjugation	Verb Pronunciation
hablar	hablar	yo hablaré	ah-blah-reh
		tú hablarás	ah-blah-rahs
		él, ella, Ud. hablará	ah-blah-rah
		nosotros hablaremos	ah-blah-reh-mohs
		vosotros hablaréis	ah-blah-reh-ees
		ellos, ellas, Uds. hablarán	ah-blah-rahn
vender	vender	yo venderé	behn-deh-reh
		tú venderás	behn-deh-rahs
		él, ella, Ud. venderá	behn-deh-rah
		nosotros venderemos	behn-deh-reh-mohs
		vosotros venderéis	behn-deh-reh-ees
		ellos, ellas, Uds. venderán	behn-deh-rahn
abrir	abrir	yo abriré	ah-bree-reh
		tú abrirás	ah-bree-rahs
		él, ella, Ud. abrirá	ah-bree-rah
		nosotros abriremos	ah-bree-reh-mohs
		vosotros abriréis	ah-bree-reh-ees
		ellos, ellas, Uds. abrirán	ah-bree-rahn

Yo hablaré con mis amigos mañana.
yoh ah-blah-reh kohn mees ah-mee-gohs mah-nyah-nah
I will speak with my friends tomorrow.

Nosotros no venderemos nuesta casa.
noh-soh-trohs noh behn-deh-reh-mohs nwehs-trah kah-sah
We will not sell our house.

¿Abrirán Uds. una cuenta?
ah-bree-rahn oo-steh-dehs oo-nah kwehn-tah
Will you open an account?

The Future Tense of Irregular Verbs

Some verbs form the future by dropping the *e* from the infinitive ending and then adding the future endings from the preceding examples.

Infinitive	Future Stem	Future Endings
cab<u>e</u>r (to fit)	cabr	é, ás, á, emos, éis, án
pod<u>e</u>r (to be able)	podr	
quer<u>e</u>r (to want)	querr	
sab<u>e</u>r (to know)	sabr	

For some verbs the *e* or *i* is dropped from the infinitive ending and is replaced by a *d*. The future endings are then added.

Infinitive	Future Stem	Future Endings
pon<u>e</u>r (to put)	pon*d*r-	é, ás, á, emos, éis, án
sal<u>i</u>r (to leave)	sal*d*r-	
ten<u>e</u>r (to have)	ten*d*r-	
val<u>e</u>r (to be worth)	val*d*r-	
ven<u>i</u>r (to come)	ven*d*r-	

The verbs *decir* and *hacer* are irregular:

Infinitive	Future Stem	Future Endings
decir (to say)	dir	é, ás, á, emos, éis, án
hacer (to make, do)	har	

333

Plans for the Day

Your Spanish hosts are sleeping in today and you feel like going out on your own to take care of some personal business. Write a list of five things you plan to do using the future tense.

What Are the Conditions?

Would you prefer to live in the city or on the beach? Would you rather take possession of furnished or unfurnished property? How about a swimming pool? Would you like to have one? The conditional is a mood in Spanish that expresses what the speaker *would* do or what *would* happen under certain circumstances. The conditional of the verb *querer* or *gustar* is frequently used to express what the speaker *would like*:

Quisiera (Me gustaría) alquilar una casa.
kee-see-eh-rah (meh goos-tah-ree-ah) ahl-kee-lahr oo-nah kah-sah
I would like to rent a house.

As a Rule
The conditional endings are the same for all verbs whether they belong to the ar, er, or ir family or are irregular. You will also notice that all of the conditional endings have accents.

Forming the Conditional

The conditional is formed with the same stem that was used to form the future, whether you are using a regular or an irregular verb. The endings for the conditional, however, are different. They are exactly the same as the *er* and *ir* verb endings for the imperfect. So, in other words, to form the conditional start with the future stem and add the imperfect endings shown in the following table.

Sample Verbs	Conditional Stem	Conditional Endings	Pronunciation
hablar	hablar	*ía*	ee-ah
vender	vender	*ías*	ee-ahs
abrir	abrir	*ía*	ee-ah
		íamos	ee-ah-mohs
		íais	ee-ah-ees
		ían	ee-ahn

Yo le hablaría.
yoh leh ah-blah-ree-ah
I would speak to him (her).

Nosotros no venderíamos nuestro coche a ningún precio.
noh-soh-trohs noh behn-deh-ree-ah-mohs nwehs-troh koh-cheh ah neen-goon
preh-see-oh.
We would not sell our car at any price.

¿Abrirían Uds. una cuenta conjunta?
ah-bree-ree-ahn oo-steh-dehs oo-nah kwehn-tah kohn-hoon-tah
Would you open a joint account?

The Conditional of Irregular Verbs

Some verbs form the conditional by dropping the *e* from the infinitive ending and then
adding the future endings just shown.

Infinitive	Conditional Stem	Conditional Endings
cab<u>e</u>r (to fit)	cabr	*ía*
pod<u>e</u>r (to be able)	podr	*ías*
quer<u>e</u>r (to want)	querr	*ía*
sab<u>e</u>r (to know)	sabr	*íamos*
		íais
		ían

For some verbs the *e* or *i* is dropped from the infinitive ending and is replaced with a *d*.
The conditional endings are then added.

Infinitive	Conditional Stem	Conditional Endings
pon<u>e</u>r (to put)	pondr-	*ía*
sal<u>i</u>r (to leave)	saldr-	*ías*
ten<u>e</u>r (to have)	tendr-	*ía*
val<u>e</u>r (to be worth)	valdr-	*íamos*
ven<u>i</u>r (to come)	vendr-	*íais*
		ían

The verbs *decir* and *hacer* are irregular:

Infinitive	Conditional Stem	Conditional Endings
decir (to say)	dir	*ía*
hacer (to make, do)	har	*ías*
		ía
		íamos
		íais
		ían

What Would You Do?

I think that everyone dreams of winning the lottery, especially when the stakes are very high. What would you do with 25 million dollars? I bet you can start rattling off a list of things immediately. Do you have visions of a fancy sports car, luxurious worldwide travel, a beautiful home with every possible amenity? Write a list of things you would do if you won *la lotería* (lah loh-teh-ree-ah), the lottery, tomorrow.

The Least You Need to Know

➤ Spanish homes are built to protect the privacy of the family and are laid out differently than homes that we are accustomed to in the United States.

➤ The future is usually formed by adding the following endings to the infinitive: *é, ás, á, emos, éis, án*. A few irregular verbs must be memorized.

➤ The conditional is formed by using the future stem (usually the infinitive) and the *er* and *ir* verb imperfect endings: *ía, ías, ía, íamos, íais, ían*. A few irregular verbs must be memorized.

Chapter 25

Money Matters

In This Chapter

➤ Banking terms

➤ Stock market terms

➤ The subjunctive

You're now prepared for an extended stay in a Spanish-speaking country. In the previous chapter you learned the necessary words and expressions to buy or rent new living quarters of any kind. You can now express the facilities you want and need in order to live the good life, whether they include a dining area to accommodate all your business staff or a backyard with an in-ground pool.

This last chapter will appeal to anyone who has to make a trip to the bank: tourists who want to change money, a businessperson seeking financial assistance, an investor in foreign affairs, or a potential home buyer. You will also learn how to use the subjunctive to express your own special wants, needs, and desires.

Banking Transactions

People visiting a foreign country stop in a bank for many reasons. Since banks are reputed to give good exchange rates, they attract tourists who want to change their money into local currency. Those with more far-reaching goals might want to establish credit and set up savings and checking accounts. Others may seek to purchase land, real estate, or a business. The most daring may choose to invest in the stock market or corporate business adventures. If you fit into any of these categories, you'll find the phrases provided in the mini-dictionary of banking terms in table 25.1 quite useful.

Cultural Tidbit

Banks in Spanish-speaking countries are open at 9 a.m. and close between 2 and 3 p.m. on weekdays, and are open from 9 a.m. until 1 or 1:30 p.m. on Saturday. Most banks have departments for changing foreign currency, and, strangely enough, tend to give better rates for traveler's checks. Remember to bring along your passport: it's the only acceptable form of identification in banks.

Money can also be exchanged at *una casa de cambio* (oo-nah kah-sah deh kahm-bee-oh). These money exchanges can be found all over the streets of Madrid and in other foreign cities as well. Some offer excellent rates while others charge exorbitant commissions. It is always wise to investigate a few first. Remember that the worst exchange rates are given by hotels, airports, and railway stations, so avoid them whenever possible.

Table 25.1   Mini-Dictionary of Banking Terms

Banking Term	Spanish Translation	Pronunciation
advance payment	el pago adelantado	ehl pah-goh ah-deh-lahn-tah-doh
automatic teller machine	el cajero automático	ehl kah-heh-roh ow-toh-mah-tee-koh
balance	el saldo	ehl sahl-doh
bank	el banco	ehl bahn-koh
bank account	la cuenta bancaria	lah kwehn-tah bahn-kah-ree-ah
bankbook	la cartilla de ahorros, la libreta de ahorros	lah kahr-tee-yah deh ah-oh-rrohs, lah lee-breh-tah deh ah-oh-rrohs
banknote	el billete de banco	ehl bee-yeh-teh deh bahn-koh

Banking Term	Spanish Translation	Pronunciation
bill	la factura	lah fahk-too-rah
borrow	prestar	prehs-tahr
branch	la sucursal	lah soo-koor-sahl
cash	el dinero en efectivo	ehl dee-neh-roh ehn eh-fehk-tee-boh
to cash	cobrar	koh-brahr
cash flow	la corriente en efectivo, los movimientos en efectivos, el flujo de efectivo	lah koh-rree-ehn-teh ehn eh-fehk-tee-boh, lohs moh-bee-mee-ehn-tohs ehn eh-fehk-tee-bohs, ehl floo-hoh deh eh-fehk-tee-boh
cashier	el cajero	ehl kah-heh-roh
change (transaction)	el cambio	ehl kahm-bee-oh
change (coins)	la moneda	lah moh-neh-dah
check	el cheque	ehl cheh-keh
checkbook	la chequera	lah cheh-keh-rah
checking account	la cuenta corriente	lah kwehn-tah koh-rree-ehn-teh
coin	la moneda	lah moh-neh-dah
credit	el crédito	ehl kreh-dee-toh
currency (foreign)	el dinero (la divisa)	ehl dee-neh-roh (lah dee-bee-sah)
customer	el cliente	ehl klee-ehn-teh
debt	la dueda	lah dweh-dah
deposit	el depósito, el ingreso	ehl deh-poh-see-toh, ehl een-greh-soh
to deposit	depositar, ingresar	deh-poh-see-tahr, een-greh-sahr
down payment	el desembolso inicial	ehl deh-sehm-bohl-soh ee-nee-see-ahl
employee	el empleado	ehl ehm-pleh-ah-doh
endorse	endosar	ehn-doh-sahr
exchange rate	el tipo de cambio	ehl tee-poh deh kahm-bee-oh
fill out	llenar	yeh-nahr

continues

Table 25.1 Continued

Banking Term	Spanish Translation	Pronunciation
final payment	el pago final	ehl pah-goh fee-nahl
guarantee	la garantía	lah gah-rahn-tee-ah
holder	el titular, el portador, el tenedor	ehl tee-too-lahr, ehl pohr-tah-dohr, ehl teh-neh-dohr
installment payment	el pago (el abono) a plazos	ehl pah-goh (ehl ah-boh-noh) ah plah-sohs
installment plan	las facilidades de pago	lahs fah-see-lee-dah-dehs deh pah-goh

interest
  simple
  compound
	el interés
	  simple
	  compuesto
		ehl een-teh-rehs
		  seem-pleh
		  kohm-pwehs-toh

interest rate	la tasa (el tipo) de interés	lah tah-sah (ehl tee-poh) deh een-teh-rehs
invest	investir	een-behs-teer
investment	la inversión	lah een-behr-see-ohn

loan
  take out a loan
	el préstamo
	  hacer un préstamo
		ehl preh-stah-moh
		  ah-sehr oon preh-stah-moh

long term	a largo plazo	ah lahr-goh plah-soh
manage	administrar, manejar	ahd-mee-nees-trahr, mah-neh-hahr
money exchange bureau	el departamento de intercambio	ehl deh-pahr-tah-mehn-toh deh een-tehr-kahm-bee-oh
monthly statement	el extracto de cuenta, el estado de cuenta, el mensual	ehl ehks-trahk-toh deh kwehn-tah, ehl ehs-tah-doh deh kwehn-tah, ehl mehn-soo-ahl
mortgage	la hipoteca	lah ee-poh-teh-kah
open account	la cuenta corriente	lah kwehn-tah koh-rree-ehn-teh
overdrawn check	el cheque sin fondos	ehl cheh-keh seen fohn-dohs
overdraft	el giro en descubierto, el saldo deudor	ehl hee-roh ehn dehs-koo-bee-ehr-toh, ehl sahl-doh deh-oo-dohr

Banking Term	Spanish Translation	Pronunciation
pay cash	pagar en efectivo	pah-gahr ehn eh-fehk-tee-boh
payment	el pago	ehl pah-goh
percentage	el porcentaje	ehl pohr-sehn-tah-heh
promissory note	el pagaré	ehl pah-gah-reh
purchase	comprar	kohm-prahr
quarter	el trimestre	ehl tree-mehs-treh
receipt	el recibo	ehl reh-see-boh
revenue	los ingresos	lohs een-greh-sohs
safe	la caja fuerte	lah kah-hah foo-ehr-teh
sale	la venta	lah behn-tah
save	ahorrar	ah-oh-rrahr
savings account	la cuenta de ahorros	lah kwehn-tah deh ah-oh-rrohs
short term	a corto plazo	ah kohr-toh plah-soh
sign (to)	firmar	feer-mahr
signature	la firma	lah feer-mah
sum	el monto, el total, la suma	ehl mohn-toh, ehl toh-tahl, lah soo-mah
teller	el cajero	ehl kah-heh-roh
total	el total, el monto	ehl toh-tahl, ehl mohn-toh
transfer	la transferencia	lah trahns-feh-rehn-see-ah
traveler's check	el cheque de viajero	ehl cheh-keh deh bee-ah-heh-roh
void (adj.)	inválido,	een-bah-lee-doh
void (v.)	anular	ah-noo-lahr
window	la ventanilla	lah behn-tah-nee-yah
withdraw	sacar, retirar	sah-kahr, reh-tee-rahr
withdrawal	la retirada	lah reh-tee-rah-dah

Transactions I Need to Make

If you're planning on a trip to the bank, the phrases in this section will be helpful in common, everyday banking situations: making deposits and withdrawals, opening a checking account, or taking out a loan.

¿Cuál es el horario de trabajo?
kwahl ehs ehl oh-rah-ree-oh deh trah-bah-hoh
What are the banking hours?

The clause in bold can be completed by tacking on any of the phrases that follow it:

Quisiera...
kee-see-eh-rah
I would like...

hacer un depósito
ah-sehr oon deh-poh-see-toh
to make a deposit

cobrar un cheque
koh-brahr oon cheh-keh
to cash a check

hacer un retiro
ah-sehr oon reh-tee-roh
to make a withdrawal

abrir una cuenta
ah-breer oo-nah kwehn-tah
to open an account

hacer un pago
ah-sehr oon pah-goh
to make a payment

liquidar una cuenta
lee-kee-dahr oo-nah kwehn-tah
to close an account

pedir un préstamo
peh-deer oon prehs-tah-moh
to apply for a loan

cambiar divisas
kahm-bee-ahr dee-bee-sahs
to change some foreign money

Some more helpful phrases to use at a bank include:

¿Recibiré un extracto de cuentas (un estado de cuentas) mensual?
reh-see-bee-reh oon ehks-trahk-toh deh kwehn-tahs (oon ehs-tah-doh deh kwehn-tahs) mehn-soo-ahl
Will I get a monthly statement?

¿Cuál es la tasa (el tipo) de cambio del dólar hoy?
kwahl ehs lah tah-sah (ehl tee-poh) deh kahm-bee-oh dehl doh-lahr oh-ee
What is today's exchange rate?

¿Tiene un cajero automático?
tee-eh-neh oon kah-heh-roh ow-toh-mah-tee-koh
Do you have an automatic teller machine?

¿Cómo se usa?
koh-moh seh oo-sah
How does one use it?

Quisiera hacer un préstamo personal.
kee-see-eh-rah ah-sehr oon prehs-tah-moh pehr-soh-nahl
I'd like to make a personal loan.

Quisiera pedir una hipoteca.
kee-see-eh-rah peh-deer oo-nah ee-poh-teh-kah
I'd like to apply for a mortgage.

¿Cuál es el plazo del préstamo?
kwahl ehs ehl plah-soh dehl prehs-tah-moh
What is the time period of the loan?

¿De cuánto son las mensualidades?
Deh kwahn-toh sohn lahs mehn-soo-ah-lee-dah-dehs
How much are the monthly payments?

¿Cuál es la tasa (el tipo) de interés?
kwahl ehs lah tah-sah (ehl tee-poh) deh een-teh-rehs
What is the interest rate?

Everyone Has Needs

If you're like me, no matter how much money you have, you always need just a little bit more to tide you over. In Spanish there are two ways to express need:

➤ Use *tener (conjugated)* + *que* + *verb (infinitive)*. Tener is an irregular verb. Refresh your memory:

yo tengo	nosotros tenemos
tú tienes	vosotros tenéis
él, ella, Ud. tiene	ellos, ellas, Uds. tienen

Yo tengo que ir al centro.   *I have to go downtown.*

Nosotros tenemos que partir.   *We have to leave.*

➤ Use the expression *es necesario que*... (ehs neh-seh-sah-ree-oh keh), it is necessary that.... *Es necesario que* and other expressions showing necessity are followed by a special verb form called the subjunctive.

343

The subjunctive is a mood, not a tense, and expresses wishing, wanting, emotion, and doubt. It is used after many expressions showing uncertainty and certain conjunctions, as well. Those applications will not be treated in this book.

Because the subjunctive is not a tense (a verb form indicating time), the present subjunctive can be used to refer to actions in the present or the future. The past subjunctive will not be treated in this book since its use is limited.

In order to use the subjunctive, certain conditions must be met:

➤ Two different clauses must exist with two different subjects.

➤ The two clauses must be joined by *que*.

➤ One of the clauses must show need, necessity, emotion, or doubt.

Es necesario que yo hable con mi amigo.
ehs neh-seh-sah-ree-oh keh yoh ah-bleh kohn mee ah-mee-goh
I (I'll) have to speak to my friend.

Es necesario que nosotros vendamos nuestra casa.
ehs neh-seh-sah-ree-oh keh noh-soh-trohs behn-dah-mohs nwehs-trah kah-sah
We (We'll) have to sell our house.

Es necesario que Uds. abran una cuenta de ahorros.
ehs neh-seh-sah-ree-oh keh oo-steh-dehs ah-brahn oo-nah kwehn-tah deh ah-oh-rrohs
You (You'll) have to open a savings account.

Present Subjunctive Formation

To form the present subjunctive of regular verbs, drop the *o* ending from the *yo* form of the present, and add opposite endings: *ar* verbs change present tense *a* to *e*; *er* and *ir* verbs change present tense *e* or *i* to *a*, (just like in the command form explained in Chapter 10) as shown in table 25.2.

Table 25.2   The Present Subjunctive of Regular Verbs

AR VERBS Conjugation of the Sample Verb—Hablar	
que yo hable	que nosotros hablemos
que tú hables	que vosotros habléis
que él (ella, Ud.,) hable	que ellos (ellas, Uds.) hablen

ER VERBS
Conjugation of the Sample Verb—Vender

que yo vend*a*	que nosotros vend*amos*
que tú vend*as*	que vosotros vend*áis*
que él (ella, Ud.) vend*a*	que ellos (ellas, Uds.) vend*an*

IR VERBS
Conjugation of the Sample Verb—Abrir

que yo abr*a*	que nosotros abr*amos*
que tú abr*as*	que vosotros abr*áis*
que él (ella, Ud.) abr*a*	que ellos (ellas, Uds.) abr*an*

Irregular Verbs in the Subjunctive

Because the subjunctive is formed by dropping endings from the *yo* form of the verb, those verbs whose *yo* form is irregular will have irregular subjunctive forms, to which the proper subjunctive endings must be added:

Infinitive	Yo form	Subjunctive Stem	Subjunctive Endings (The Same for All)
conocer (to know)	conozc*o*	conozc	*a, as, a, amos, áis, an*
decir (to say)	dig*o*	dig	
hacer (to make, do)	hag*o*	hag	
oír (to hear)	oig*o*	oig	
poner (to put)	pong*o*	pong	
salir (to go out)	salg*o*	salg	
traer (to bring)	traig*o*	traig	
venir (to come)	veng*o*	veng	

Spelling Change Verbs in the Present Subjunctive

Verbs ending in *car*, *gar*, and *zar* have the following changes in the present subjunctive to maintain the proper pronunciation:

➤ For *car* verbs, *c* changes to *qu* in all forms of the subjunctive and *a* changes to *e* in the ending:

Buscar—to Look For	
que yo bus*que*	que nosotros bus*que*mos
que tú bus*que*s	que vosotros bus*qué*is
que él (ella, Ud.) bus*que*	que ellos (ellas, Uds.) bus*que*n

➤ For *gar* verbs, *g* changes to *gu* in all forms of the subjunctive and *a* changes to *e* in the ending:

Pagar—to Pay	
que yo pa*gue*	que nosotros pa*gue*mos
que tú pa*gue*s	que vosotros pa*gué*is
que él (ella, Ud.) pa*gue*	que ellos (ellas, Uds.) pa*gue*n

➤ For *zar* verbs, *z* changes to *c* in all forms of the subjunctive and *a* changes to *e* in the ending:

Cruzar—to Cross	
que yo cru*ce*	que nosotros cru*ce*mos
que tú cru*ce*s	que vosotros cru*cé*is
que él (ella, Ud.) cru*ce*	que ellos (ellas, Uds.) cru*ce*n

Stem-Changing Verbs in the Present Subjunctive

As a Rule
These spelling changes are the same that you would expect to find in the yo form of the preterite tense of verbs ending in *car*, *gar*, and *zar*. Refer to Chapter 21.

For verbs ending in *ar* and *er*, the same change occurs in the stem vowel in the subjunctive that occurred in the stem vowel in the present tense (refer to Chapter 12). The stem vowel does not change in the nosotros and vosotros forms. Remember to change to the opposite vowel in the ending for the subjunctive (*ar* verbs change *a* to *e*; *er* verbs change *e* to *a*):

Pensar—to Think

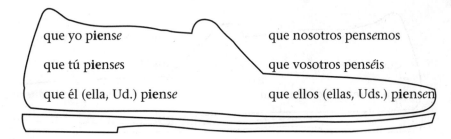

que yo p**ie**ns*e*   que nosotros pens*emos*

que tú p**ie**ns*es*   que vosotros pens*éis*

que él (ella, Ud.) p**ie**ns*e*   que ellos (ellas, Uds.) p**ie**ns*en*

Volver—to Turn

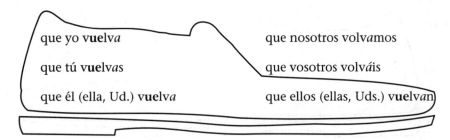

que yo v**ue**lv*a*   que nosotros volv*amos*

que tú v**ue**lv*as*   que vosotros volv*áis*

que él (ella, Ud.) v**ue**lv*a*   que ellos (ellas, Uds.) v**ue**lv*an*

For verbs ending in *ir*, the same change occurs in the stem vowel in the subjunctive that occurred in the stem vowel in the present tense (refer to Chapter 12). Additionally, the stem vowel changes from *e* to *i* or *o* to *u* in the nosotros and vosotros forms. Remember to change to the opposite vowel in the ending for the subjunctive (*ar* verbs change *a* to *e*; *er* verbs change *e* to *a*):

Sentir—to Feel

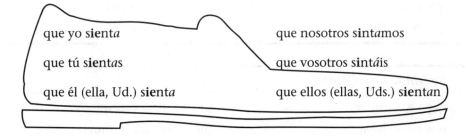

que yo s**ie**nt*a*   que nosotros s**i**nt*amos*

que tú s**ie**nt*as*   que vosotros s**i**nt*áis*

que él (ella, Ud.) s**ie**nt*a*   que ellos (ellas, Uds.) s**ie**nt*an*

Dormir—to Sleep

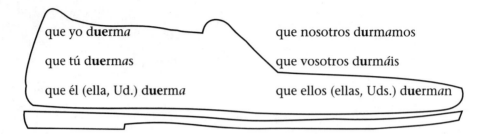

que yo d**uerm**a   que nosotros d**urm**amos

que tú d**uerm**as   que vosotros d**urm**áis

que él (ella, Ud.) d**uerm**a   que ellos (ellas, Uds.) d**uerm**an

Pedir—to Ask

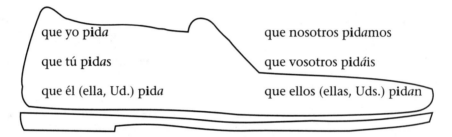

que yo p**id**a   que nosotros p**id**amos

que tú p**id**as   que vosotros p**id**áis

que él (ella, Ud.) p**id**a   que ellos (ellas, Uds.) p**id**an

Some verbs ending in *iar* and *uar* (refer to Chapter 12) require an accent on the *i* (*í*) and the *u* (*ú*) in all forms of the subjunctive except nosotros and vosotros. In the vosotros form, the *e* of the subjunctive ending takes the accent.

Guiar—to Guide

que yo gu**í**e	que nosotros gu**i**emos
que tú gu**í**es	que vosotros gu**i**éis
que él (ella, Ud.) gu**í**e	que ellos (ellas, Uds.) gu**í**en

---

Continuar—to Continue

que yo contin**ú**e	que nosotros contin**u**emos
que tú contin**ú**es	que vosotros contin**u**éis
que él (ella, Ud.) contin**ú**e	que ellos (ellas, Uds.) contin**ú**en

The Present Subjunctive of Irregular Verbs

Some verbs follow no rules and must be memorized. The ones that will prove to be most useful are

Dar—to Give

que yo dé	que nosotros demos
que tú des	que vosotros deis
que él (ella, Ud.) dé	que ellos (ellas, Uds.) den

Estar—to Be

que yo esté	que nosotros estemos
que tú estés	que vosotros estéis
que él (ella, Ud.) esté	que ellos (ellas, Uds.) estén

Ir—to Go

que yo vaya	que nosotros vayamos
que tú vayas	que vosotros vayáis
que él (ella, Ud.) vaya	que ellos (ellas, Uds.) vayan

Saber—to Know

que yo sepa	que nosotros sepamos
que tú sepas	que vosotros sepáis
que él (ella, Ud.) sepa	que ellos (ellas, Uds.) sepan

Ser— to Be

que yo sea	que nosotros seamos
que tú seas	que vosotros seáis
que él (ella, Ud.) sea	que ellos (ellas, Uds.) sean

So Many Things to Do and So Little Time

I have a million things to do today and I bet you do, too. The only way to escape the hassles and obligations of our daily routine is to go on vacation. When you return, however, it's back to the grind. Express what these people have to do using *tener que + infinitive* and then *es necesario que + subjunctive*:

Example: **él/trabajar**

> *Él tiene que trabajar.*
>
> *Es necesario que él trabaje.*

nosotros/preparar la cena	él/pedir la cuenta
ella/aprender español	Uds./continuar a estudiar
ellos/vivir en Puerto Rico	tú/graduarse
yo/cerrar esa cuenta	ellas/dar un paseo
vosotros/no perder su cartera	nosotros/estar a tiempo
tú/no mentir	yo/ir al centro
Ud./no dormir tarde	vosotros/saber jugar al tenis
Ud./ser más responsable	

Impersonal Expressions of Wishing, Emotion, Need, and Doubt That Require the Subjunctive

Es necesario que is a very common expression used with the subjunctive. There are, however, several other common expressions that you might use that will require the subjunctive. In order to speak properly, you should become familiar with them:

Phrase	Pronunciation	Meaning
Es aconsejable que	ehs ah-kohn-seh-hah-bleh keh	It is advisable that
Es bueno que	ehs bweh-noh keh	It is good that
Es difícil que	ehs dee-fee-seel keh	It is difficult that
Es dudoso que	ehs doo-doh-soh keh	It is doubtful that
Es fácil que	ehs fah-seel keh	It is easy that

Phrase	Pronunciation	Meaning
Es importante que	ehs eem-pohr-tahn-teh keh	It is important that
Es imposible que	ehs eem-poh-see-bleh keh	It is impossible that
Es increíble que	ehs een-kreh-ee-bleh keh	It is incredible that
Es indispensable que	ehs een-dees-pehn-sah-bleh keh	It is indispensable that
Es malo que	ehs mah-loh keh	It is bad that
Es mejor que	ehs meh-hohr keh	It is better that
Es posible que	ehs poh-see-bleh keh	It is possible that
Es preciso que	ehs preh-see-soh keh	It is essential that
Es probable que	ehs proh-bah-bleh keh	It is probable that
Es una lástima que	ehs oo-nah lahs-tee-mah keh	It is a pity that
Más vale que	mahs bah-leh keh	It is better that

The Least You Need to Know

➤ Spanish banks are modern and efficient and provide the same services as ours.

➤ Use *tener (conjugated)* + *que* + *verb (infinitive)* to express that the subject needs or has to do something.

➤ The subjunctive is used to express need, wishing, emotion, and doubt. To form the present subjunctive of most verbs, drop the *o* from the yo form. For *ar* verbs add these endings: *e, es, e, emos, éis, en*. For *er* and *ir* verbs add: *a, as, a, amos, áis, an*. Spelling-change verbs, stem-changing verbs, and irregular verbs require special changes.

Answer Key

Chapter 3

How Much Have You Learned?
1. The piano is big.
2. The actor is horrible.
3. The information is terrible.
4. The teacher is sincere.
5. The tiger is cruel.
6. The cereal is delicious.

Yes, You Can Write in Spanish
1. El presidente es elegante.
2. La computadora es interesante.
3. La información es importante.
4. El hotel es grande.
5. El color es magnífico.

You've Got it Now
Juan prepares the menu.
The mechanic repairs the car.
The tourist uses the information.
The program ends.
Martha celebrates her birthday.
José adores the program.

Give Your Opinion
El programa es excelente.
El parque es popular.
El plato es famoso.
El restaurante es grande.
El teatro es moderno.
El programa es magnífico.

El actor es dinámico.
El hotel es confortable.

Chapter 4

The ABCs of Using a Dictionary
1. bien
2. el pozo
3. el grito
4. llorar
5. solamente

Chapter 5

You're Off and Running (sample responses)
1. en coche
2. en metro
3. en coche
4. en autobús
5. en avión
6. a pie
7. en barco
8. en barco
9. en coche
10. en metro

What Time Is It?
1. adiós
2. inmediatamente, en seguida
3. tarde
4. temprano

Chapter 5

Is Everything All Right?
sueño
calor
hambre
sed
miedo
razón

What's Doing Around the World
1. En Madrid hace calor.
2. En Sevilla hace frío y nieva.
3. En Córdoba hace mal tiempo.
4. En México ilueve.
5. En Panama hace buen tiempo.
6. En Argentino hace viento.
7. En Columbia hace sol.
8. En Peru hace frío.

Chapter 6

Practice Those Plurals
el lápiz
el regalo
el collar
el paquete
la revista
la loción

What Have You Learned About Gender?

1. female
2. male
3. male

Chapter 7

Tú vs. Vosotros

a doctor? Ud.

your cousin? tú

your friend? tú

a salesman? Ud.

a woman? Ud.

two female friends? vosotras

two male friends? vosotros

a policeman? Ud.

your friends? vosotros

Eduardo? él

Anita? ella

Sara y Beatriz? ellas

Gloria? ella

Arturo? él

Juan y Miguel? ellos

Roberto y Lupita? ellos

Alba? ella

Blanca? ella

Cristina y Manuel? ellos

Paco? él

Julio y Amalia? ellos

Conjugation 101

1. anuncia
2. buscan
3. notamos
4. ando
5. nadáis

Conjugation 102

1. corres
2. comen
3. bebemos
4. responde
5. aprende
6. debo

Conjugation 103

1. vivís
2. aplaude

3. escriben
4. omites
5. asiste
6. abro
7. descubrimos
8. reciben

Ask Away (sample responses)

1. ¿Nosotros hablamos demasiado? ¿no? ¿verdad? ¿Está bien? ¿Hablamos nosotros demasiado?
2. ¿Él asiste..? ¿no? ¿verdad? ¿Está bien? ¿Asiste él...?
3. ¿Uds. comprenden mucho? ¿no? ¿verdad? ¿Está bien? ¿Comprenden Uds. mucho?
4. ¿María escribe...? ¿no? ¿verdad? ¿Está bien? ¿Escribe María...?

Chapter 8

Using Ser and Estar

1. somos
2. es
3. están
4. son
5. está

What's Happening Now?

Yo estoy leyendo.

Yo estoy escuchando música.

Yo estoy comiendo.

Yo estoy cantando.

Yo estoy hablando español.

Yo estoy mirando una película.

Yo estoy durmiendo.

Ask as Many as You Can (sample responses)

1. ¿De dónde es Roberto? ¿Con quién viaja? ¿Dónde viaja con su familia? ¿Cómo viaja? ¿Cuánto tiempo pasan en España? ¿Dónde pasan un mes? ¿Qué desean visitar? ¿Cuándo regresan?
2. ¿Cómo te llamas? ¿De dónde eres? ¿A quién buscas? ¿Por qué? ¿Qué deseas practicar? ¿Cuándo hablas inglés? ¿Cómo es el inglés? ¿Cómo eres tú?

Chapter 9

What's in an Apellido?

apellido paterno—Vega

Fernández

apellido materno—Pérez

Rueda

Ana Fernández de Vega

Rueda

Diego Vega Fernández

María Vega Fernández

What Do You Prefer? (sample responses)

Mis actrices favoritas son...

Mi canción favorita es...

Mis restaurantes favoritos son...

Mi deporte favorito es...

Mi color favorito es...

Mi película favorita es...

Can You? (sample responses)

Buenos días. Me llamo...

¿Ud. conoce a mi hermano, Jorge?

Le presento a mi hijo, Miguel.

Mucho gusto en conocerle.

El gusto es mío.

Using Tener

1. tenemos cuidado
2. tiene lugar
3. tiene éxito
4. tienen dolor del estómago
5. tengo suerte
6. tienes prisa

Complete the Descriptions (sample responses)

1. importante
2. buenas
3. inteligente
4. magníficas
5. divertidas

Personal Ads

1. A 47-year-old North American lawyer and art gallery director who is tall, attractive, and sophisticated seeks a loving, young, educated, English-speaking 28–42-year-old woman with long hair, for romance, matrimony, and a family.

2. A 6' 166 lb. 28-year-old Chilean man who likes romantic music, dancing, sports, and studying seeks a 25–35-year-old woman who is understanding, happy, intelligent, and honest for friendship.

3. A 40-year-old working woman who is nice and caring seeks a Brazilian man with same qualities for friendship and a serious relationship.

4. A 37-year-old divorced Dominican woman with 2 children seeks a 35–40-year-old 5'10' or taller, nonsmoking, hard-working, fun man with a good sense of humor.

Chapter 10

Airline Advice

A. Hand luggage must be kept in special compartments or under the passenger's seat during take-off and landing. Many compartments are available to travelers.

B. Don't keep valuable things in your luggage: money, jewels or your passport.

C. Don't put fragile items or those that can deteriorate in your luggage. They are not protected in case of damage.

Signs Everywhere

c

e

a

f

b

d

What's the Message

1. You may not bring dangerous items aboard such as certain gases—butane, oxygen, propane, corrosives, acids, dry cell batteries, flammable liquids and solids, radioactive materials, explosives, weapons, pyrotechnical materials, mercury, and magnetic materials.

Using Commands

Verb	Ud.	Uds.	Meaning
ir	*vaya*	*vayan*	*go_*
continuar	*continue*	*continuen*	*continue*
seguir*	¡Siga!	*sigan*	*continue*
bajar	*baje*	*bajen*	*go down*
caminar	*camine*	*caminen*	*walk*
subir	*suba*	*suban*	*go up*
pasar	*pase*	*pasen*	*pass*
tomar	*tome*	*tomen*	*take*
doblar	*doble*	*doblen*	*turn*
cruzar*	¡Cruce!	*cruzcen*	*cross*

Chapter 11

Using ¿Qué? and ¿Cuál?

¿Cuál es su nombre?

¿Cuál es su dirección?

¿Qué lee Ud.?

¿Cuál es su nacionalidad?

¿Qué metro va a la Ciudad de México?

What's Your Number

cuarenta y cinco, sesenta y siete, ochenta y nueve

trescientos veinticinco, once, setenta y dos

Chapter 12

Just in Case

What to do in case of a fire

1. If the fire is in your room: Go to the exit and close the door to your room. Follow the lights along the floor. Tell the reception desk.

2. If you hear the fire alarm: Go to the exit and close the door to your room. Follow the lights along the floor. If there is smoke in the corridors or the stairway is impassible, stay in your room, go to the window and make yourself visible while awaiting the arrival of the firemen.

Using Ordinal Numbers

tobacco—planta baja

flowers—planta 1

records—sótano 1

toys—planta 2

travel items—planta 3

park—sótano 2, 3, & 4

interpreter—planta baja

photos—sótano 1, planta 2

travel agency—planta 3

keys—planta 1

Using AR and ER Verbs

1. piensas
2. almorzamos
3. entiendo
4. vuelven
5. pensáis
6. cuesta
7. descendemos
8. cerráis

Using IR Verbs

1. prefiero
2. dormimos
3. repiten
4. mentís
5. muere
6. reís

Using UIR, IAR, and UAR Verbs

1. envio
2. incluimos
3. continúa
4. contribuyen
5. actúas
6. guiáis
7. continúa

Chapter 13

What's the Date?

el cinco de agosto

el ocho de agosto

el veintidos de agosto

el quince de agosto

el seis de agosto

el treinta y uno de julio

Using Dar

1. dan un paseo
2. dáis gritos
3. damos gracias
4. doy un abrazo
5. das con

Chapter 14

Making Suggestions (sample responses)

Quiero ir a la corrida de toros. ¿Qué piensas?

Vamos a ir al carnival.

Partamos por el castillo.

¿Por qué no vamos al circo?

Where Are You Going?

Voy a España.

Voy a China.

Voy a México.

Voy a Rusia

Voy a Italia.

Voy a Inglaterra.

Voy a Francia.

Voy a los Estados Unidos.

Chapter 15

What Do You Put On? (sample responses)

Work—Yo llevo un vestido, medias, zapatos, un reloj, un collar, dos pulseras y dos anillos.

Beach—Yo llevo un bikini y sandalias.

Formal dinner—Yo llevo un traje, una camisa, calcetines, zapatos y un reloj.

Friend's house—Yo llevo una camisa, los jeans, calcetines, los tenis, un reloj y dos anillos.

Skiing—Yo llevo un pantalon, un suéter, calcetines, zapatos, un abrigo, una bufanda y guantes.

Putting Gustar to Work

1. (No) me gusta el sombrero rojo.
2. (No) me gusta la camisa pequeña.
3. (No) me gusta la camiseta grande.
4. (No) me gustan los zapatos verdes.

Using Direct Object Pronouns

1. (No) Lo compro.
2. (No) Los quiero.
3. (No) La escojo.
4. (No) Las tomo.
5. (No) Lo considero.
6. (No) Los detesto.

Using Indirect Object Pronouns

Cómprele un abrigo. No le compre una chaqueta.

Cómpreles vestidos. No les compre faldas.

Cómpreles sombreros. No les compre guantes.

Cómprele una camiseta. No le compre una bolsa.

Cómpreles casetas. No les compre discos.

Cómprele una pulsera. No le compre un reloj.

What Do You Think? (sample responses)

Esta corbata larga, de rayas es horrible.

Estos pantalones cortos de tartán son prácticos.

Esta camisa de lunares es demasiado chillona.

Esta pequeña camiseta de rayas es elegante.

Chapter 16

Where Are You Going?

Voy a la abacería.

Voy a la pastelería.

Voy a la carnicería.

Voy a la frutería.

Voy a la pescadería.

Voy a la tienda de licores.

Voy a la confitería.

Voy a la lechería.

Your Likes and Dislikes (sample responses)

Me encanta el pescado.

Me gusta la carne.

Me encantan los productos lácteos.

Me disgustan las frutas.

Me encantan las legumbres.

Me gustan las bebidas.

Me encantan los postres.

What's in the Fridge (sample responses)

una botella de agua mineral, un saco de galletas, una caja de dulces, un pan, panecillos, una botella de gaseosa.

Chapter 17

Which Restaurant?

La Casita—grilled meats.

La Princesa—seafood.

Restaurante de Madrid—private rooms, music.

Cena Romantica—romantic dinner for 2 with wine, music and a complimentary rose for women.

El rincón—good selection of dishes at reasonable prices. Live music.

La Cava—private rooms, fish, meat dishes, and roasts.

How Was It? (sample responses)

¡Qué sopa tan excelente!

¡Qué bistec tan delicioso!

¡Qué vino tan sabroso!

¡Qué ensalada tan magnífica!

¡Qué postre tan rico!

Chapter 18

Shall We Play? (sample responses)

Me gusta la equitación.

Detesto la vela.

Me encanta la natación.

Me gusta el fútbol.

Me encanta el golf.

Me gusta el tenis.

Do the Inviting

¿Quieres ir al parque?

¿Puedes acompañarme a la pista?

¿No quieres acompañarme a la piscina? a la playa?

¿No puedes ir a la pista?

¿Queres ir a la montaña?

¿Puedes acompañarme al campo?

Will You or Won't You? (sample responses)

Shopping—Con mucho gusto.

Visit the ruins—No estoy libre.

Jog—No me interesa.

Movie—Por supuesto.

Restaurant—Tal vez.

Disco—¿Por qué no?

How Do You Do It? (sample responses)

Hablo español rápidamente.

Cocino bien.

Pienso inteligentemente.

Trabajo cuidadosamente.

Bailo lentamente.

Nado bastante mal.

Chapter 19

Please Do My Laundry

They are not responsible for buttons or other adornments on clothing. In case of loss or damage, the hotel will give up to 10 times the cost of the service. They are not responsible for synthetic materials or items left for more than 3 months. They are closed Saturdays, Sundays, and holidays. Emergency service will cost 50% more.

I Need These Shoes

It will pick up and deliver your shoes to your address.

It's My Watch (sample responses)

Mi reloj no funciona. Está parado. Necesito una batería. ¿La tiene Ud.? Necesito mi reloj en seguida.

I Can't Wait to See My Pictures

Photo Stop—makes your vacation pictures more beautiful, 25% larger and develops them more quickly at a better price. They take credit cards and give discounts and a free album.

Compare Yourself (sample responses)

Soy menos grande que mi hermano.

Soy más gorda que mi madre.

Soy tan encantadora como mi hermana.

Bailo mejor que mi esposo.

Trabajo tan diligentemente como mi amiga.

Escucho más pacientemente que mi hijo.

Chapter 20

I Hurt (sample responses)

Flu—Tengo dolor de cabeza. Me duele todo el cuerpo. Yo toso y estoy agotado. Me siento mal.

Allergy—Yo toso y estornudo. Yo no puedo dormir.

Sprained ankle—Me duele el tobillo. Tengo una torcedura y una inflamación. No puedo caminar.

Migraine—Tengo dolor de cabeza. Tengo náuseas. Me siento mal.

I'm Not a Hypochondriac

Hace dos semanas que yo toso. Toso desde hace dos semanas.

Hace tres días que tengo dolor de cabeza. Tengo dolor de cabeza desde hace tres días.

Hace un mes que me duele el estómago. Me duele el estómago desde hace un mes.

Practicing Reflexive Verbs (sample responses)

Yo me despierto.

Yo me levanto.

Yo me desvisto.

Yo me baño.

Yo me visto.

Yo me preparo el desayuno.

Yo me cepillo los dientes.

Yo me peino.

Commanding with Reflexives

Despiértense Uds. No se despierten Uds.

Levántense Uds. No se levanten Uds.

Báñense Uds. No se bañen Uds.

Apúrense Uds. No se apuren Uds.

Vístanse Uds. No se vistan Uds.

Péinense Uds. No se peinen Uds.

Cepíllense Uds. los dientes. No se cepillen Uds. los dientes.

Diviértanse Uds. No se diviertan Uds.

Chapter 21

What's On Sale

1. Band-Aids
2. anti-dandruff shampoo
3. aspirin
4. mouthwash
5. perfumes/floral fragrances

Talk About Yesterday

1. trabajó
2. comió
3. escribiste
4. leí
5. anduvimos
6. jugué
7. tuvieron
8. me equicoqué
9. oyeron
10. dijisteis
11. durmieron
12. pagué

Ask Questions

1. ¿Carlos, hiciste una visita al museo?
   Sí, hizo una visita al museo.
2. ¿Pablo y Jorge, dieron Uds. un paseo?
   No, no dimos un paseo.
3. ¿María, pescaste en el mar?
   No, no pesqué en el mar.
4. ¿Isabel y Pilar, almorzaron Uds. al centro.
   Sí, almorzamos al centro.
5. ¿Adela, trajiste regalos a tus primos?
   Sí traje regalos a mis primos.
6. ¿Francisco y Rafael, sirvieron Uds. refrescos a sus amigos?
   No, no servimos refrescos a nuestros amigos.

What Didn't You Do Today (sample responses)

No comí el almuerzo.

Fui al centro.

No estudié mucho.

Hice mucho trabajo.

Me levanté temprano.

No oí las noticias.

No telefoneé a mis padres.

Busqué un nuevo apartamento.

Chapter 22

While You Were Out

On July 11th, 1975 at 4:25 P.M., Roberta Cruz from Aerolíneas, México called. Her number is 12-34-56. She wants you to call her back as soon as possible. Ana took the message for you.

Preterite or Imperfect?

1. Eran
2. Estaba
3. salí
4. Tomé
5. llegué
6. Entré
7. subí
8. Saqué
9. necesité
10. observé
11. estaba
12. sabía
13. Tenía
14. Estaba
15. robó
16. Empujé
17. entré
18. escuché
19. marchaba
20. gritaron

Chapter 23

Would You Use Saber or Conocer?

1. saben
2. sé
3. conoce
4. sabemos
5. conoces
6. conoce
7. saben
8. conocéis

Putting the Present Perfect to Work

1. nosotros hemos ido
2. ellos han jugado
3. tú no has trabajado

4. yo he leído
5. Ud. no ha escrito
6. vosotros no habéis corrido
7. Uds. no han traído
8. ella no ha vuelto

Chapter 24

Buying Furniture

Your furniture will be guaranteed for 5 years and recovering for 2 years should there be any problem with the manufacturing.

They will give free decorating consultation and will come to give free estimates and take measurements.

You will be given a guarantee against all risks for one year.

Your old furniture will be removed.

All guarantees are free throughout Spain.

Decisions, Decisions, Decisions

A safe place to live within your price range. It's near downtown, recreational facilities, restaurants, malls, main highways, beaches and has a wonderful view of Puerto Rico. The residences are modern, have elegant facades, 3 bedrooms, and a bathroom.

A Choice Is Made

4 bedrooms
4 and a half bathrooms
Maid's quarters, separate entrance for family and workers, an office, 2 fireplaces, a terrace, and private layout.

Plans for the Day

1. Iré al centro comercial.
2. Telefonearé a mi familia.
3. Saldré con mis amigos.
4. Haré un viage.
5. Abriré una cuenta.

What Would You Do? (sample responses)

Yo me compraría un nuevo coche deportivo y una casa muy grande. Yo daría mucho dinero a los pobres. Yo viajaría por todo el mundo. Yo iría en España con toda mi familia. Yo no trabajaría.

Chapter 25

So Many Things to Do and So Little Time

1. Nosotros tenemos que preparar…
   Es necesario que preparemos…
2. Ella tiene que aprender…
   Es necesario que aprenda…
3. Ellos tienen que vivir…
   Es necesario que vivan…
4. Yo tengo que cerrar…
   Es necesario que cierre…
5. Vosotros no tenéis que perder…
   Es necesario que no perdáis…
6. Tú no tienes que mentir.
   Es necesario que no mientas.
7. Ud. no tiene que dormir…
   Es necesario que no duerma…
8. El tiene que pedir…
   Es necesario que no pida…
9. Uds. tienen que continuar…
   Es necesario que continúen…
10. Tú tienes que graduarte.
    Es necesario que te gradues.
11. Ellas tienen que dar…
    Es necesario que den…
12. Nosotros tenemos que estar…
    Es necesario que estemos…
13. Yo tengo que ir…
    Es necesario que vaya…
14. Vosotros tienen que saber…
    Es necesario que sepáis…
15. Ud. tiene que ser…
    Es necesario que sea…

Index

O

P

Q

R

to hug (dar un abrazo), 157
to know, be acquainted with (conocer), 314
to know facts, how to do things (saber), 314
to me (me), 164
to pack (hacer la maleta), 112
to pay a visit (hacer una visita), 112
to run into (dar con), 157
to take a trip (hacer un viaje), 112
to take a walk, go for a ride (dar un paseo), 157
to thank (dar las gracias a), 157
tocar (to play a musical instrument), 242
today (hoy), 155
toiletry store (una perfumería), 282
tomato (tomate), 218
tomorrow (mañana), 155
tonto (silly), 167
too much (demasiado), 205
torero (bullfighter), 161, 179
tormenta eléctrica (electrical storm), 149
tortillas
    tortilla española, 217
    tortilla mexicana, 217
    types of food, 216
Tourist Card (Tarjeta Turística), 111
tourist tickets (un metrotour de tres días/cinco días), 111
traer, 112
train (el tren), 110
transitive verbs, 29
transportation idioms, 35
travel idioms, 35
traveler's check (el cheque de viajero), 341
tronar, 147
Tuesday (martes), 150
to turn (volver), 347
two weeks from tomorrow (dos semanas de mañana), 155
types of mail delivery, 312
types of movies and television, 239
types of phone calls, 296

U

ugly (feo), 167
-uir ending verbs, conjugating, 289
último(a), last, 154
un alquiler de coches (car rental agency), 115
un billete de diez viajes (metro ticket packs), 111
un billete sencillo (metro ticket), 111
un gato (car jack), 116
un horror (a horror), 167
un metrotour de tres días/cinco días (tourist tickets), 111
un partido de... (a game of...), 233
un rincón español (Spanish corner), 8
una goma de repuesto (spare tire), 116
una tarjeta de abono transportes (monthly commuter pass), 111
to understand, 135
uno (one), 121
usher (un guía), 240

V

valer, 112
variants of uno (one) for numbers or nouns, 121
variar (to vary), 141
vegetables, 198
vender, 286
venir (to come)
    conjugating, 285
    for yo, 113
una venta (regional inn), 210
ver (to see), 162, 291
el verano (summer), 152
verbal sentences, 51
verbs

-ar
    common ar verbs, 62
    conjugating, 55
    past tense, 286
    spelling changes for present tense, 134
basics of grammar, 28
car ending, 287
cognates, 24
conditional tense, 334
conjugating, 28, 112
directional, 101-102
-er
    common er verbs, 63
    conjugating, 56
    past tense, 286
    spelling changes for present tense, 134
future tense, 332
-gar ending, 287
gerunds, 73
imperfect past tense, 304
infinitives, 55
intransitive, 29
-ir
    common ir verbs, 64
    conjugating, 58
    past tense, 286, 289
irregular, 54
    conditional tense, 335
    imperfect past tense, 305
    subjunctive form, 345
past participles, 317
present perfect tense, 316
preterite past tense, 286
reflexive, 29, 277
regular, 54
simple verbal sentences, 51
spelling changes within stem of verb, 134
subjects, 52
subjunctive, 344
transitive, 29
-uir ending, 289
-zar ending, 288
¿verdad? tag, 60
vergüenza, shame, 12
viernes (Friday), 150
el vino (wine), 225

Lifestyle

The Complete Idiot's Guide to Learning French on Your Own
ISBN: 0-02-861043-1 ▪ $16.95

The Complete Idiot's Guide to Dating
ISBN: 0-02-861052-0 ▪ $14.95

The Complete Idiot's Guide to Hiking, Camping, and the Great Outdoors
ISBN: 0-02-861100-4 ▪ $16.95

The Complete Idiot's Guide to Cooking Basics
ISBN: 1-56761-523-6 ▪ $16.99

The Complete Idiot's Guide to Learning Spanish on Your Own
ISBN: 0-02-861040-7 ▪ $16.95

The Complete Idiot's Guide to Gambling Like a Pro
ISBN: 0-02-861102-0 ▪ $16.95

The Complete Idiot's Guide to Choosing, Training, and Raising a Dog
ISBN: 0-02-861098-9 ▪ $16.95

You can handle it!

When You're Smart Enough to Know That You Don't Know It All

For all the ups and downs you're sure to encounter in life, The Complete Idiot's Guides give you down-to-earth answers and practical solutions.

The Complete Idiot's Guide to Trouble-Free Car Care
ISBN: 0-02-861041-5 ▪ $16.95

The Complete Idiot's Guide to the Perfect Wedding
ISBN: 1-56761-532-5 ▪ $16.99

The Complete Idiot's Guide to Getting and Keeping Your Perfect Body
ISBN: 0-286105122 ▪ $16.99

The Complete Idiot's Guide to First Aid Basics
ISBN: 0-02-861099-7 ▪ $16.95

The Complete Idiot's Guide to the Perfect Vacation
ISBN: 1-56761-531-7 ▪ $14.99

The Complete Idiot's Guide to Trouble-Free Home Repair
ISBN: 0-02-861042-3 ▪ $16.95

The Complete Idiot's Guide to Getting into College
ISBN: 1-56761-508-2 ▪ $14.95

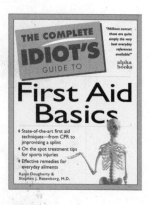